THE FUTURE OF SERVICE-LEARNING

About the Cover Artist

The influence of southern folk culture and many diverse life experiences are incorporated into the eclectic painting of William "Bill" Hemmerling. Bill was born in Chicago and moved to Ponchatoula, Louisiana, in 1977. Upon retirement in 2002, he finally found time to paint from the heart. His philosophy about painting was this: "One day when I let God out of the box I built, he danced with me." Unfortunately, Bill died in 2009 before this book was released.

Bill was constantly searching for and using found or recycled materials for his one-of-a-kind creations. His love of people and his humble, offbeat nature brought excitement and energy to his internationally known and appreciated folk art.

Bill donated proceeds from his paintings to a number of causes, including helping to rebuild Xavier University after Hurricane Katrina, Habitat for Humanity, and Hospice. In 2008, he generously agreed to donate proceeds from a limited edition giclee reproduction of one of his paintings to the service-learning program of co-editor Marybeth Lima. These proceeds will provide construction funds for dream playgrounds designed by public school and college students.

For more information about Bill Hemmerling, see www.billhem merling.com

Photo by Kevin Duffy

THE FUTURE OF
SERVICE-LEARNING

New Solutions for Sustaining
and Improving Practice

Edited by

Jean Strait and Marybeth Lima

Foreword by Andrew Furco

STERLING, VIRGINIA

Sty/us

COPYRIGHT © 2009 BY STYLUS PUBLISHING, LLC.

Published by Stylus Publishing, LLC
22883 Quicksilver Drive
Sterling, Virginia 20166-2102

Library of Congress Cataloging-in-Publication-Data
The future of service learning : new solutions for sustaining and improving practice / edited by Jean R. Strait and Marybeth Lima ; foreword by Andrew Furco.
   p.   cm.
Includes bibliographical references and index.
ISBN 978-1-57922-364-9 (cloth : alk. paper)
ISBN 978-1-57922-365-6 (pbk.. : alk. paper)
1. Service learning.   I. Strait, Jean R. (Jean Renee),
1965–   II. Lima, Marybeth, 1965–
LC220.5.F87   2009
361.3'70973—dc22   2009007530

13-digit ISBN: 978-1-57922-364-8 (cloth)
13-digit ISBN: 978-1-57922-365-6 (paper)

Printed in the United States of America

All first editions printed on acid free paper
that meets the American National Standards Institute
Z39-48 Standard.

Bulk Purchases

Quantity discounts are available for use in workshops and for staff development.
Call 1-800-232-0223

First Edition, 2009

10   9   8   7   6   5   4   3   2   1

Jean would like dedicate this book to her family:
Suzi, Kyle, Abby, Buddy, Grandma Susie, Dad and Sally, John and Barb.
I am the person I am today because
you gave of yourselves to me.

Marybeth would like to dedicate this book to Jan Shoemaker,
the heart and soul of service-learning at LSU and an alchemist.
She finds carbon in the rough
and molds, blends, and polishes
to create gems of community engagement.

A portion of the proceeds of this book will be donated by the authors and
Stylus Publishing to a service-learning program in New Orleans called *Each One
Teach One*. Funds will be used to partner New Orleans 5–8 grade students with
Hamline University and Avalon student mentors to encourage students to stay
in school and improve academic achievement.

CONTENTS

ACKNOWLEDGMENTS

From Jean:

I would like to thank my family for giving me extra time to create Each One Teach One (EOTO). Tony Wilson, Denny Hilton (The Depot House), Luscious Newell, James Peppersack, Steven Martin, and Deb Brown are quiet heroes and true inspirations for the work we do in New Orleans. On our down days you lift our spirits. Special thanks to student leaders Margaret Selva, Joyce Jones, Jenna Londy, and Adam Vetvick for their unwavering dedication to children; and the crew that I call EOTO (Ana Panone, Jenna Peterson, Koomie Kirmi, Rachel Smolinski, Selam and Hiwot Melka, and my favorite biking graduate student, Aaron Kadera); the amazing Hamline University, Avalon High School and Martin Luther King Science and Technology middle school students for showing us everything is possible when someone believes in you. Someday, we will be reading about the work they are doing to change the world!

Special thanks to Marybeth Lima, co-editor extraordinaire, for her excellence in editing and for keeping me sane in this process. You made this collaboration fun. Let's do it again soon.

From Marybeth:

I enjoy writing acknowledgments because they manage to capture a slice of life in a way that nothing else does. The work in this book was completed in a short time frame, and my acknowledgments are geared toward the individuals who have held me up and pulled me through accordingly.

Thanks to my service-learning collaborators whose work in the trenches enables me to continue mine. They include home girls Jan Shoemaker, Debbie Normand, Carol O'Neil, Roxanne Dill, Julie Smith, Judy Weaver, and

Lisa Frost, and homeboys Joe Howell, Bill Hemmerling, and Russ Carson. I also thank those in leadership positions whose support is critical for my work, including Richard Bengston, Dan Thomas, Ken Koonce, David Constant, Catherine Fletcher, and Charlotte Placide. Staff support is also extremely important, and I acknowledge the work ethic and dedication of Angela Singleton, Donna Elisar, and Rhonda Shepard.

Family and friends remain my rock and my root. I especially thank Lynn Hathaway, my life partner, for her keen insights, heartfelt wisdom, and unwavering love and support—you are a true inspiration. My parents and my brother do not actively push me to do better, but their presence in my life encourages me to do so just the same. Life is rich when you have friends to depend on, and I couldn't ask for a better crew; thank you Carol Lee Moore, Ann Christy, Diana Glawe, Sue Nokes, Leslie Morreale, Cristina Sabliov, Kristi Davis, Dorothy Gammel, Connie Kuns, Emily Toth, Sherry Desselle, and Elaine Maccio. Carmen Board and Shaqing "Ching" Guo help me to sustain my sanity and my health through yoga and acupuncture, respectively.

My co-editor, Jean Strait, is the driving force behind and the leader of this project. Her dedication, attitude, and work ethic are unparalleled. I wish that collaborating with others was always as easy—thank you Jean, for your indefatigable efforts, attention to detail, and high standards.

From Both:

Thanks to John Von Knorring, president of Stylus Publishing, for your vision and expediency in making this publication a reality, and to Linda Zuk for her superlative handling of our manuscript throughout the production process.

FOREWORD

Service-learning first gained attention in the 1980s. At that time there was next to no literature on the subject, and few persons could define service-learning or had much interest in the practice. With the establishment of the Corporation for National and Community Service in 1993, service-learning began to gain popularity within the K–12 and higher education systems in the United States. The earliest articles and volumes on service-learning appeared in the late 1980s and early 1990s; these publications were dedicated primarily to explaining the philosophy and essence of the pedagogy. Indeed, throughout the 1990s, almost every book or article on service-learning included a substantial section that focused on defining service-learning, mostly because the term had minimal currency beyond those who practiced it.

During this early period in service-learning's development, debates raged within the field regarding what types of experiences qualified or did not qualify as service-learning. This early literature even included debates about whether or not the written term should include a hyphen! It also did not take long for variants of the term to appear in the literature. By 1997, terms such as *academic service-learning, community service-learning, service-learning internships,* and *co-curricular service-learning* were part of the lexicon; each term supposedly characterized a particular, nuanced type of service-learning experience. The quest to define in words the character and essence of service-learning persisted in the literature throughout the 1990s.

As more government agencies, community organizations, and educational systems adopted service-learning initiatives, and service-learning became more widely understood, the tenor and focus of the service-learning literature began to shift. There was not only growing interest in what service-learning was, but also in what service-learning did. By the mid- to late 1990s, the literature began to pay more attention to the elements of quality practice and the impacts of service-learning on students. A number of curricular guides and case study volumes were produced, such as Edward Zlotkowski's

Successful Service-Learning Programs (1998), which provided examples of different approaches and models for high quality service-learning. About this time, research studies of service-learning began to be published, and groundbreaking journals and books, such as the *Michigan Journal of Community Service-Learning* and Eyler and Giles' (1999) *Where's the Learning in Service-Learning,* set the stage for examining service-learning's impacts on students and others who provide service.

By the new millennium, the service-learning literature was beginning to include more discussions on service-learning's impacts on community-based participants and other service-learning stakeholders. Several publications produced by Campus-Community Partnerships for Health and the Council of Independent Colleges set the stage for more robust conversations about the community's role in service-learning. Also at this time, the literature was tackling issues of sustainability and institutionalization, as service-learning programs that had operated throughout the 1990s, mostly on soft money, were now facing greater funding competition for a very limited pool of service-learning dollars; effective strategies for sustaining service-learning programs were in great demand.

Although the focus of service-learning literature has shifted over the years as service-learning has matured and evolved, the literature on service-learning has primarily highlighted the positive aspects of service-learning, often giving short shrift to the challenges, complexities, and pitfalls of engaging in the practice. In addition, there is not yet enough literature in the field that has examined issues pertaining to more advanced, mature service-learning practice.

Today, although service-learning continues to grow and flourish, it is now being presented less as a separate initiative and more as part of a broader civic engagement agenda. In many ways, the development of this civic engagement movement has opened the door for more circumspection about the value and virtues of service-learning. Recent publications from Stanley Fish, Dan Butin, and others have helped members of the field take a harder look at service-learning, its complexities, and its position in formal education.

The service-learning field can benefit from more in-depth analyses of both the merits and shortcomings of service-learning, especially now as President Barack Obama begins his presidency with a call for the expansion of youth community engagement and citizen service initiatives. Having a fuller understanding of the many different facets of service-learning and how to build a long-term agenda for advanced service-learning practice can prepare service-learning practitioners, participants, and partners for the development of the highest quality service-learning programs possible.

The Future of Service-Learning: New Solutions for Sustaining and Improving Practice expands and extends the dialogue on the challenges and complexities of service-learning. The experienced service-learning practitioners and researchers contributing to this volume take readers beyond the basics of service-learning, providing a refreshing look at the intricacies and complexities of the service-learning enterprise. They are not afraid to reveal the shadow side of service-learning as they examine some of service-learning's pitfalls and potential liabilities. Their collective contributions create an important volume that paints a realistic portrait of what is required to establish, maintain, and sustain advanced service-learning initiatives. Although in the end, readers will walk away embracing service-learning for all the benefits it can offer its participants, they will do so armed with a clearer understanding of what it really takes to do advanced service-learning well.

Andrew Furco
University of Minnesota, Twin Cities

PART ONE

FOSTERING INTERDEPENDENT RELATIONSHIPS

I

INTRODUCTION

Critical Questions and Directions for the Next Generation of Practitioners

Jean Strait

I t is hard to believe the journey for this book began a year ago. In May 2007, both of us were nominated for the Thomas Ehrlich Award for Faculty Service-Learning, given by Campus Compact. Marybeth was the award winner that year, and I was a finalist. We were brought together for the formal presentation of the award and asked to serve on a panel of finalists as part of a featured presentation at the annual American Association of Colleges and Universities in January 2008. During the panel, an exciting discussion ensued on what may happen in the field of service-learning in the next decade. As we were finishing the presentation, Jon von Knorring, president and publisher of Stylus Publishing, approached us and asked about taking these topics and this conversation to a larger audience through the creation of a book. What follows here is an ongoing conversation about what the issues and challenges will be for what we call the next generation of service-learning leaders.

Why the next generation? Much valuable work has occurred over the last 20 years. Pioneers and leaders of this movement are moving into academic administration, and many are either retiring or are close to retiring. Who will pick up the work? How are we engaging our junior faculty in service-learning and community-based learning? Is this work being valued by institutions and communities? Now that a generation of K–12 students has moved into college and university settings, what is the next step or level of engagement for them?

As we attempt to look at these and other questions, our world continues to evolve into a more globalized society. World problems become everyone's problems. We will have to work together to solve them, and no one country will be able to do it alone. At the time of this writing, President Obama is calling on all citizens to serve. What will this citizenry service look like? How will it affect our schools, communities, economy, and world? What will the new global citizen look like? Truly, time will tell. However, I believe that the service-learning field will have to grapple with the topics presented in this book to grow and evolve in ways that will help continue to bring about positive change in our society.

As we work to become a more global community, we increasingly create further opportunities to share our practices in service-learning. Such opportunities enable us to engage in dialogue that helps interrogate our existing understandings and build a collective intelligence through collaboration. In doing so, service-learning models and our interpretation of them as learning opportunities become subject to different pedagogical and professional contexts that may offer different insights. *Service-learning* is a term used primarily in the United States to depict a mutually beneficial partnership where students provide service and, through the experience, gain valuable learning. The word *service* means to help. However, in international contexts, service can have a more complex or even negative connotation.

For the last decade, *international service-learning* is a term that has been used to denote the work that students from the United States undertake in international contexts with international organizations. Examples of such work and international connections can be found in models created in South Africa (Bender, 2008), East Africa (Johnson-Pynn & Johnson, 2005), Ireland (Murphy, 2008) and Hong Kong (Ngai, 2006). Through such opportunities students' service-learning experiences have brought focus to bear on issues of social justice, intercultural competence, and environmental education. At the same time, the impact of service-learning on life careers has also received attention.

Perhaps significantly, the engagement with international partnerships connected to service-learning activities offers opportunities to consider the definition of service-learning more broadly, particularly in response to the question of "whose learning?" Rather than viewing its international dimension as simply referring to U.S. students engaging in service-learning opportunities in other countries, a broader consideration now embodies the many different models and methods used by international students and practitioners outside the United States in international settings.

Of course, in going beyond geographic, cultural, and professional boundaries we must acknowledge the potential different interpretations of service-learning that may arise. The questions we ask, then, become these:

What is international service-learning?
How is it configured?
What is the purpose?
What models exist and how can those models be replicated?

Service-learning across international settings and developed in complex social and professional contexts may look different in different countries. Although this may pose potential challenges, practitioners must remember that there are essential elements of service-learning, such as reciprocity and reflection. Perhaps we can begin to create international models that use common themes. Once such themes are identified, a more systematic process of developing international models through comparison, analysis, and international collaboration can begin.

This book is divided into three themes. Part I addresses institutional and administrative issues of service-learning. In chapter 2, Strong, Green, Meyer, and Post discuss where service-learning is located on campus and the reasoning and rationale of service-learning placement institutionally. The authors also provide us with several examples of public, private, 2-year, and 4-year institutions, showing how each structure best reflects the needs of the institution served. They take on the current debates of centralized or decentralized engagement and academic or student service leadership, offering recommendations for each.

Chapter 3 authors Gilbert, Johnson, and Plaut tackle sustainability of service-learning programs. With the current economy and multiple ways to define service-learning, some see cutting programs as an effective way to curb spending. The authors stress the voices of community partners, the formation and sustaining of essential partnerships, generation of respect for community knowledge, commitment to building community, and the identification of best practices/attributes that partnerships have in common.

Andy Furco and Barbara Holland, two highly regarded leaders in service-learning research, bring us chapter 4, which covers administrative and institutional issues. These two pioneers have contributed more than 20 years of service to the field. They offer advice to administrators who are taking on service-learning at their institution and present five maxims that can aid in advanced levels of institutionalization of service-learning.

Part II of the book examines service-learning as a springboard for research. In chapter 5, Lorilee Sandmann brings her expertise and leadership skills to bear on promotion and tenure issues in service-learning. She helps move this issue forward by framing service-learning and community engagement as scholarship and provides ways to document and evaluate community-engaged scholarship. She concludes the chapter by using the first-generation work to make recommendations for the second generation. Chapter 6, by Barbara Jacoby, asks tough questions about service-learning. Jacoby's experience allows her to take on complex issues, such as: What counts as service-learning? What value does it bring to institutions? Is service-learning appropriate for all students? What are the issues of globalization of service-learning? She also cautions us to continue to be reflective practitioners, using inquiry-based methods to study service-learning.

Chapter 7 is written by Dr. Joe Erickson, a founding member of the International Center for Service-Learning in Teacher Education at Clemson University and co-editor of the volume *Learning With the Community: Concepts and Models for Service-Learning in Teacher Education*, part of the American Association of Higher Education series on service-learning in the disciplines. An avid practitioner and researcher of service-learning, Dr. Erickson has been contributing to this field for more than 20 years. His institution, Augsburg College in Minneapolis, Minnesota, was one of the first to have a community-based learning center. Experience has led him to investigate the psychological effects of service-learning in chapter 7.

Marybeth Lima takes a highly practical path in chapter 8 to conclude this section. Here she gives us a blueprint for funding, including how to find funding and how to maximize it for service-learning projects and ideas. This chapter can serve as a template for many future practitioners.

Part III, the final section of the text, discusses the future evolution of service-learning. Our colleagues at Leeds Metropolitan University bring us two models of reflective practice that they researched in London, France, and Ireland. Like service-learning colleagues around the world, international practitioners examine the key components of service-learning models and are beginning to implement and research these elements. Here, we offer two models that centralize critical reflection as one potentially defining theme. The first model is Irish Educationalists and the Open Spaces for Dialogue and Enquiry (OSDE) model. The second is English Pre-service Teachers and Internationalization. Both models are unique because they take one component of service-learning—reflection—and use a technique known as critical reflexivity to develop models that connect experiential learning with dialogic, reflective pedagogies and that may offer opportunities for international comparison. This has never been done before. In the next 10 years, we expect that international associations will adopt common terms and that these associations will also call for essential components of service-learning in all contexts to be identified and used. Dr. Tan, Dr. Murphy, and Christine Allan are pioneering this research in Ireland and the United Kingdom. The account in chapter 9 will no doubt lead us to implement and analyze service-learning in global contexts in more systematic ways and to think deeply about the wider opportunities for interconnecting students and professional learning.

In chapter 10, Jean Strait explores using service-learning in online formats and offers a practical framework for enhancing online learning formats by engaging students in service-learning in their own communities. She also discusses how service-learning can be used to provide service locally or globally, as with the *Each One, Teach One* project where students mentored Ninth Ward New Orleans students online and helped them to stay in school and complete projects.

The biggest evolutional changes in service-learning include who is doing the service, what kind of service is done, and exactly what items students are learning. In chapter 11, Tania Mitchell of Stanford University and David Donahue of Mills College bring us the untouched issue of underrepresented populations in service-learning. One of the unspoken realities of service-learning is that it is often carried out by white middle-class students. Mitchell and Donahue challenge the field to address different perspectives and kinds of consciousness. Students of color have very different experiences in service-learning classes, experiencing a dichotomy about the community and service.

In chapter 12, Dr. Rob Shumer guides us through the process of student-led evaluation. He contends that students learn valuable skills to produce reports and systems to help improve communities and the lives of young people who reside there. Dr. Shumer also emphasizes the critical importance of research that engages citizens in the study of their lives, their institutions, and their communities. In chapter 13, Walter Enloe brings us a community-generated vision for a charter school, governed by its students, showing the unique civic engagement possibilities when all participants are involved in citizenship in the community. Dr. Enloe is an expert on Hiroshima, Nagasaki, and the Community Peace Project. He uses this exclusive background to help create and shepherd this "living democracy" for Avalon High School and supports learning environments that allow for passionate, self-motivated, lifelong learners.

In the Epilogue, Marybeth Lima concludes the book by addressing the need for development of students as complex problem solvers. As the service-learning field continues to struggle with specific issues, it will also help move forward potential solutions for global problems and the development of human skills necessary to avert global problems. In 2000, Thomas Ehrlich argued that moral responsibility and civic responsibility are inseparable. If we want a future citizenry that lives these two as one, we must begin today to be more intentional about teaching those principles as one. We must be willing to show students what integrity is and how it can be used to best serve communities and each other.

We hope you find the following chapters not only useful, but inspiring. Our goal is for this text to be used as a guidebook and handbook for many generations of service-learners. We hope you enjoy reading and using it!

References

Bender, G. (2008). Exploring conceptual models for community rngagement at higher education institutions in South Africa. *Perspectives in Education, 26*(1), 81–95.

Johnson-Pynn, J., & Johnson, L. (2005). Successes and challenges in East African conservation education. *Journal of Environmental Education, 36*(12), 25.

Murphy, T. (2008). Democratic schooling practices in the Republic of Ireland: The gaps between the rhetoric and reality. *Irish Educational Studies, 27*(1), 29–39.

Ngai, S.S. (2006). Service-learning, personal development, and social commitment: A case study of university students in Hong Kong. *Adolescence, 41*(161), 165.

2

FUTURE DIRECTIONS IN CAMPUS-COMMUNITY PARTNERSHIPS

Location of Service-Learning Offices and Activities in Higher Education

Elizabeth Carmichael Strong, Patrick M. Green, Micki Meyer, and Margaret A. Post

Over the last 10 years, tremendous growth has occurred in the number of young educators working in the field of service-learning. Many of us came to the work of service-learning because of a direct experience we had as undergraduates, graduate students, or young professionals. Whether we regularly volunteered at a social service agency in college, were active in building new partnerships with a local organization, or conducted graduate-level community-based action research projects, these community relationships shaped our commitment to this field. Through these experiences, we came to believe that one critical pathway to realizing a more just society is participation in campus–community partnerships as engaged scholars, teachers, and practitioners. We learned that both teaching and learning could happen in the community context, and that—on the bridge between the classroom and our local communities—we are able to build mutually beneficial and transformative relationships.

This inspiration roots our commitment to bringing the resources of colleges and universities to bear on the most pressing concerns of the cities and towns in which we live and learn. Our educational experiences prompt us to seek professional opportunities where we could participate in educating young people about civic engagement. Today, we each hold positions in different types of colleges and universities where we are responsible for facilitating these pathways. As scholar–practitioners, we seek strategies to strengthen our institutions' ability to do this work effectively and sustainably, while also extending the knowledge resources of institutions to the process of community problem solving. Building on the work of other leaders in service-learning, this chapter explores our practice in the institutionalized, community-based learning structures of higher education and focuses on the benefits, challenges, and opportunities to move our work toward deeper, transformational learning inherent in campus–community partnerships.

Institutionalization is a familiar topic among educators creating sustainable models, structures and engaged departments that fully support service-learning at every level of the institution. Institutionalization occurs when colleges and universities align mission, curriculum, resources (human and fiscal), and faculty reward structures to support and enhance community-engaged activities. Institutionalization on college campuses does not happen overnight. It requires long-term strategic planning that involves diverse voices and ongoing efforts through organizational change to create shared capacity and common goals. Although learning outcomes associated with service-learning and strategies for faculty involvement and curriculum design have received significant attention in the literature, *how* to institutionalize service-learning is also a theme that has generated numerous articles and publications. In addition, from Campus Compact's Professional Development Institutes to other national and regional conferences, best practices for institutionalizing service-learning have been communicated on many fronts. Presently, many colleges and universities have an office or center responsible for service-learning.

A review of the service-learning literature reveals that commonly accepted organizational practices include: (a) hiring a full-time professional dedicated to service-learning, (b) establishing a centralized office to coordinate service-learning, (c) funding the office and its staff with institutional funds, and (d) housing it under the chief academic officer's or provost's office (Bringle & Hatcher, 1996, 2000; Furco, 2002; Holland, 1997). As scholar–practitioners in the field, we have built upon this foundation of best practices for institutionalizing service-learning. The focus of this chapter is not on the theories, rubrics, or heuristics of institutionalizing service-learning, but rather on the practice of service-learning in institutions. We focus on practical insights from current organizational approaches to community-based learning with an eye toward the institutional dynamics and contemporary trends that assist the implementation of service-learning. Our rationale is rooted in a collective understanding that engaged learning is central to the undergraduate experience today, and that our institutions can adopt structural arrangements that facilitate sustainable service-learning programs.

Location, Location, Location

Should service-learning be located under student affairs, academic affairs, or be university wide? Where does service-learning find its home in higher education? Does reporting structure and physical location increase or decrease the value of service-learning? The answers to these questions appear to depend on who responds. Limited research suggests that centralizing service-learning under the chief academic office aids in institutionalizing it in the academy, especially in regard to obtaining buy-in from faculty (Bringle & Hatcher, 2000). Yet research on the institutionalization of service-learning recognizes various placements of service-learning in the academy. For example, Furco's *Self-Assessment Rubric for the Institutionalization of Service-Learning in Higher Education* (2002) emphasizes the need for a coordinating center or office of service-learning and the support of faculty and academic departments, but it does not specify a preferred location for service-learning offices in the academy. Because research is limited on this subject, it is not clear whether location changes the perception of service-learning by students and community partners. Likewise, we know that if the variables of staff support, easy access, and clear direction remain constant between student affairs and academic affairs offices, office placement does not necessarily affect the appeal or outcome of service-learning experiences.

Faculty, however, adopt the pedagogy more readily when it is found under the academic affairs umbrella (Bringle & Hatcher, 2004). Faculty members seek the blessing of academic affairs to legitimize their work in research, teaching, and service. Even those faculty members who pursue community-based scholarship must reconcile their interests with institutional tenure policies. When a service-learning office is tied to the chief academic officer, research suggests that service-learning gains a greater degree of institutionalization on campus (Bringle & Hatcher, 2000). Moreover, such placement is critical in underscoring its pedagogical value to faculty members' careers.

The first step—and key to supporting the work—is the decision to invest in sustaining an office of service-learning. After that choice is confirmed, a number of institutional structures for service-learning in higher education exist. Decisions about location, reporting lines, and organizational scope often depend on institutional mission and organizational culture. Many centers and offices—whether using the name *community service, community-based learning, service-learning,* or *public service*—work toward student involvement in the community through a variety of tools of experiential education. Currently, the most common structural elements are as follows:

- Centers and offices for service-learning/community-based learning, community or public service, and volunteerism
- Centers and offices of community-based research
- Centers and offices for community partnerships and/or public engagement
- Service-learning faculty councils (often advisory to a center or office)
- Dedicated staff or faculty positions, often housed within a center or office

Table 2.1 further distinguishes the primary structures and functions of service-learning offices in the college or university setting.

According to the 1999 Service-Learning Needs Assessment of UCLA's Service-Learning Clearinghouse Project, 70% of all service-learning centers were housed in academic affairs offices and 30% were placed in student affairs offices. In National Campus Compact's 2005 member survey, 40% of service offices, or persons with service-learning responsibility, reported to a student affairs office, while 34% reported to academic affairs. The remaining 16% either reported to more than one office or to a specific center, office, department, or person. These findings from past surveys indicate a variety of placements in student affairs and academic affairs programs.

However, Bringle and Hatcher (2004) note the importance of establishing and maintaining the academic integrity of civic engagement in academic affairs and apart from student affairs. According to the National Service-Learning Clearinghouse's *Institutional Structures for Service-Learning in Higher Education* (2008), "Many offices initially housed within Student

TABLE 2.1
Primary Structures and Functions of Service-Learning Placement

Divisional location	⇨ Academic or student affairs
Subunit structure	⇨ Centers or offices within departments
Function	⇨ Oversight, management, and implementation of: • Service or community-based learning • Community or public service programs/volunteerism • Community-based research • Institution-wide community engagement initiatives
Types of staffing	⇨ Full-time administrator ⇨ Full-time faculty ⇨ Program coordinator ⇨ Administrative support staff ⇨ Volunteer student leaders or work-study positions

Affairs have either shifted to Academic Affairs or developed a dual affiliation in order to secure greater administrative support and credibility for service-learning." Recent literature and research on service-learning emphasizes that the location of service-learning varies by institutional priorities but calls attention to the significant support by academic affairs (National Service-Learning Clearinghouse, 2008).

From the Edge to the Center: Examples of the Engaged Campus

As colleges and universities continue to provide quality experiences for 21st-century realities, many administrators and faculty see community engagement as a vehicle driving learning. Some campuses have committed to moving community-based learning experiences from the edge of the educational experience to the center. They have realigned academic curriculum with the necessary resources, personnel, and budgets to reflect a commitment to engaged learning and campus–community partnerships that facilitate such learning. This institutional commitment (known as *institutionalization*) provides campuses the unique opportunity to enhance and grow service-learning offerings for students in hopes of creating an engaged campus that is in unison with community interests and needs.

Creating a fully engaged campus is no easy task. Campuses need to match mission and values with specific resources, organizational structures, and curriculum, which often leads to reshuffling priorities, offices, and roles on campus. Everyone on campus—administrators, faculty, students, and staff alike—is a key stakeholder in building and sustaining campus–community learning partnerships. Faculty, practitioners, and students are recruited, selected, and rewarded for their involvement whether it is through scholarship, teaching, direct service, or outreach. Executive leadership and other administrators are called to make consistent statements about the institution's commitment to community engagement, while also backing up those commitments with the tangible resources and support to realize the vision of the engaged campus.

The colleges and universities discussed in the following subsections serve as exemplars of the engaged campus. They illustrate various benefits and challenges of structural arrangements drawn directly from our experience as scholar–practitioners. Many of these campuses were selected for the 2008 Carnegie Classification for Community Engagement. In addition, these examples represent a cross section of university types and geographical regions and are based on the work of National Campus Compact's Engaged Scholars for New Perspectives in Higher Education (ESNPHE). ESNPHE is composed of a group of scholar–practitioners engaged in dialogue about the future of service-learning and community engagement in the 21st century. At each institution, the Engaged Scholars serve primarily as "boundary crossers." Often, they wear multiple hats as faculty, administrators, scholars, and community practitioners.

We provide these institutional examples, and our reflections on their benefits and challenges, to highlight the range of approaches that colleges and universities have used to institutionalize community-based experience, including service-learning. No one example is a blueprint model: There is no "right" way to construct such a center because each depends upon many variables unique to its institution. Rather, we draw upon these examples to illustrate what we believe are the central opportunities and potential barriers to strengthening our work for the long term. Table 2.2 compiles our findings about the example colleges into an easy-to-read format for comparison.

College of the Holy Cross

The College of the Holy Cross is an undergraduate, liberal arts college in the Jesuit tradition with a time-honored commitment to service and social

TABLE 2.2
Research Findings from Example Institutions

Institution	Institutional Type	Service-Learning Location/Reporting	Description of Service-Learning	Service-Learning Leadership	Staff Structure	Year Established
College of the Holy Cross	Private, Catholic (liberal arts undergraduate in the Jesuit tradition)	Primary: Academic Affairs Secondary: Center for Interdisciplinary Studies	Community-based learning	Director responsible for program leadership, faculty and curriculum development, and oversight of community-based learning partnerships	⇧ Director ⇧ Full-time AmeriCorps VISTA volunteer ⇧ Part-time administrative assistant	2001
De Anza Community College	Public (2-year undergraduate general and vocational education)	Primary: Academic Services Secondary: Institute of Community and Civic Engagement	Community service-learning	Director responsible for program leadership, faculty and curriculum development, and oversight of community-based learning partnerships	⇧ Director ⇧ Part-time student administrative assistant ⇧ Part-time student program coordinators ⇧ Part-time curriculum faculty trainers	2006
Loyola University of Chicago	Private, Catholic, Jesuit, doctorate-granting, research intensive	Primary: Academic Affairs Secondary: Center for Experiential Learning under the Office of the Provost	Service-learning and community-engaged learning	Director primarily responsible for program development, faculty development, curriculum development, and community partnerships with significant support from and collaboration of service-learning coordinator	⇧ Director ⇧ Service-learning coordinator ⇧ Academic internship coordinator ⇧ Full-time AmeriCorps VISTA volunteer as community-based Federal work-study coordinator ⇧ Graduate assistant	2007

TABLE 2.2 (Continued)

Institution	Institutional Type	Service-Learning Location/Reporting	Description of Service-Learning	Service-Learning Leadership	Staff Structure	Year Established
Missouri State University	Public, comprehensive	Primary: Academic Affairs	Academic community-based learning	Associate director responsible for student and faculty program leadership, faculty development, oversight of community-based partnerships	⇧ Associate director ⇧ Program coordinator ⇧ Administrative assistant ⇧ Two graduate assistants	1996
Otterbein College	Private, independent comprehensive liberal arts college affiliated with the United Methodist Church	Primary: Student Affairs Secondary: Center for Community Engagement	Academically based community service	Director of Center for Community Engagement responsible for community outreach, partnerships, coordination of service-learning course development, extracurricular community service, and community-based undergraduate research	⇧ Director ⇧ Assistant director ⇧ Program coordinator ⇧ Faculty service-learning liaison ⇧ AmeriCorps VISTA volunteer	1994 Community Service 2003 Center for Community Engagement
Rollins College	Private, liberal arts	Primary: Office of Community Engagement Secondary: Academic Affairs, Office of the Dean of Faculty for Arts and Sciences	Community engagement*	Director responsible for vision and leadership; curricular and co-curricular programming, including curriculum development; oversight of community partnerships; funding; and college priorities in community engagement activities	⇧ Full-time director ⇧ Full-time assistant director ⇧ Graduate assistant ⇧ Community and office coordinator ⇧ Four Federal Work-Study student assistants	2001

Community engagement is the umbrella term for activities that involve direct service, civic engagement, and community-based research. *Service-learning* is used to describe a pedagogical approach to community engagement through academic courses linked to curriculum.

16

justice. It serves 2,600 undergraduate students. Located in Worcester, Massachusetts—a midsized, postindustrial city in central Massachusetts—Holy Cross involves more than a quarter of the student population in cross-curricular, engaged learning experiences. In each division of the institution, staff are charged with providing some dimension of experiential education, specifically community involvement in Worcester. Four major program areas include (a) service-learning courses, (b) academic and summer internships, (c) more than 40 student-led volunteer programs through Student Programs for Urban Development (SPUD), and (d) community work study. These programs are each directed by different offices, predominantly housed in either the divisions of academic affairs or student affairs. Moreover, the executive leadership of the institution has long supported community involvement by actively promoting its value as integral to the Holy Cross mission of educating young people to be mentors for others.

To oversee service-learning, the Donelan Office of Community-Based Learning (CBL) was established in 2001 with a gift from alumnus Joseph P. Donelan ('72). It is part of the Center for Interdisciplinary and Special Studies in Academic Affairs and works with faculty to design CBL curriculum; arrange community partner sites; and monitor and evaluate the pedagogical and community-based experiences of faculty, students, and community partners. Many students who participate in CBL courses also participate in internships and volunteer programs, all of which contribute to their engaged learning experience at Holy Cross.

Because multiple areas of Holy Cross are involved in community engagement, the Community Engagement Committee acts as a central coordinating structure for these initiatives and includes members from all divisions, including Academic Affairs (Donelan Office of Community-Based Learning, academic internships, and the teacher education program), Athletics, the Chaplain's Office (volunteer and immersion programs), summer internship program, the President's Office (community work study), and Student Affairs. The group meets monthly, reports to the president, and is chaired by the director of the Donelan Office.

De Anza Community College

Located 45 miles south of San Francisco, De Anza Community College occupies a 112-acre site in Cupertino in the heart of Silicon Valley. Serving a diverse population of more than 23,000 students per year, De Anza regularly ranks as one of the top three institutions in California in terms of the number of students it transfers to the University of California and California State University systems. De Anza's Institute of Community and Civic Engagement advances education for democracy by empowering students to be agents of change in the social, economic, and political realities of their lives, communities, and beyond.

Housed in Academic Services, which reports to the Vice President of Instruction, De Anza's Institute of Community and Civic Engagement provides faculty and students the tools for purposeful engagement in creating social change. Academically, community service-learning (CSL) is a form of experiential education in which students apply knowledge, skills, critical thinking, and good judgment to pressing local community needs. At De Anza, CSL is either infused in academic courses or can be attached as additional credit in general education courses in all disciplines. Students can also obtain a Leadership and Social Change certificate of achievement by taking a series of CSL courses and engaging in community-based learning special topics courses. Co-curricular programs include Youth Voices United for Change, a leadership conference that connects high school and college students to community-based youth and student organizations, and the Community Scholars in Residence Program, which brings community organizers and leaders to De Anza College as co-educators to provide lectures, workshops, and team-teaching opportunities with students and staff.

Loyola University Chicago

Loyola University Chicago is the largest Jesuit Catholic university and the largest Catholic Research institution in the nation. It is situated in a major metropolitan area—the city of Chicago—with three campuses in Chicago and one campus in Rome. The institution is committed to the promise of "preparing people to lead extraordinary lives." Loyola University Chicago was founded in 1870 and enrolls more than 15,600 students, including more than 10,100 undergraduates hailing from all 50 states and 82 foreign countries. Community engagement is a focus in Loyola's mission: "We are Chicago's Jesuit Catholic University—a diverse community seeking God in all things and working to expand knowledge in the service of humanity through learning, justice and faith," and Loyola's vision: "to seek new knowledge in the service of humanity in a world-renowned urban center as members of a diverse learning community that values freedom of inquiry, the pursuit of truth and care for others" (www.luc.edu/).

Several departments and centers at Loyola engage in community-based learning and service work. University Ministry, part of the Division of Mission and Ministry, houses the co-curricular community service program and the Alternative Break Immersion program. The Center for Urban Research and Learning (CURL) is the university hub for community-based research, offering faculty fellowships, graduate fellowships, and undergraduate research fellowships for engaged research with community partners. A number of academic departments are engaged in community work, including the schools of nursing, education, social work, medicine, and various academic departments such as psychology and sociology.

The Center for Experiential Learning (CEL), under the Office of the Provost, is an academic support service for faculty, students, and staff and houses the service-learning program, the academic internship program, the community-based Federal Work-Study Program, and undergraduate research. The CEL is the university's central structure for community-engaged learning and engaged scholarship. The CEL staff consists of a director, service-learning coordinator, academic internship coordinator, AmeriCorps VISTA volunteer (who coordinates the community-based Federal Work-Study Program), and a graduate assistant.

Missouri State University

Founded in 1905 as Missouri State Normal School, Missouri State University has grown into one of the nation's leading public, multi-campus, metropolitan universities. With an enrollment of nearly 21,000 students, Missouri State University is the second largest university in Missouri and offers approximately 150 undergraduate programs and more than 40 graduate programs. Missouri State's statewide mission of public affairs frames the work of this academic community. The university is devoted to educating students well; addressing important questions through front edge research; and helping the region, Missouri, and the nation imagine and create a better future.

The Office of Citizenship and Service-Learning (CASL) was established by Missouri State's Faculty Senate through a senate action in 1996, one year after Missouri Governor Mel Carnahan signed into law Senate Bill 340, which gave Missouri State a statewide mission in public affairs. CASL was established under Academic Affairs as a program intended to strengthen the university's bonds with the community and to provide Missouri State students with opportunities to practice citizenship. Three primary goals of CASL are to (a) support faculty in their careers of scholarship, which includes both their activities in teaching and research; (b) ensure and enhance the quality of students' service-learning experience; and (c) develop and maintain long-term, reciprocal, positive relationships with community partners. CASL program oversight is provided by an ad hoc committee of the faculty senate, which ensures the program's fidelity with program guidelines and maintains a strong relationship with faculty. The office reports to the Associate Provost for Student Development and Public Affairs and is located in the Plaster Student Union, the living room of the university. CASL staff includes an associate director, program coordinator, administrative assistant, and two graduate assistants. Staff members collaborate with the Campus Volunteer Center, Student Community Action Team, Student Affairs, and the Center for Social Issues Institute.

Otterbein College

Otterbein College, located in Westerville, Ohio, has been an engaged campus since its founding in 1847 as an institution for teachers, preachers, and early missionaries traveling to Sierra Leone in Africa to build orphanages and for professors and students working together in the abolitionist and prohibitionist movements of the 19th and 20th centuries. Efforts to engage with the community are scattered across more than a century of the history of Otterbein, with early course-based service projects evolving in the education and health departments, active student service groups emerging in Student Affairs, and undergraduate research projects permeating the disciplines.

Community engagement became centralized in 2003 in the Center for Community Engagement (CCE) housed in the Student Affairs division. The CCE acts as gateway to the community, brokering partnerships and acting as a portal to resources to support community efforts. The CCE brings together student volunteerism, service-learning, and community-based research by housing several campus initiatives including service-learning courses, community-based research fellows, student service scholarship opportunities, and faculty-in-residence programs.

Rollins College

In Winter Park, Florida, Rollins College serves as home for 1,750 undergraduate arts and science students and an additional 1,500 M.B.A. and evening students. As expressed through the words of Rollins Vice President for Academic Affairs and Provost Dr. Roger Casey, "The mission of Rollins is to educate students for global citizenship and responsible leadership and the heart of this mission is community engagement." Community engagement is a fundamental piece of the Rollins student and faculty experience.

The Office of Community Engagement (OCE) at Rollins serves as the clearinghouse for campus–community partnerships in learning. OCE fosters, encourages, and promotes student, faculty, and staff involvement in local and global communities. Through service-learning courses, community-based research, leadership development, community service, and innovative programs and resources, the Office of Community Engagement is deeply committed to fostering a lifelong commitment to social justice, civic engagement, and social responsibility in every member of the Rollins community. This is done through three strategic priorities: the scholarship of engagement, the engaged campus, and community partnerships and development.

OCE is housed in Academic Affairs under the Dean of Faculty in the College of Arts and Sciences. Office structure includes a director, who oversees staffing, academic partnerships, and the strategic vision and plan for community engagement; an assistant director, who works with office programs, events, and student organizations focused on service and community partnerships; an administrative assistant, who oversees budget and day-to-day administrative operations; a graduate assistant, who works with assessment and on the ground with faculty and students in campus–community partnerships; and three Federal Work-Study students. OCE works closely with a number of programs and areas on campus that focus on community and learning, including the Community Engagement Fellows Team, Arts and Sciences Faculty Governance, Faculty-Student Collaborative Research Program, and the Offices of Multicultural Affairs, Student Involvement and Leadership, International Programs, Academic Internships, and Explorations First Year Programs.

Benefits and Challenges of Service-Learning Office Placement

The preceding examples invite scholar–practitioners to ask how service-learning practice fits into institutions' civic missions and to evaluate in ongoing ways how programmatic efforts reflect those missions. In the examples, the criticality of where service-learning is located is apparent, as is the fact that its structural arrangements can be guided by an institution's lived commitment to community engagement. The ways in which engaged learning is embedded in a range of institutional structures and in collaboration with varying stakeholder groups reveal how an institution understands this commitment (a theme that is also highlighted by the Community Engagement classification of the Carnegie Foundation for the Advancement of Teaching). The examples provided substantiate the premise that institutional mission, decisions about structure and organization of service-learning and community engagement, and their integration across the institution drive sources of support, especially institution-wide and departmental funding streams.

From the examples, three particularly relevant themes emerge about the benefits and challenges of the location, structural arrangement, and institutionalization of service-learning. As higher learning institutions attempt to organize and reshuffle existing structures, it is important to consider how benefits and challenges can affect stakeholders and the long-term viability of service-learning as both a pedagogy and a field of study. Here are the three themes:

1. Academic affairs or student affairs?

Most community engagement structures mentioned in this chapter house centers or offices in traditional academic affairs departments. However, these centers and offices are closely connected with student affairs departments, staff, and administrators.

Historically, community engagement offices that provided students with opportunities for community service and co-curricular field experiences evolved through student affairs departments and divisions. From the mid-1990s through today, colleges and universities created parallel service-learning offices that reported through academic affairs and that focused on academic service-learning curriculum, development, and outcomes. Service-learning offices were separate from existing volunteer and community service centers and efforts in student affairs units.

However, over time we have learned that when service-learning is housed within academic affairs, faculty are able to influence and direct service-learning curriculum on campus. With the direct involvement of and reporting to senior academic affairs administration, especially in scholarship and research, service-learning in this context gains a different kind of academic legitimacy. When community engagement is housed in student affairs, practitioners must engage in intentional partnerships with academic affairs to cultivate learning beyond the classroom. Opportunities for professional development in engaged pedagogies and practices that include both faculty and staff allow for curricular and co-curricular enhancement and provide a pathway for powerful partnerships in education to be forged across divisions.

As the field evolves with growing legitimacy, awareness, and support of community engagement across the academy, and more intentional efforts are geared toward community needs and assets, colleges and universities are thinking more strategically about placement. Offices that have student learning and community needs at the heart of their mission recognize the value of campus movements that involve both academic and student affairs educators. Reflection, learning, and sustainability are the bridges between academic affairs and student affairs partnerships in community engagement.

2. *Centralized versus decentralized debate.*

As the practice of service-learning has evolved, centralizing engagement has become a hot topic. Many colleges and universities, even large research institutions, are beginning to merge multiple areas of community engagement under one umbrella, including leadership education, international programs, community service and volunteerism, internships, and experiential education. Shifts in understanding engagement as a fundamental part of the college experience have led educators and administrators to consolidate program areas to create synergy around civic learning and outcomes. In addition, competing pressures such as budget constraints and cuts, especially at large public institutions, have catalyzed this shift. Moreover, some institutions are beginning to rethink the boundaries between student affairs and academic affairs and are attempting to provide more centralized and integrated approaches to campus–community partnerships that cross the divisional divide.

The benefit of a centralized structure for community engagement is that service-learning centers and offices, along with their campus neighbors, can serve as an epicenter for campus–community partnerships. Community partners, faculty, staff, and students can clearly identify the office as the key point of entry for engagement. A centralized infrastructure can provide a convening space on campus, one that is situated at the crossroads of academic programming and other dimensions of campus life. With this type of structural arrangement, duplication of campus efforts and silos can more readily be identified and redirected. There is a clear point of entry into the college community for community agencies, providing greater possibilities for effective partnerships and sustainability across curricular and co-curricular pathways. With these benefits, however, can also come the expectation that *everything* related to campus–community partnerships must have coordination, oversight, and funding from the same office.

Because of the nature of large institutions and their need to serve multiple stakeholders, decentralized approaches to community engagement are also common. The benefit of a decentralized structure is that each department and center has responsibility for a specific program. Many times, departments and centers are natural collaborators because of the nature of their work and civic outcomes. The challenge of a decentralized structure is the absence of a central mechanism to report, communicate, and evaluate or assess the community-engaged work of the institution. Often duplications of programs and efforts exist. Community partners many times can become confused on how best to connect with the university. Students also can have difficulties connecting the dots of their educational experiences when involved in multiple departments.

According to the National Service-Learning Clearinghouse (2008), some key questions to consider when evaluating the most appropriate structure for an institution include the following:

- Where is service-learning (and other kinds of civic and community engagement) already happening on campus? Who is actively involved and/or supportive?
- What is working well, and what improvements would you or others like to see?
- How can service-learning be tied to other major campus initiatives or objectives?
- How are community partnerships developed and maintained?
- Where can new or existing service-learning efforts offer meaningful leadership opportunities for students? For community partners?

Add to this list these questions:

- What structure will most effectively promote the mission of the institution?

- What structure will most effectively promote the learning outcomes in the curriculum and the objectives of the program?

3. *Attempts to build synergy in service-learning office placement.*

How can universities successfully pull together various program areas focused on campus–community partnerships in learning? How can educators effectively partner when historically many have experienced sensitivity about territory and expertise? The example institutions reveal that many campuses are beginning to understand the importance of tending to organizational structure and placement of service-learning, community engagement, and community service programs. Housing them in the same facility alone is consistent with the belief that proximity can lead to greater collaboration and relationship building. Faculty and community partners are able to access multiple areas of expertise and resources clearly and effectively through one point of entry. Students are able to connect their community engagement experiences by getting involved in multiple campus efforts and partnerships in the curriculum and co-curriculum. Faculty, academic affairs administrators, and student affairs educators are able to engage in powerful ways through these kinds of opportunities for relationship building and expertise sharing.

Some colleges and universities that are unable to physically house community engagement areas together are starting to create campus-wide committees and advisory boards that cut across academic and student affairs. Often chaired and co-chaired by senior-level administrators and/or faculty, these boards are responsible for serving as a clearinghouse for all academic courses, community-based research, programs, activities, and events between the campus and community. Boards have also been created to streamline assessment of outcomes and activities and move the strategic vision of curricular and co-curricular community engagement forward.

Moving Ahead: Recommendations for the Future of Service-Learning

To move service-learning into the 21st century we must take a step back to reflect on and argue the *why* of service-learning. Through service-learning, students can identify the complex systems and structures of our world in their lived experiences, linking course theory to practice. We also understand and recognize that this learning may take place in environments, including structures of higher education, which are inherently equally complex and unjust.

Thus, in order to meet the challenges of global community, service-learning offices of today cannot operate in a context of division and silos. Often, competition and conflict arise on college campuses between areas with similar involvement in the community, including volunteer offices, civic and public service departments, community-based research centers, experiential learning, and leadership education programs. To cultivate greater collaboration and support, senior administrators should publicly celebrate campus collaboration and be actively involved in bringing areas together in partnership. As we have demonstrated, this can happen through physical office placement or by creating campus-wide advisory boards for community engagement that serve as an umbrella for all campus–community partnerships. A clearly structured and unified campus moving in one direction provides greater opportunity for progress and social change in the global community.

To that end, many service-learning offices connect academic affairs, student affairs, and the community. Faculty and administrative staff alike must learn strategies that cross divisional lines and bring together multiple stakeholders to discuss opportunities for campus–community partnerships. As the field has grown, we have witnessed service-learning offices becoming a critical point of entry to the campus for the community. Colleges and universities can therefore be strategic in physical placement of service-learning offices to provide the best opportunity for on-campus partnerships and synergy.

Even with strategic placement of a service-learning office or center at an institution, the academy must work to move beyond boundaries and divisions by asking difficult questions about knowledge, expertise, insight, and perceived power on college campuses.

Critical questions to consider while analyzing structures of service-learning on campus may include:

- Is the current structure of service-learning meeting the most pressing issues and opportunities in the community through collaborative and sustainable methods?
- Does the current placement of offices that house service-learning activities (structure) simultaneously meet the needs of students and faculty (function)?

- What area of campus has the most influence in service-learning to create policy, utilize resources, and build capacity? Who is best positioned to engage students in service while meeting critical learning outcomes and goals?
- How can resources (human and fiscal) focused on campus-community partnerships be shared among offices and departments in order to meet 21st century realities?
- How can data collected by offices that house service-learning activities be used to create greater opportunities for shared community-engaged scholarship among multiple areas of campus?
- Are offices of service-learning held accountable for cross-campus partnerships and collaboration through annual review? Are there systems in place to enable community partners to evaluate current structures of service-learning, placement of offices, and campus effectiveness in creating progress in the community?
- How can colleges/universities create environments and celebrate opportunities for synergy among all constituencies (faculty, staff, students, and community partners) in order to create sustainable systems that aim for institutionalization and the common good?

Fundamental to this approach are underlying questions of motivation: Why do we do what we do? Who are the educators on college campuses today and at the academy of tomorrow? How can we work for justice in our communities *and* educate young people for engaged citizenship? These questions guide our broader philosophical orientation to the structural dilemmas we face and, in practice, shape our approach to responding to these challenges.

To take seriously the call for mutually beneficial and reciprocal relationships with our community partners, the work of such an office should be *interdisciplinary, interdepartmental,* and *interrelational.* This suggests a new set of critical questions be used on a regular basis to evaluate and assess service-learning at institutions:

Interdisciplinary
- What disciplinary outcomes are associated with service-learning?
- What personal development outcomes are associated with service-learning?

- What civic development outcomes are associated with service-learning?
- What career development outcomes are associated with service-learning?

Interdepartmental

- What coordinating entity on campus is supportive of and engaging in service-learning?
- What academic departments are supportive of and engaging in service-learning?
- What student affairs departments are supportive of and engaging in service-learning?
- What administrative departments are supportive of and engaging in service-learning?

Interrelational

- What relationships have been formed through service-learning with community partners as co-educators?
- What relationships have been formed through service-learning with faculty as co-educators?
- What relationships have been formed through service-learning with student affairs staff as co-educators?
- What relationships have been formed through service-learning with other university staff as co-educators?
- What relationships have been formed through service-learning with students as co-educators?

As we move into a new era in higher education, colleges and universities that seek to grow community-engaged learning have an opportunity to promote the work of educators in all areas of campus, especially those with the knowledge, skills, and capacity for building bridges to the community. Therefore, recognizing service-learning as interdisciplinary, interdepartmental, and interrelational frames it through a multidimensional lens and situates it more solidly in both an academic and community context.

Summary of Recommendations

Based on our assessment of the benefits and challenges we face as scholar–practitioners, and from this multidimensional perspective, we make the following recommendations to generate new conversations about the future of service-learning in higher education and to promote sustainable organizational practices. Table 2.3 also provides a set of examples to accompany each recommendation.

- Create venues for interdepartmental collaboration in the academy.
- Extend education space to the community, recognizing that the four walls of the classroom extend to the community partner organization.
- Create models of community–university co-education in which classes are held at the community site and community partners are invited into the classroom in recognition of the fact that community partners are co-educators.

TABLE 2.3
Example Facilities Implementing Recommendations

Recommendation	Examples
Interdepartmental collaboration	College of the Holy Cross De Anza Community College Loyola University Chicago Missouri State University Otterbein College Rollins College
Community education space on campus	College of the Holy Cross Loyola University Chicago Rollins College
Community–university co-education with community partners as co-educators and co-researchers in participatory community-based research	Loyola University Chicago Missouri State University Rollins College
Integration of civic-oriented learning outcomes with curriculum	Loyola University Chicago Missouri State University Otterbein College
Cross-campus community partnerships	De Anza Community College Missouri State University Rollins College
Campus-wide dialogues and education forums about value and impact of campus–community partnerships	Otterbein College Rollins College
Community partner representation on advisory boards	Loyola University Chicago Missouri State University

- Identify shared locations in the community that can serve as meeting spaces for campus–community synergy in creating progress toward the common good.
- Strategically plan from an outcomes-based perspective by articulating clear, developmental learning outcomes in the institution's core curriculum (e.g., to develop citizenship or to develop leadership skills in the community).
- Focus on community partnerships that can be developed across campus units so that community partners connect with multiple departments, offices, and programs.
- Promote campus dialogue about who bears the onus of learning in the community context and develop action steps for how multiple stakeholders (faculty, professional staff, students, and community partners) can share in that responsibility.
- Develop opportunities for shared funding (federal, private, and institutional) to meet goals of both campus and community.
- Invite community partners to participate in advisory boards, as co-educators in the classroom and as co-researchers in participatory community-based research, thus operating *in*, *with*, and *for* the community through collaboratively developed partnerships.

Although many institutions are striving toward deeper and more meaningful learning and collaboration with the community, further research needs to be conducted on campuses that fully align resources, efforts, and effectiveness through an interdisciplinary, interdepartmental, and interrelational framework.

These recommendations suggest a new perspective that operates from an asset-based community development approach. If higher education institutions establish and support service-learning offices, the scaffolding to support such offices must be the mission-driven learning objectives as well as the community needs to which the service is directed. In other words, we need to operate within the community, not just within the institution.

As scholar–practitioners, we have noted the ongoing institutionalization of service-learning across campuses. Yet the practice has consistently been to promote service-learning from the institutional point of view—involving faculty, engaging students, establishing full-time and dedicated staff. If service-learning emphasizes the reciprocity between service in the community and learning, as well as the mutually beneficial relationship among the student learners, university, and the community, then we need to situate service-learning from a community development point of view.

To accurately position service-learning in a community development model, we need to approach service-learning projects, site placements, and community-based work from a community capacity-building perspective. In other words, with the community members we must answer the question: "How does this community work build the capacity of the community or organization?" For example, Kretzmann and McKnight (2005) provide the Asset-Based Community Development (ABCD) model as an asset-mapping tool to understand the communities and organizations in which we are working. In this model, we are challenged to identify the assets of the community and its organizations from a strength-based perspective.

Our work in service-learning often operates from a needs-based perspective because we continuously frame such work through community-defined needs rather than community-identified assets and capacity. As long as we position community-based work strictly from a needs-based perspective, we diminish reciprocal relationships and establish a hierarchical dynamic reflective of the ivory tower reaching down to the community. When we approach service-learning through the lens of community development and capacity building, we are open to what the community organization and neighborhoods around us can teach us. It is then that we become more civically engaged, and as citizens, we move from working *for* to working *with* the community and *in* the community.

Conclusion

Service-learning educators have the responsibility to be reflective as well as reflexive in meeting 21st century realities through purpose, practice, and partnership. Sustainable models that support service-learning at every level of the institution include institutional structures that build synergy among educators, share critical resources, and enable community partners to serve in key roles in the learning experience. As the field of community-engaged learning and practice continues to grow and evolve, colleges and universities committed to analyzing and evolving service-learning structures, curriculum, and activities will be better equipped to respond to the greatest challenges and opportunities in campus–community partnerships and engaged scholarship.

References

Abes, E., Jackson, G., & Jones, S. (2002, Fall). Factors that motivate and deter faculty use of service-learning. *Michigan Journal of Community Service-Learning, 9*, 5–17.

Bringle, R., & Hatcher, J. (1996, March/April). Implementing service-learning in higher education. *Journal of Higher Education, 67*(2).

Bringle, R., & Hatcher, J. (2000, May/June). Institutionalization of service-learning in higher education. *Journal of Higher Education, 71*(3), 273–290.

Bringle, R., & Hatcher J. (2004). Advancing civic engagement through service-learning. In M. Langseth & W. M. Plater (Eds.), *Public work and the academy: An academic administrator's guide to civic engagement and service-learning* (pp. 125–145). Bolton, MA: Anker Press.

Campus Compact. (2005). *Campus compact annual membership survey* [electronic version]. Retrieved October 7, 2008, from www.compact.org/about/statistics/2005/

Colby, A., Ehrlich, T., Beaumont, E., & Stephens, J. (2003). *Educating citizens: Preparing America's undergraduates for lives of moral and civic responsibility.* San Francisco: Jossey-Bass.

Furco, A. (2002). *Self-assessment rubric for the institutionalization of service-learning in higher education* (Rev. ed.). Berkeley: Service-Learning Research and Development Center, University of California.

Holland, B. (1997, Fall). Analyzing institutional commitment to service: A model of key organizational factors. *Michigan Journal of Community Service-Learning, 4*, 30–41.

Hoy, A., & Meisel, W. (2008). *Civic engagement at the center: Building democracy through integrated cocurricular and curricular experiences.* Washington, DC: Association of American Colleges and Universities.

Kretzmann, J. P., & McKnight, J. L. (2005). *Discovering community power: A guide to mobilizing local assets and your organization's capacity.* Evanston, IL: Institute for Policy Research. Retrieved April 14, 2009, from www.sesp.northwestern.edu/abcd/kellogg/

National Service-Learning Clearinghouse. (2008). *Institutional structures for service-learning in higher education* [electronic version]. Retrieved October 8, 2008, from www.servicelearning.org/instant_info/fact_sheets/he_facts/inst_structure/

Torres, J., & Sinton, R. (Eds.). (2000). *Establishing and sustaining an office of community service.* Providence, RI: Campus Compact.

Zlotkowski, E. (Ed.). (2002). *Service-learning and the first-year experience: Preparing students for personal success and civic responsibility* (Monograph No. 34). Columbia: University of South Carolina, National Resource Center for the First-Year Experience and Students in Transition.

Zlotkowski, E., Longo, N., & Williams, J. (Eds.). (2006). *Students as colleagues.* Providence, RI: Campus Compact.

3

CULTIVATING INTERDEPENDENT PARTNERSHIPS FOR COMMUNITY CHANGE AND CIVIC EDUCATION

Melissa Kesler Gilbert, Mathew Johnson, and Julie Plaut

Τhis chapter explores an approach to service-learning that focuses on deepening a sense of interdependence as the foundation for powerful partnerships. These partnerships still reflect other generally recognized good practices such as shared goals, trust, respect, clear communication, and joint decision making. By building as well on a sense of common fate, common responsibility, and the need for common spaces, these partnerships will more likely result in the societal, institutional, and personal transformation desired by community partners at the Community-Campus Partnerships for Health (CCPH) summit and by so many campus-based faculty and staff involved in service-learning (CCPH, 2007, p. 13). It is clearly not neat or short-term work. Public policy theorists Barbara Crosby and John Bryson (2005) argue that solutions to the emergent, complex, and usually ill-defined problems in our society require "networked organizations," which are composed of internal networks of individuals and units or departments, and are also integrated into "a variety of external networks that are fluid and chaotic" (p. 5). Although we may yearn for coherence rather than chaos, the experiences and reflections shared here suggest that authentic civic and community engagement will never be static. Our efforts grow and benefit everyone involved the most when they provide common spaces in which stakeholders can develop and act on relationships grounded in a deep sense of interconnectedness.

Toward an Interdependent Partnership Paradigm

In recent years, service-learning has been variously considered a field, a pedagogical method, and a movement. These conceptual models suggest somewhat different priorities for scholars, practitioners, and advocates of service-learning. The W. K. Kellogg Foundation, for instance, has sought to advance service-learning in part by supporting the development of Melinda Fine's field-building framework, which defines a field as "an area of specialized practice that encompasses specific activities carried out by trained practitioners in particular settings" and outlines key elements for establishing a new one: distinct identity, standard practice, knowledge base, leadership and membership, information exchange, resources, and committed stakeholders and advocates (Fine, 2001, p. 1). Shelley H. Billig and Janet Eyler (2003) draw on that framework to call for more rigorous research to inform practice and to justify an increased investment of resources in service-learning. Barbara Holland and Andrew Furco, among others, focus on institutionalization of service-learning as a form of engaged teaching and learning in higher education that emphasizes integration of service-learning into colleges' and universities' cultures, policies, programming, and budgets, as well as departmental curricula and expectations of faculty (Holland, 1997; Furco, 2003). Although those drawn to the idea of service-learning as a transformative movement worry that institutionalization will limit possibilities for change, Dan Butin (2006) suggests that "disciplining" service-learning—creating an academic home for critical dialogue and scholarship, as was done in women's studies—will foster more powerful change in higher education than would likely arise from a social movement striving to stand apart from academic norms (p. 59).

These conceptions of service-learning share a primary focus on the place and status of service-learning within educational institutions. At the same time, they all rest on principles of good practice that include the importance of mutually beneficial partnerships characterized by shared planning and leadership, clear roles, consistent communication, evaluation, and account-ability. Yet strengthening campus–community partnerships is one of three major areas for improvement identified by Amy Driscoll, who directs the Community Engagement Classification process for the Carnegie Foundation for the Advancement of Teaching. Based on applications for the elective clas-sification received in its first round in 2006, Driscoll observes, "Most institu-tions could only describe in vague generalities how they had achieved genuine reciprocity with their communities" (Driscoll, 2008, p. 41). Two years later, the press release announcing the second-round recipients high-lighted the need "for more attention to the intentional practices of develop-ing reciprocal relationships between higher education and the community. . . . Building reciprocity into a partnership with community requires inten-sive development of mechanisms for mutual understanding, ongoing feed-back, and time and attention to a relationship of respect" ("Carnegie Selects," 2008). Because the colleges and universities applying for this rec-ognition tend to be fairly advanced in their commitment to civic and community engagement—195 of the 236 applications were successful—this persistent gap between principles and practice is troubling.

The problem stems in part from what Driscoll (2008) calls "both inter-nal and external perceptions of the campus as an 'ivory tower' " (p. 41). Most higher education institutions lack the strong shared identity and commit-ment to community development and cultural preservation evident in the missions and traditions of Tribal and historically Black colleges and universi-ties (Zlotkowski et al., 2005). As long as campus and community partners see themselves as essentially separate, brought together by individual rela-tionships and mutual interest in a particular collaborative project, their investment in each other will be somewhat limited. To move from "transac-tional" to "transformational" partnerships, Sandra Enos and Keith Morton (2003) argue, campus and community partners must "come to understand that they are part of the same community, with common problems, common interests, common resources, and a common capacity to shape one another in profound ways" (p. 20). Although partners grounded in a deep, transfor-mational relationship bring distinctive perspectives, backgrounds, and knowledge to their common work, "their relationship becomes based on interdependence rather than mutual dependence," a sense of "a shared con-text," and a new, collectively created understanding of the issues they have decided to address together (Enos & Morton, 2003, p. 30).

Several recent projects highlighting the voices of community partners also underscore the importance of stronger relationships between campus staff and faculty and community-based organization leaders. Analysis of a series of focus groups with community partners in California revealed a stronger concern for relationships as "foundational" or "essential" than appears in statements of best practice produced by higher education stakeholders (Sandy, 2007, pp. 11–12). Community-Campus Partnerships for Health (CCPH) convened a summit of experienced community partners to offer critical analysis of current patterns and recommendations for improvement (CCPH, 2007). Both reports call for greater respect of community knowledge and commitment to building community capacity, more equitable distribution of power and resources, more dialogue among stakeholders to increase mutual understanding, and more involvement of faculty and deeper institutionalization so collaborative efforts outlast changes in funding or personnel.

It is interesting to note that neither report suggests any effort to cultivate a sense of interdependence among partners. Of course, there are very real differences in the power, priorities, resources, and cultures that campuses and community-based organizations bring to collaborative efforts. Service-learning practitioners within higher education, like community partners, often see their work as a process of negotiating and building bridges across distinct campus and community identities. Yet we are inexorably bound to one another. We operate within the same set of social, economic, and political systems, and we share an interest in and a responsibility for creating the conditions that allow people to thrive—public safety, participatory democracy, environmental sustainability, widespread access to higher education, as well as shelter, food, and other basic needs. As campuses stretch to co-create knowledge and actions that contribute to positive community change, community partners stretch to co-educate the students engaged in such efforts.

Common Fate

Reimagining community transformation prompts us to develop new networks of partners who recognize that we share in a common fate that requires a shared vision. The Community Impact Statement process developed by community and campus leaders involved with the Phillips Neighborhood Healthy Housing Collaborative and the University of Minnesota's

GRASS Routes initiative takes an important step toward dialogue about their common fate by inviting stakeholders to identify their common traits as well as their differences. They pose the question, "What are the attributes that the partnership participants have in common (e.g., being parents, caring for children, wanting to prevent certain diseases)?" (Gust & Jordan, 2008, p. 3). This question demands that all participants negotiate their own situatedness in their community before trying to work collectively on a common struggle. There is great value in trying to build this deeper sense of connection, perhaps in part emotional, but also practical in realizing we all face the dangers and costs of social problems and we share the responsibility for creating and changing the conditions that allow those problems to persist.

The core partnership model that now informs Otterbein College's community engagement efforts is an example of one effort to recognize a community's common fate, reimagine that community, and "extend and deepen the energy and synergy" of the partnerships sharing the responsibility for change (Enos & Morton, 2003, p. 30). In 2001, community partners who served on an advisory board for an Otterbein grant from the Consortium for the Advancement of Private Higher Education (CAPHE) argued that the college needed to "drill deeper" at their sites to develop "core partnerships" instead of continuing to focus on increasing the number of partners associated with the college and the overall breadth of its service programs. The board recognized that the college's well-being was interconnected with the local school systems and urged local stakeholders to focus efforts on the development of a common vision for K–16 partnerships that would address youth literacy, risky behaviors, drop-out rates, college awareness, and opportunity issues.

When the college founded the Center for Community Engagement in 2003, affiliated faculty, staff, and community partners identified three strategies to support sustainable, meaningful, and transformative partnerships with local schools and nonprofits who were also vested in educational transformation (Gilbert, Weispfenning, & Kengla, 2007). The first strategy in this model is the development of what John McKnight terms community *connectors*—applied at Otterbein as a faculty site-liaison who knows a particular partner organization well, recognizes the assets of each partner, teaches at least one service-learning course at that site, and stewards the college's relationship with the partner (McKnight, 2003, p. 13). CCPH also notes the importance of this role, suggesting that campuses need "a community-aca-demic liaison familiar with both community and academic contexts, which can play a 'translational role' between each partner" (CCPH, 2007, p. 6). In the core partnership model, the liaisons also mobilize other students and fac-ulty to become involved by communicating a sense of common values and purpose that connect the community and the college.

The second strategy is the creation of a *collective body* of program plan-ners at each core partnership site, intentionally including representatives of all stakeholders, especially those who usually have less voice (e.g., students, youth, and clients of the partner organizations). At some sites, this body takes the form of a traditional advisory board, but at others people come together as social change alliances and coalitions. The different ways in which partners formally or informally come together often reflect the way in which community partners envision their work. At a local middle school, a Creative Literacy Alliance was formed as the action arm of a teacher-training program that also incorporated a student poet-in-residency initiative. This community of practice valued an alternative critical pedagogical stance that argued for poetry across the curriculum and youth voice assembled to raise awareness about issues facing teens today. Where an understanding of a com-mon fate leads participants to a social justice framework, the collective bodies tend to come together in nonhierarchical, dynamic forms. More traditional advisory boards are often formed at community sites where the common goals are more practical, logistical, and formally linked to static existing infrastructures. However, to be successful, all forms of collective bodies need to be able to translate community change goals into possibilities for student transformation and student learning objectives into possibilities for commu-nity transformation.

The third strategy for a reimagined core partnership is *concerted commit-ment*—ensuring that at every core partner site student volunteers, service-learners, and community-based researchers from the campus are readied to participate fully when short- and long-term projects are identified by the col-lective planning body. While ensuring that streams of volunteers, resources, and expertise are shared, attention also needs to be directed at efforts to build new capacities at partner sites. In 2003, the principal of a local elementary school was the first Otterbein community partner to establish an advisory board where teachers, parents, and students from the school and faculty and students from Otterbein met monthly to plan, assess, and imagine the relationships possible between the school and the campus. When they gathered in a community of practice dedicated to student learning at both institutions, they identified curriculum needs, posed innovative strategies, mapped out training programs for students, and evaluated new programming. Both partners were surprised to learn during these meetings that they shared common learning outcomes for their students, including developing an appreciation for diversity, citizenship skills, and quantitative literacies. Over time, the school grew to be a community partner where multiple collaborative programs were running concurrently, fully sharing a concerted commitment to jointly realized programs. Otterbein student scholars, trained as part of a developmental Cardinal*Corps* leadership team, ran an after-school program for youth, six service-learning courses were taught at the school, and undergraduate math education students led a research program on cognitively guided instruction (CGI). Teachers from the school were earning graduate credit from the institution for their participation in research programs as they were trained in new techniques for teaching reading and mathematics.

In this situation, both partners experienced what Enos and Morton (2003) call "interdependence rather than mutual dependence" (p. 30). The school flourished with students available to tutor, mentor, and facilitate enrichment activities where youth experienced a richer academic and social environment. Otterbein students inhabited a vibrant school landscape where they were encouraged to explore, learn, grow, and deepen their commitment to their community. Two years after its inception, the partnership began to be fully transformational when the school began to struggle with accommodating increasing numbers of English-as-a-Second-Language students in its classrooms and students who were redistricted from lower income communities outside of the district limits. The partners developed programs together to explore and embrace the new diversity and internationalization of the school. They developed after-school programs to explore different cultures, students in Otterbein's Growing Up in America integrated studies course were paired in mentoring relationships with youth immigrants from Somalia, and Otterbein faculty and teachers developed Family Fun Nights to assist new immigrant families through the transition to a new educational pathway for their children. Both Otterbein and elementary school students have been transformed through this partnership, where new knowledge has been co-created and a new vision for K–16 education has been realized.

The core partnership model and sense of common fate and purpose demanded that the relationship move beyond one campus and one elementary school to extend the synergetic spirit of this work throughout the district. Westerville City Schools have now established six core partner schools with Otterbein at the elementary, middle, and high school levels to address literacy, health and wellness, and diversity programming. Otterbein has been recognized by the school system as its "Business Partner of the Year" and was credited with helping one school increase its passage rates on the Ohio Achievement Test.

Developing *core* partnerships requires a willingness to wrestle with difficult questions. Higher education institutions that are actively engaged in their communities often receive daily requests to join or support organizations addressing a wide range of local, regional, national, or global issues through service, organizing, research, or advocacy. How does a campus decide with whom to partner and what issues they will address? Who in the community can influence or make these decisions? How do we effectively balance the need to develop deep, sustainable core partnerships with the need to evolve and address new ideas that emerge from faculty, student, and community stakeholders? Community-building theorist Peter Block (2008) suggests that when we ask, "Who do we want in the room?" and "What is the new conversation that we want to occur?" we are creating a new social fabric "one room at a time" (p. 11). To answer these questions, he argues, we must converge on a series of core insights, including a focus on community gifts, associational life, transformation that occurs through language, the context that governs our conversations, and our willingness to "speak into the future" (Block, 2008, p. 11). This case study of Otterbein's K–16 campus–school partnership speaks to the necessity of recognizing community assets as well as the goals each partner brings to the relationship when trying to answer important questions. The core partnership model is one way to develop a common language, grounded in a common fate, that can be co-translated to speak to the big questions our future poses. The question is not "Who do we want in the room?" but "Who are we already bound to in the work we need to accomplish?" Our futures depend on our capacity to unpack our interdependence and articulate our convergent and common responsibilities.

Common Responsibility

According to research by Marie Sandy (2007) and Laurie Worrall (2005), partners' commitment to supporting students' civic, academic, and professional development may grow over time as their involvement in service-learning continues. Sharing responsibility for the ongoing development of college students as future leaders is critical to sustaining innovative service-learning. The community partners who attended the CCPH summit and contributed to the resulting report distinguished between community-based research and service-learning, deeming the latter less compatible with "community participatory approaches, authentic partnerships, community capacity building or social change" (CCPH, 2007, p. 12). Their concern seems to arise primarily from the prevalence of one-term service-learning courses that require students to spend relatively little time in the community, do not have faculty directly involved in the community, and are not part of any larger ongoing effort. Some campuses committed to enhancing the outcomes of service-learning for communities and students have developed longer-term student engagement programs and initiatives that allow for deeper, authentic partnerships and invite students to join faculty, campus staff, and community partners as co-leaders and colleagues. Even as these programs explicitly focus on supporting students' development, they ideally engage *all* stakeholders in a continuous and collaborative acting out of Kolb's experiential learning cycle (Kolb, 1984).

At Siena College and other schools in and beyond the Bonner Foundation Network, students make a multiyear commitment to service in exchange for financial assistance. These students serve as Core Student Service Leaders (CSSLs), typically committing to 8 to 10 hours of service per week in a multiyear site placement. In addition to remaining at a core partner site over the term of their placement, CSSLs attend weekly meetings on campus to discuss their service and to plan campus and community-based events that highlight the service needs of their site placements and the social-structural issues that create the needs. During these meeting times, CSSLs also participate in and lead a developmental training program designed to build the skills necessary to move from basic direct-service volunteering to more sophisticated forms of service such as program and strategic planning, program leadership, board service, and resource development. Finally,

CSSLs form a student leadership framework, often alongside the more traditional student leadership framework, and in some cases replacing the more traditional student government model. Within a specific campus–community relationship, the CSSL student leadership framework builds on the core partnership model by organizing service initiatives, placements, and activities focused on a shared set of common responsibilities for the social issues pertinent to the core partner site. Beyond the specific campus–community relationship, CSSL student leadership then connects the individual campus and community to the national student service movement through regular participation in Bonner Network meetings and other national youth conferences.

Although the CSSL model began primarily as a student development endeavor through Student Affairs (at West Virginia Wesleyan, Alleghany, and other institutions), an academic pathway has been initiated to complement the CSSL developmental pathway. Variously referred to as a major, minor, or certificate, and piloted with support from the Bonner Foundation and the Funds for Improvement of Post Secondary Education, these programs usually contain a sequence of courses from an entry course, to policy-based courses, community-based research courses, traditional service-learning courses, and a capstone. These academic pathways give students an opportunity to intentionally connect their service with academic content and rigor. Thus, although powerful for its ability to create student ownership and student leadership and to contribute to the sustainability of core partnerships, without academic integration, the CSSL model can go only so far in advancing service-learning practice.

The benefits of a CSSL program to the development of academic service-learning are clear. Students become full stakeholders and leaders in the campus–community relationship. CSSLs become a critical ally in the classroom as a voice for connection to community partners and at the community site as a voice for connection with the campus. Faculty at CSSL program institutions comment consistently that the presence of a CSSL in their course raises the level of sophistication and quality of engagement in service-learning activities. CSSLs often bring community needs and concerns to the attention of institutional actors (faculty, administrators, other students) and frequently become academic service-learning leaders. At Allegheny College, for example, the CSSL program has led to the development of a two-semester sequence of coursework designed to prepare students to be academic assistants to faculty engaged in service-learning pedagogy. The CSSL model illustrates how the growth, development, and sustainability of service-learning rest on the intentional common responsibility and co-evolution of all stakeholders.

Finally, a few institutions, in collaboration with their community partners, have found students' intensive, long-term development at core partnership sites so fruitful that they have created additional year-long postgraduate leadership positions. Both Siena and West Virginia Wesleyan are involved in partnerships that utilize AmeriCorps VISTA funding to support positions at key community agencies, whereas the College of New Jersey provides fellowships for a cohort of Bonner Program alumni. These recent graduates are deeply connected in the community, helping to develop new site-based teams of student volunteers and assisting in capacity-building innovations with community partners that sustain their interdependence.

Common Spaces

Networked communities of practice require common spaces where community participants who share a common fate and recognize their common responsibility can gather, explore, share, and unite in social and civic change. Social theorists Sara Evans and Harry Boyte (1992) argue that social change requires spaces that embrace the "participatory, egalitarian, and open character of public life" (p. xxvi). They call these places "free spaces" and suggest they

> are the environments in which people are able to learn a new self-respect, a deeper and more assertive group identity, public skills, and values of cooperation and civic virtue. . . . settings between private lives and large-scale institutions where ordinary citizens can act with dignity, independence, and vision. . . . where people experience a schooling in citizenship and learn a vision of the common good in the course of struggling for change." (Evans & Boyte, 1992, pp. 17–18)

Otterbein College has found significant value in creating these kinds of free spaces, stretching its collaborative efforts to reimagine educational communities beyond the margins of the campus and beyond the singularity of the core campus–school partnership. With support from Learn and Serve America, a program of the Corporation for National and Community Service, Otterbein College, Ohio Campus Compact, and the University of Cincinnati, the Great Cities ~ Great Service (GCGS) Consortium was founded, composed of 13 colleges and universities situated in each of Ohio's nine urban centers.* The consortium partners with local schools and community-based organizations around a common goal of helping urban youth understand and pursue pathways to postsecondary education. Youth and college students across the state come together in alliances to lead service projects for community change in their neighborhoods. Great Cities includes multiple campuses, creating complex networks of service that come together in common spaces much like the ones Evans and Boyte challenge us to consider. The youthLEAD model that grounds the consortium emphasizes youth voice and leadership through service; it was inspired by a Girl Scout leader who came to an organizing meeting at Otterbein to help plan a new program for scouts whose mothers were incarcerated. She taught the group that these girls should not be labeled "at-risk," for they were, in her words, "at-promise" and could teach college students about resistance, passion, and a will to survive.

The consortium is bound together in a community of practice to harness the promise of Ohio's youth. A common sense of purpose brings together these institutions that normally compete with one another for enrollment. Consortium partners work together to create innovative service-learning courses and student-led programs at their institutions that are in dialogue with similar programs across the state. As a consortium, GCGS was able to create a statewide "gateway to change" where "partnerships forged by one campus with local youth-serving agencies can benefit institutions across the state by providing models, curriculum, assessment data, resources, and funding leverage" (Gilbert et al., 2007, p. 73).

In a recent survey of GCGS consortium members, participants confirmed these benefits. They reported learning new strategies for working with youth and gaining access to "expertise" that was not available on their own campus, but was available through other consortium members and partners. GCGS has been able to forge broader relationships with organizations like the YMCA, Ohio College Access Network, Project Grad, the National Middle School Association, and Gear-Up satellite sites that have shared extensive knowledge across the partnership. They have also gained "legitimacy" for

---

* The Great Cities ~ Great Service Consortium housed at Otterbein College is funded, in part, through a higher education consortium grant (grant #06LHHOH001) from the Learn and Serve America program of the Corporation for National and Community Service.

programs through their affiliation with state and national initiatives. Campuses have institutionalized new service-learning initiatives, replicated each others' model courses on their own campuses, and leveraged additional external funds to sustain their work well beyond the time constraints of the grant. The consortium's partnership with Ohio Campus Compact ensures its longevity as a statewide initiative supported by an established network of higher education institutions with strong leadership potential. However, the greatest benefit shared by the participants was the annual exchanges and gatherings with colleagues that they found "invigorating" and that provided spaces for "new ideas and new connections."

Data from GCGS community partners also provide evidence that networks focused on a common goal and grounded in a sense of common fate and responsibility have the potential to make significant community change. More than 8,000 college students and 12,000 urban youth have participated in community service programs to strengthen their local neighborhoods through GCGS, creating camps for youth engineers, intergenerational linkages, nursing clubs, environmental initiatives, near-peer mentoring programs, literacy projects, anti-bullying campaigns, and diversity challenge days. Each of these programs has created a sustainable collective body between a campus and a youth-serving agency (e.g., an alliance, coalition, club, or association) and has incorporated a college student and youth development model to ensure that the initiative is educating future leaders for social change. The spaces created across the state for transformational change are embodied in the commitments made by partners. In a survey of GCGS school- and youth-serving agencies, 100% of the partners said that their organization was committed to providing ongoing support to the new service-learning program initiated by GCGS. More than 90% of the community partners involved in the GCGS had established new connections through the consortium and improved their ability to meet community needs. Teachers across the state who have been involved in the youthLEAD programs have also reported a deeper awareness of the capacities of the students labeled at-risk in their classrooms.

In similar fashion, Siena, together with two other smaller liberal arts colleges in New York's Capital Region (St. Rose and Sage), and several community partners have begun building the Campus Community Consortium for the Capital Region (4CR) with Learn and Serve America support through New York and Pennsylvania Campus Compacts. Although currently at a much earlier stage than the Otterbein experience, the power of network community is already evident. Each of the three institutions struggled through fits and starts with developing service-learning, which resulted in islands of individual faculty practice for many years. Through co-founding 4CR, joint participation in faculty development activities, resource sharing, and a common commitment to a shared community beyond any of the three campuses, the formation of the network has greatly advanced redevelopment and institutionalization of service-learning on the three campuses and created a new sense of "stakeholdership" in the institutions on the part of community partners. "We are in it together," noted a key academic stakeholder. "Our institutions, our community, our faculty and students. We are becoming a community of the whole rather than a community of parts."

Thus far, 30 faculty members across the three institutions have committed to and are developing a broad array of service-learning courses particular to their institutional cultures and community partnerships, while at the same time coordinating and collaborating across schools through the network. Participant evaluation from a recent 2-day Problem-Based Service-Learning training at which faculty, administrators, and community partners were participants allowed that *networking* with faculty and community partners from throughout the community and particularly across institutions was "the most rewarding part of the training" *and* "the most likely to contribute to your continued development and implementation of service learning."

Consortia of higher education institutions, just like campus–community partnerships, are often muddied by tensions that emerge from divergent priorities, a lack of transparency about those priorities, limited or unequal resources, conflicting risk management or recognition policies, and different campus/community calendars. These challenges can easily stagnate innovation and effectiveness and can sometimes lead to participants pulling out of consortia. However, service-learning practitioners James Birge, Brooke Beaird, and Jan Torres (2003) suggest that U.S. institutions "share a common tradition of responding to the needs of society" and can "move beyond competition to collaboration in addressing the local, national, and global issues" (p. 149). They offer successful incentives and strategies, modeled by GCGS, to encourage institutions to build effective partnerships. For example, whereas distinct academic cultures that define each campus can often pose challenges for working together, GCGS has brought distinctive campus identities to bear on the partnership. The University of Cincinnati, a large state-funded research institution, offers consortium partners a wealth of community partnership experience, with partners ranging from medical facilities to museums and city zoos. On the other hand, a small liberal arts institution like Otterbein models innovative practices in bridging the student affairs/academic affairs divide for consortium partners. Many of the perceived barriers to partnerships were grounded in stereotypes about each institution, including perceptions about prestige, power, and purpose that needed to be addressed collectively (Birge et al., 2003, p. 141). When GCGS campus constituents came together to share and reflect on their successful and innovative work at regional gatherings, their common commitment to students, student leadership, the youthLEAD model, and community wellness broke down any notions that campuses were too different to be able to speak a common language.

GCGS participants confirmed that most inherent challenges to collaboration were "minor compared with the benefits." However, they were troubled about the consortium's inability to regularly gather everyone in the same room at the same time because of members' dispersion across the state. Participants felt that this work demanded more common spaces for interaction and dialogue—a problem one member felt could be easily solved through modern technologies and virtual community spaces. Social media, online exchanges, and other means of communication may serve as helpful tools for those seeking to build deep collaborative relationships. Such technologies may also remind users of our global interconnectedness.

Where new technologies, common spaces, and consortia intersect we may find more encompassing definitions of community and enter into conversations with a greater ability to change the future. A consortium's structural complexity, extensive community connectedness, and inherent diversity are essential elements to healthy, sustainable change. Sustaining service-learning by addressing community possibility in partnership with other institutions of higher education encourages us to share limited resources, develop more diverse best practices, and create more systemic community-building efforts. These partnerships pool and distribute resources to meet common needs, making them more efficient while building a cadre of committed faculty colleagues, student leaders, and community partners across institutions.

Carrying the Conversation Forward

Community organizer and educator Marshall Ganz reminds us that public work requires public narratives that weave together three key stories: "Our *Story of Self* allows others to experience the values that move us to lead. Our *Story of Us* makes common cause with a broader community whose values we share. And a *Story of Now* calls us to act, so we can shape the future in ways consistent with those values" (Ganz, 2007, pp. 9–10). By telling our stories and listening to others' stories, we can build relationships that acknowledge our commonalities and our differences; help us wrestle with the challenges and feelings of isolation, despair, uncertainty, or outrage that might emerge; and create a vision and collaborative plan for change.

In the CCPH report on community partners' perspectives on community–higher education partnerships, the one hint at a vision of interdependence comes in an appendix containing stories participants wrote about imagining the future as they hoped it would look. One participant shared, "We have seen many people become really serious about addressing the power imbalances that exist in our society. . . . Maybe it's because enough people figured out that if we didn't do this, we were not going to survive as a planet or a species" (CCPH, 2007, p. 15). As we build a new paradigm of interdependence, an ecological lens on this work that questions the survival and evolution of service-learning may be valuable, offering a more integrated, interdependent acknowledgment that we all exist as part of the same ecosystem and face the costs and consequences of environmental degradation, poverty, illiteracy, prejudice, crises in health care and access, and other social ills. An ecosystems approach may help partners working for social change, partners who may now inhabit their own niches, recognize their interdependence. An understanding of the "geography" of service-learning may also help us build new or improve existing partnerships and consortia, allowing us to map where our work overlaps, where our needs intersect, where our vision is shared, where gaps exist, and where our collaborative possibilities merge. New technologies such as geographic information system (GIS) have the potential to map service-learning programs to the distinctive contours of our communities (Gilbert & Krygier, 2007).

In these times, we feel a sense of urgency about cultivating this interdependence to help us diversify, bridge social capital, negotiate globalization, and resolve human conflict. The interdependent paradigm for creating high-quality service-learning offered here encourages us to foster new networked communities of practice to sustain our work, communities that are interconnected, where a sense of common fate and common responsibility "inspires people to contribute" and people "support what they create" (Wheatley, 2006, p. 68). All stakeholders in service-learning are already and necessarily *in relation* to one another, in complicated ways. We share the same societal and systemic contexts even as we hold different identities and positions, compete for resources, and seek to develop and sustain collaborative work.

Conclusion

Service-learning coexists as a field, a movement, a complex set of interdependent relationships sharing a common fate and a common vision for the common good. We need to recognize that change, adaptability, and evolution is inherent in the sustainability of our work, and we have to continue to build the alliances, associations, networks, and social enterprises necessary for transforming education and community. Journalist David Bornstein (2007), author of *How to Change the World: Social Entrepreneurs and the Power of New Ideas*, calls people from the "citizen sector" who are tackling widespread social problems by advancing systemic change *"restless* people" (p. 1). Service-learning is a restless pedagogy that has the potential to advance energetic, imaginative, alive, and relentless work to transform our communities through a network of partnerships.

References

Billig, S. H., & Eyler, J. (2003). The state of service-learning and service-learning research. In S. H. Billig (Ed.), *Deconstructing service-learning: Research exploring context, participation, and impacts* (pp. 253–264). Charlotte, NC: Information Age Publishing.

Birge, J., Beaird, B., & Torres, J. (2003). Partnerships among colleges and universities for service-learning. In B. Jacoby (Ed.), *Building partnerships for service-learning* (pp. 131–150). San Francisco: Jossey-Bass.

Block, P. (2008). *Community: The structure of belonging.* San Francisco: Berrett-Koehler.

Bornstein, D. (2007). *How to change the world: Social entrepreneurs and the power of new ideas.* New York: Oxford University Press.

Butin, D. (2006). Disciplining serving learning: Institutionalization and the case study for community studies. *International Journal of Teaching and Learning in Higher Education, 18* (1), 57–64.

Carnegie selects colleges and universities for 2008 community engagement classification. (2008). Retrieved April 26, 2009, from www.carnegiefoundation.org/news/sub.asp?key=51&subkey=2821

Community-Campus Partnerships for Health. (2007). *Achieving the promise of authentic community-higher education partnerships: Community partners speak out!* Seattle: Community-Campus Partnerships for Health.

Crosby, B., & Bryson, J. (2005). *Leadership for the common good: Tackling public problems in a shared power world.* San Francisco: Jossey-Bass.

Driscoll, A. (2008, January/February). Carnegie's community-engagement classification: Intentions and insights. *Change,* 38–41.

Enos, S., & Morton, K. (2003). Developing a theory and practice of campus-community partnerships. In B. Jacoby (Ed.), *Building partnerships for service-learning* (pp. 20–41). San Francisco: Jossey-Bass.

Evans, S. M., & Boyte, H. C. (1992). *Free spaces: The sources of democratic change in America.* New York: Harper & Row.

Fine, M. (2001). What does field-building mean for service-learning advocates?. Retrieved May 13, 2009, from http://thrivable.wagn.org/wagn/Field_Building+Elements_of_a_Field

Furco, A. (2003). *Self-assessment rubric for the institutionalization of service-learning in higher education.* Providence, RI: Campus Compact.

Ganz, M. (2007). What is public narrative? Practicing Democracy Network. Retrieved April 26, 2009, from www.hks.harvard.edu/organizing/tools/toolshome.shtml

Gilbert, M. K., & Krygier, J. (2007). Mapping campus-community collaborations: Integrating partnerships, service-learning, and GIS. In D. Sinton (Ed.), *Understanding place: GIS and mapping across the curriculum* (pp. 63–75). Redlands, CA: ESRI Press.

Gilbert, M. K., Weispfenning, J., & Kengla, J. (2007). A geography of collaborative K–16 partnerships for the common good. In S. Van Kollenburg (Ed.), *Leading for the common good: Programs, strategies, and structures to support student success* (pp. 70–74). Chicago: The Higher Learning Commission.

Gust, S., & Jordan, C. (2007). *Community impact statement.* Draft included with personal communication, S. Gust, August 4, 2008.

Holland, B. (1997). Analyzing institutional commitment to service: A model of key organizational factors. *Michigan Journal of Community Service Learning,* 4, 30–41.

Kolb, D. A. (1984). *Experiential learning: Experience as the source of learning and development.* Upper Saddle River, NJ: Prentice Hall.

McKnight, J. (2003). *Regenerating community: The recovery of a space for citizens.* The IPR Distinguished Public Policy Lecture Series: Institute for Policy Research. Northwestern University.

Sandy, M. (2007). *Community voices: A California Campus Compact study on partnerships, final report.* San Francisco: California Campus Compact.

Wheatley, M. (2006). *Leadership and the new science: Discovering order in a chaotic world.* San Francisco: Berrett-Koehler.

Worrall, L. (2005). Discovering the community voice: The community perspective of the service-learning program at DePaul University (Illinois). *Dissertation Abstracts International, 66*(05). (UMI No. AAT 3175659)

Zlotkowski, Ed., et al. (2005). *One with the community: Indicators of engagement at minority-serving institutions.* Providence, RI: Campus Compact.

4

SECURING ADMINISTRATOR SUPPORT FOR SERVICE-LEARNING INSTITUTIONALIZATION

Andrew Furco and Barbara Holland

In our 2004 publication "Institutionalizing Service-Learning in Higher Education: Issues and Strategies for Chief Academic Officers" (Furco & Holland, 2004), we sought to make the case that a key strategy for institutionalizing service-learning is to connect service-learning to institutional priorities and key initiatives. We suggested that the best way to institutionalize service-learning is not to promote service-learning for its own sake, but to use service-learning as a strategic vehicle to accomplish other important institutional priorities. We wrote, "Perhaps one of the most serious pitfalls in the institutionalization of service-learning is the establishment of service-learning as an independent, separate program. Academic leaders and faculty must articulate their primary goals for their campus and then explore the ways in which service-learning can be used to help meet the objectives of those goals" (p. 35). As service-learning has matured in recent years to become a more essential and indicative aspect of the civic engagement movement, the importance of viewing service-learning less as a distinctive outreach program and more as an integral strategy for advancing broader institutional goals has become even more apparent.

When service-learning operates on the margins of a college or university, verbal support and some resources to support the program are usually sufficient to continue operating service-learning activities. Despite relying heavily on external funding, most programs are able to continue over several years, maintaining a fairly steady level of operation. However, a more advanced level of institutionalization means that service-learning is more strongly connected to and associated with mainstream institution-wide priorities, thus requiring new levels and different kinds of internal support, sustained commitment, and leadership from senior administrators. Having the support of senior administrators who understand service-learning concepts and practices in all dimensions is key to securing the full institutionalization and long-term success of service-learning. But to gain the administrators' full support, service-learning program leaders inevitably will need to respond to administrators' questions about the effectiveness, efficiency, and potential liabilities of service-learning.

Building on the institutionalization strategies presented in our 2004 chapter, we present five maxims that can help service-learning directors, faculty, and practitioners secure the support of senior administrators in ways that can further the institutionalization of service-learning. The maxims focus on strategies for securing service-learning institutionalization, thus ensuring that the mature service-learning initiatives make the critical shift from a sustained place on the margins to a more institutionalized place in the academy's mainstream. Although the maxims are universal in their application, how they are operationalized is highly dependent on specific institutional missions, cultures, histories, and community contexts, as well as on the institutional purposes service-learning is intended to serve.

Deindividualizing Service-Learning

Today, service-learning is used to advance many different higher education goals, including improving town–gown relationships, fulfilling the civic missions of institutions, fostering interdisciplinary learning communities, improving instruction through authentic and active learning, strengthening the outreach missions of institutions, helping students achieve student learning and development goals, internationalizing the curriculum, strengthening multicultural and diversity awareness, and a host of other institution-wide goals (Brackin & Gibson, 2004; Furco & Holland, 2004; Zlotkowski, 2002). As service-learning has become a more widely used strategy to advance key institutional priorities, it has gained legitimacy and visibility in the academy. This is evidenced by the substantial number of higher education institutions that now have formalized service-learning initiatives, centers, awards, and strategic plans. For example, among the 195 institutions that received the Carnegie Community Engagement designation, service-learning (as opposed to internships, study abroad, etc.) is the most common instructional mode for engaging students in field-based activities. However, having a robust set of service-learning opportunities on a campus does not necessarily mean that service-learning is institutionalized. The full institutionalization of service-learning occurs when it is integrated completely into the overall academic culture of the academy (Bringle & Hatcher, 2000; Holland, 1997; Prentice, 2002).

On the organizational margins, service-learning endeavors can operate and perhaps expand without much attentive administrative oversight. But when service-learning begins to move beyond the more marginal "critical mass" and "quality building" stages of institutionalization to the more advanced, institutionally mainstream stage of "sustained institutionalization" (Furco, 2002), executive leaders are likely to begin to pay more attention to developments in service-learning. In turn, they begin to apply more scrutiny to the financial, organizational, and political implications of service-learning. It is at this time that some senior administrators may begin to ask more questions about service-learning potential, liabilities, and overall value to core academic and scholarly activities. This is especially true if administrators perceive service-learning to be reliant primarily on the work of a few advocates.

Given that entrepreneurship is part of the culture of higher education, executive leaders are not prone to stifle the work of members in the academy who passionately advocate for particular innovations. However, when these advocates begin to suggest that an innovation should infiltrate broader, more institutionalized practices in ways that might challenge the status quo, administrative leaders may begin to question the breadth of internal support, the costs to and the returns on investment, and potential liabilities of the practice. These leaders are also likely to consider the resistance that might arise from less supportive members of the campus who might now be asked to accept the innovation as a more central feature of the institution's work.

The substantial growth of service-learning in higher education over the last two decades can be attributed to the support it has received from passionate advocates of the practice (Butin, 2006). Although skepticism about service-learning's academic legitimacy has persisted, proponents of service-learning have remained fervent in their efforts to prove its merits and to make service-learning more central to the academy's core work. Surely, this passionate and persistent advocacy has helped raise the visibility of service-learning in higher education. However, the passionate support service-learning has enjoyed can become a problem when service-learning begins to become part of the academic culture.

First, when a few people advocate strongly for any good idea, the idea can become so much associated with the individuals or small group that it can easily be dismissed as a personal agenda or ambition. Advocates who are overly focused on their own ideas may eventually be tuned out in group discussions because everyone can anticipate what the proponents will say. Administrators are naturally cautious about appearing to support an idea that may be seen as a boutique program with few supporters.

Second, there have been cases where institutional leaders were interested in advancing service-learning, but then met resistance from passionate service-learning advocates who had a specific model and vision for the program, and in turn, did not trust others to do service-learning "the right way." Third, administrators are likely to feel they can support service-learning as long as knowledgeable and experienced service-learning practitioners are present to ensure quality service-learning. But they will also worry about what will happen if and when those expert advocates move on to other institutions or retire. If key experts leave, the critical mass for service-learning would suddenly erode and create an administrative dilemma—find new leadership that can continue to keep the advancement of service-learning on track, or pull support away from service-learning. Thus, as service-learning gains prominence and becomes more infused into core educational practices, administrators' concerns about levels of support, costs, and stability of service-learning may increase if the program appears to rely on one or a few individuals. Savvy executive leaders know that relying on a small group of individuals to carry out a large-scale institutional initiative is a risky prospect. For service-learning to be successful and survive through the stages of development toward full institutionalization, it must be owned by and associated with the institution as a whole, not a few individuals.

Therefore, the first maxim for securing ongoing administrative support for service-learning is: *Service-learning is an institution-based not an individual-based practice.* Service-learning should not be associated primarily with particular individuals; rather, it must be associated with broader institutional practices (e.g., a vehicle for students to achieve a required learning outcome). Specifically, service-learning should be strongly associated with other programs and initiatives at the institution. For example, when people hear the term *service-learning*, campus-wide programs and initiatives (e.g., freshman seminars, capstone experiences, multicultural development) rather than individuals or specific units should come to mind.

This is not to say that there should not be a service-learning director with accountabilities for quality performance, but he or she should not be perceived as being the owner of the idea of service-learning or its sole advocate. Too often, campuses see the advancement of service-learning stalled when the service-learning director leaves or the faculty member who used service-learning in a particular program decides to use a different pedagogy. This can cause administrators to lose confidence in the strength and long-term potential of service-learning.

Institutions can avoid this situation by finding points of synergy between service-learning and particular institutional goals, and then tying service-learning to the practices that are being employed to achieve those goals by involving a wide array of institutional voices. For example, if an institutional goal is to ensure that all students have multicultural, international, or capstone experiences, then service-learning could be used as one vehicle (or the vehicle) for facilitating these experiences for students. This would require negotiation and cooperation among a number of units across the institution. It would seat service-learning less as a separate program that feeds the passions of advocates and more as a campus-wide strategy that helps the institution and its members accomplish more universally accepted goals. With this approach, the future institutionalization of service-learning moves from being reliant primarily on the success and longevity of the individuals who passionately advocate for it to being fed by the growing need to have service-learning present at the institution because it serves as a key and effective strategy for accomplishing universal, broader-based institutional goals. This strategy is likely to confer wider buy-in for service-learning as well as open up options that will help service-learning to flourish.

Deemphasizing Service-Learning

During the initial stages of service-learning implementation and development, much emphasis is placed on solidifying service-learning's institutional identity. Service-learning centers are established. Service-learning program requirements are proposed. Service-learning course criteria are developed. Much time is spent on defining service-learning; articulating the specific programmatic features that produce high-quality practice; and marketing the concept of service-learning to faculty, students, community partners, and campus leaders.

However, as service-learning gains institutional prominence and becomes associated with campus-wide initiatives, the institutionalization process reaches a tipping point at which a shift in focus occurs. Once this tipping point is reached, the final stage of institutionalization (sustained institutionalization) begins. At this stage, the service-learning institutionalization work needs to shift away from supporting and promoting service-learning for its own sake to supporting and promoting broader, campus-wide initiatives that can be advanced by service-learning. To become fully institutionalized into the academy, service-learning must ultimately morph from being an innovative idea for a distinct purpose into being a widely understood tool that has beneficial impacts on campus-wide institutional and community goals.

Throughout the course of the year, campus administrators are flooded with proposals from various units and individuals who seek greater campus support, resources, and/or visibility for their respective programs and initiatives. When determining how to proceed with these proposals, administrators consider the extent to which an investment in the proposed programs will benefit the greater institution. Although administrators are typically interested in supporting innovations and other entrepreneurial initiatives proposed by units and individuals, such endeavors are likely to receive only initial seed support. Unless the programs demonstrate that they have substantial value added to the overall success of the institution, they are unlikely to receive support over an extended period of time.

Thus, the second maxim for garnering administrator support for service-learning institutionalization is: *Service-learning exists to facilitate the advancement of key institutional priorities.* This maxim centers on deemphasizing service-learning as the focal initiative, especially as it matures and becomes more infused in the culture of an institution. Therefore, instead of working to garner institutional support specifically for service-learning projects, courses, or activities, leaders of more mature service-learning initiatives should focus on seeking support for activities that help forge linkages between service-learning and specific campus priorities (e.g., multicultural and diversity enhancement programs, interdisciplinary teaching and learning initiatives, learning communities opportunities). This support emphasizes the role that service-learning plays in facilitating the advancement of key institutional priorities and, in turn, ultimately helps make service-learning indispensable.

Part of institutionalization is that the idea transitions from being an innovation to becoming ordinary business. Because of the broad applicability of service-learning, those responsible for service-learning can benefit from making explicit connections to a host of other curricular strategies and learning initiatives such as capstones, internships, international exchange, cooperative education, e-learning, or undergraduate research. Identifying which of these or other initiatives are campus priorities, and then articulating the ways in which service-learning can help advance those initiatives can make service-learning a substantially more attractive prospect to discerning administrators. Good ways to create these connections are for service-learning advocates to join committees working on these related initiatives, propose an evaluation to learn how students use these programs in combination, work collaboratively to define different forms of experiential learning, or propose new models or efforts that would combine some of these experiences (such as international service-learning).

By deemphasizing service-learning as a stand-alone program and emphasizing it more as a strategy that can help meet or complement important campus-wide priorities, advocates are likely to garner the level of administrative support needed to institutionalize service-learning fully in the academy.

Emphasizing Strategic Visioning

Two of the best indicators of institutionalization are inclusion of service-learning in the base budget and in the strategic plan of the institution. Getting into the budget depends not only on evidence (as described in the next section), but also on fit with the strategic agenda of the whole institution. If service-learning is to move to the core, and if doing so requires connecting service-learning to important institutional objectives, then the strategic plan becomes the road map for finding and demonstrating those connections. Leaders of service-learning initiatives should look carefully at the current strategic plan of their institution and/or the primary division or unit in which they are located organizationally. If a planning process is under way, leaders of the service-learning initiative can volunteer to join a working group.

Whatever the context for planning, every service-learning and civic engagement unit should have a strategic plan for its work and an action plan for how service-learning will be connected to key institutional priorities. Having a clear, succinct strategic plan for service-learning facilitates measurement of outcomes, helps others understand the concept and its purposes, and demonstrates links to other institutional initiatives and a focused use of program funds. Focus is important because leaders rarely support a "let every flower bloom" approach; concentrated attention to specific models and outcomes helps administrators visualize how service-learning might evolve across the institution over time.

This third maxim, *The institutionalization of service-learning is a calculated future,* suggests that time must be taken to envision what the institution will look like in the future and the ways in which service-learning will feature prominently in that vision. Service-learning must not only evolve as the institution evolves, but must be tied to specific elements of the institution's short-range and long-range strategic plan. Whereas the second maxim focuses on identifying ways service-learning can be an approach to achieving institutional priorities, this maxim is about developing and implementing a strategic action plan that defines the steps that will guide the development and growth of service-learning in the coming years.

Along with providing a road map for benchmarking the development and institutionalization of service-learning over time, the plan helps service-learning appear on the institution's main radar. By seeing service-learning as a part of the overall institutional plan, administrators are more likely to view service-learning as a permanent fixture in the academy and, in turn, gain confidence in service-learning's long-term prospects. Most administrators are aware that innovations and reform efforts in higher education typically have short shelf lives; therefore, the presence of a plan that articulates service-learning's place in the academy's future can help overcome resistance among administrators who fear service-learning may be just another educational fad. To this end, the plan should include chronologies, timelines, and benchmarks that characterize a set of specific action steps that will be taken to strengthen service-learning's short- and long-term contributions to institutional priorities.

Showing Evidence of Success

Regardless of the prominence and importance of the institutional priority(ies) to which service-learning is connected, long-term institutional support ultimately depends on demonstrating the initiative's effectiveness through convincing evidence. Although a growing body of research reveals service-learning's positive impacts on the academic, social, cultural, and civic development of students, as well as benefits to the institution and community, campus leaders will want to know whether the service-learning efforts on their campus are having positive impacts. Whereas national and other broad studies of the impacts and value of service-learning are important in garnering administrative support in the earlier stages of institutionalization, the more advanced stages of institutionalization require the presentation of data that show the benefits of service-learning activities operating at the institution.

Higher education leaders are hungry for good data on campus-wide impacts of any initiative intended to address specific institutional concerns (recruitment, retention, diversity and harmony, growth in research, etc.). They are also interested in knowing how particular programs raise their institutional rankings, increase faculty productivity, help the institution garner grants, and/or strengthen the overall reputation of the institution. When making decisions about which programs to support, administrators are likely to give more serious consideration and make a greater investment in those programs that have in place a comprehensive assessment plan that measures the program's costs, benefits, and impacts in the context of broad, overarching institutional concerns.

Thus, the fourth maxim for securing administrators' support for advanced service-learning institutionalization—*Evidence above passion*—calls for the establishment of a comprehensive assessment plan that measures the impacts of service-learning on the outcomes and issues that are of interest to campus leaders. Although many faculty members who use service-learning conduct formal assessments of the impact of service-learning on their students, they typically use these data to identify the strengths and limitations of their particular service-learning courses, and the ways in which the courses have affected their students. These assessments often reveal useful findings on how much the students enjoyed and learned from the experience, but do not typically provide the kinds of information that institutional leaders need most. Classroom-based assessments are limited in utility because they tend to focus on specific courses and types of service-learning experiences. They also rely primarily on faculty-developed measures that have not been validated on a sample beyond the students in the faculty members' courses. Therefore, establishing a comprehensive, campus-wide assessment system that can measure service-learning's impacts across courses and student experiences can produce the evidence needed to show campus leaders that service-learning has broad, institutional value.

As administrators consider making more substantial investments in service-learning, they will want to see that data show the ways in which service-learning is helping to advance key institutional priorities (e.g., student retention, students' achievement of particular learning outcomes, the advancement of interdisciplinary learning experiences). Continued support from campus administrators is more likely if they see that a genuine, concerted effort is being made to assess objectively and systematically the strengths and limitations of service-learning. Campus service-learning managers and leaders should consider working with their campuses' institutional assessment offices or committees to incorporate comprehensive measures of service-learning into their institutions' overall assessment plan. The comprehensive assessment plan should include assessment strategies that collect data from students, faculty, alumni, and community voices. If they can prove positive effects of service-learning on key institutional priorities, this could become the evidence administrators need to justify making larger and/or longer-term investments in service-learning.

Building a Broad Constituency

The preceding four maxims all lead to a final maxim: *Service-learning grows through a strong political base.* Achieving the full institutionalization of service-learning ultimately requires garnering political support from key constituencies in the community and within the academy. Service-learning leaders must tap the political force of these constituencies as they consider the maxims. For example, each maxim creates opportunities to demonstrate links to other departments and units, especially those working on student learning and development and those working on external community connections and public image. For service-learning to find its place in the institutional toolbox, these units are key to building a broader constituency.

Creating a strategic plan for service-learning is also an opportunity to involve other units such as academic administrators, student leaders, or members of governance committees related to curriculum, student development, assessment, or external relations. Such involvement will expand the core of influential voices who understand service-learning and its potential purposes. Similarly, developing an assessment or evaluation plan presents opportunities to involve other internal experts in service-learning implementation. And one must not forget the political power of external constituencies; developing a community advisory panel can be important both in signaling external commitment to the program as well as in contributing to the development of quality data for assessing community impacts.

Because administrators must be concerned with the institution as a whole, they are likely to view service-learning as one possible program among many that can contribute to the overarching goals of the campus. Therefore, administrators are not likely to be convinced about the merits of service-learning by hearing how wonderful it is from the service-learning director or service-learning faculty. The more often that senior administrators hear about the virtues and value of a program from different corners of the institution and from those who perhaps have little or no vested interest in seeing service-learning succeed, the more convinced they will be of the program's merits. Having community members and students share powerful stories about how service-learning enhanced their lives or having alumni express the value that service-learning had for them in their postcollegiate life can provide administrators with the kinds of testimony that may convince them that service-learning is something that produces important and often intangible outcomes for the betterment of the institution, the members of the academy, and the community.

Conclusion

One of the major forces for institutionalizing service-learning continues to be leadership. Campus leaders, therefore, play an important role—both rhetorical and symbolic—in shaping the ultimate outcome of service-learning for their institutions. They, in partnership with faculty and community partners, set the tone for how extensively service-learning is infused in the institutional culture. Obtaining buy-in and maintaining support from campus administrators, especially during the more advanced stages of service-learning institutionalization, is essential for ensuring that service-learning continues to thrive as an important and vital institutional practice. The five maxims we offer in this chapter can help achieve this outcome.

The five maxims are especially important during the more advanced stages of service-learning institutionalization, when higher stakes surround service-learning's success or failure. An institution's mission, culture, history, and community context inevitably shape how each maxim is operationalized. In operationalizing these maxims, service-learning leaders should analyze how other innovations at their institutions are gaining traction and administrative support, and then identify the particular leverage points that are helping those innovations succeed. This kind of careful and strategic analysis is needed to keep service-learning institutionalization on track. The full institutionalization of service-learning does not happen automatically, and neither does it come easily. But through the implementation of the key strategic steps identified in the maxims, the full institutionalization of service-learning can be realized.

References

Brackin, P., & Gibson, J. (2004). Service learning in capstone design projects: Emphasizing reflection. *2004 ASEE Annual Conference Proceedings.*

Bringle, R. G., & Hatcher, J. A. (2000). Institutionalization of service learning in higher education. *Journal of Higher Education, 71*(3), 273–290.

Butin, D. W. (2006). The limits of service-learning in higher education. *Review of Higher Education, 29*(4), 473–498.

Furco, A. (2002). Institutionalizing service-learning in higher education. *Journal of Public Affairs, 6,* 39–67.

Furco, A., & Holland, B. A. (2004). Institutionalizing service-learning in higher education: Issues and strategies for chief academic officers. In M. Langseth & S. Dillon (Eds.), *Public work and the academy* (pp. 23–39). Bolton, MA: Anker Publishing Company.

Holland, B. (1997). Analyzing institutional commitment to service: A model of key organizational factors. *Michigan Journal of Community Service Learning, 4*(1), 30–41.

Prentice, M. (2002). Institutionalizing service learning in community colleges. Research Briefs. *Broadening Horizons,* 1–12.

Zlotkowski, E. (Ed.). (2002). *Service-learning and the first-year experience: Preparing students for personal success and civic responsibility.* Columbia: University of South Carolina, National Resource Center for the First-Year Experience and Students in Transition.

PART TWO

INFRASTRUCTURE FOR SUSTAINABLE SERVICE-LEARNING

5

COMMUNITY ENGAGEMENT

Second-Generation Promotion and Tenure Issues and Challenges

Lorilee R. Sandmann

Acadeademe-based conversations on service-learning and community engagement invariably turn to laments about the trials of faculty members who seek rewards and recognition for their efforts in this burgeoning field, particularly through the key areas of promotion and tenure (P&T). Well-meaning senior mentors often discourage junior faculty members from pursuing an engagement agenda, with the rationale that such a course may put their chances of academic advancement at risk. Are these concerns warranted? That is, are faculty being passed over for promotion and tenure because of their roles in service-learning and community engagement, or is this a widely held perception not based in actual practice? Even if such concerns are not groundless, the focus on them may be a red herring that draws attention away from a central issue: the parameters of contemporary faculty work.

Promotion and Tenure—Red Herring or Real?

For the past decade, I have teamed with Amy Driscoll to create and direct the National Review Board for the Scholarship of Engagement, which provides external peer review and evaluation of the scholarship of engagement as input in faculty promotion and tenure decisions. In this capacity, I have reviewed a number of faculty dossiers. Additionally, I have worked with many campuses to institutionalize community engagement. Experiences with individual faculty, as well as institutional leaders who are trying to make systemic changes, have given me insights into the complexity of issues around the diverse expressions and results of learning partnerships with community. I have gained an appreciation of the challenges involved in demonstrating the value of this work, given the entrenched, deeply rooted, yet personal practices related to promotion and tenure decisions.

This chapter reviews findings on this topic based on research and practice in what I call the first generation of service-learning and community engagement. Next, I discuss ways of making community engagement count for promotion and tenure, specifically, issues around framing, documenting, and evaluating the work. Finally, to help individual faculty and particularly institutional leaders, this chapter offers challenges and recommendations for the second generation.

For purposes of this discussion, service-learning is considered an expression of community engagement. The Carnegie Foundation for the Advancement of Teaching (n.d.) defines community engagement as "the collaboration between higher education institutions and their larger communities (local, regional/state, national, global) for the mutually beneficial exchange of knowledge and resources in a context of partnership and reciprocity." Educators who define their work within the engagement movement tend to draw from service-learning pedagogy, community-based participatory research, and public scholarship as a set of powerful strategies for generating knowledge and practices that are applicable to alleviate social problems affecting communities outside the walls of the academy (Bringle, Games, & Malloy, 1999). Engagement, in this context, has an explicit community-based dimension and is distinguished from engagement as the term is used by the National Survey of Student Engagement, which measures student engagement in learning.

Learning From the First Generation

This section summarizes research related to community engagement work in the professoriate, current trends in promotion and tenure systems supporting such work, and findings from the examination of actual cases that were advanced for promotion and tenure decisions.

Engagement as Faculty Work

A growing body of literature reflects the perception of faculty engagement as a form of faculty work that defies categorization (Giles, 2008; Sandmann, 2008; Sandmann, Saltmarsh, Giles, & O'Meara, 2008; Ward, 2003); involves integration of faculty roles (Bloomgarden & O'Meara, 2007; Colbeck, 1998; Moore, 2006; Ward, 2003); involves both personal and professional values and commitments (Kuntz, 2005; Moore, 2006; Neumann, 2006; O'Meara, 2008); and engages faculty in ways outside the norm of disciplinary peers, across institutional boundaries (Sandmann & Weerts, 2008; Weerts & Sandmann, 2007, 2008), including involvement in interdisciplinary work (Lattuca, 2005) and in activism on and off campus (Kuntz, 2005).

Further, growing insight into faculty's extrinsic and intrinsic motivations for engaged work is emerging (O'Meara, 2003, 2008; Peters & Alter, 2006). Researchers have found faculty motivation for engagement and outreach (O'Meara, 2002), and service-learning in particular (Abes, Jackson, & Jones, 2002), to be largely intrinsic. Studies have shown that many faculty members pursue these engagement activities regardless of external rewards. For example, faculty members choose to use service-learning in their belief that, as a pedagogical strategy, it increases student understanding of course materials and contributes to student personal development (Abes et al., 2002; Bringle, Hatcher, & Games, 1997; Hammond 1994). However, research also indicates that faculty are motivated differently in early career (more extrinsic rewards emphasized) compared with mid or late career (more intrinsic rewards when gaining tenure is no longer an issue) (O'Meara, 2003). It has been found that today's new generation of academics may be characterized as not wanting to be buried with a heavy *curricula vitae*; rather, they want to engage in knowledge activities that address meaningful global and local issues by working in collaborative, interdisciplinary, democratic modes (Rice, 1996; Trower, 2006). Therefore, what types of institutional and professorial changes are needed to support and develop engaged learning and scholarship?

Promotion and Tenure Systems That Support Engagement

Many advocates argue that if community engagement is to be truly supported as faculty work, formal changes to higher education academic reward systems are needed. "No matter how clear the mission statement or presidential proclamation to connect the campus with the community," observes

Ward (2005), if community engagement is "unrewarded or seen by faculty as distracting from the pursuit of those kinds of things that count on a dossier, either those public service efforts will be set aside, or the faculty member will be. Either way community approaches to scholarship will not be strengthened" (p. 228). Institutions "must define in their promotion and tenure guidelines and faculty handbooks what this work looks like, and how it will be evaluated and rewarded" (p. 229).

Academic reward systems in higher education institutions reflect a continuum of such changes. Using the framework of Boyer's (1990) seminal work in *Scholarship Reconsidered*, some institutions have chosen to give Boyer no consideration; others have embedded Boyer's conceptualization of scholarship into their departmental guidelines, and still others have revised institutional guidelines within the categories of teaching, research, and service. Finally, a set of reform-minded institutions have "Boyerized" their promotion and tenure systems, replacing the traditional categories with the scholarship of discovery, the scholarship of integration, the scholarship of application, and the scholarship of teaching (Rice & Sorcinelli, 2002).

When Braxton, Luckey, and Helland (2002) explored the extent to which Boyer's four scholarship domains were advanced, they found that all domains had attained the most basic or structural level of institutionalization. However, they also found that the scholarships of discovery and teaching had attained procedural-level institutionalization (being a regular part of workload), but only the scholarship of discovery achieved incorporation-level institutionalization (faculty values and assumptions support the activity). Similarly, in an empirical study surveying 729 chief academic officers, O'Meara (2005) found that over the past 10 years, two out of three had changed their institution's mission and planning documents, amended faculty evaluation criteria, and provided incentive grants or developed flexible workload programs as a basis for a broader definition of scholarly work. However, only one-third of the chief academic officers reported increases in the scholarship of integration, student contact with faculty, and scholarship focused on civic engagement and professional service. Variations were found by institutional type, but most institutions exhibited an asymmetry toward research or discovery. Such institutional priorities may reflect external factors. For example, master's institutions that seek to increase their standings in ranking systems often experience a "mission drift" that pushes faculty to emphasize discovery or research to the exclusion of other forms of scholarship (O'Meara, 2005, p. 276).

More direct evidence regarding support for community engagement through promotion and tenure systems is provided by an analysis of the first set of Carnegie classified community-engaged institutions (reporting on this topic was an option in the first group of applications). These applications reflect a trend toward significant revision of specific institutional policies that accommodate community engagement. Most respondents felt they had a clear way to ensure that engagement was included, evaluated, and counted in a promotion and tenure application process. In their review, Saltmarsh, Giles, Ward, and Buglione (2009) found that such changes were taking place over time; that is, more campuses had become involved in the often lengthy process of revising their promotion and tenure guidelines than had revised their guidelines and adopted new policies. The policies adopted by the latter group establish conceptual clarity around community engagement, address engagement across faculty roles, and are grounded in reciprocity.

Closer examination, however, reveals just how deeply rooted traditional categories of evaluation are even among institutions achieving Carnegie community-engaged status. In her analysis, Holland (2009) notes that among those institutions implementing formal (administrative) changes acknowledging engagement, most had made conservative revisions indicating how faculty dossiers should present evidence of engagement. Driscoll (2008) observes of the applicants, "most institutions continue to place community engagement and its scholarship in the traditional category of service and require other forms of scholarship for promotion and tenure" (p. 41).

P&T Decisions on Community Engagement

Although many reports suggest that lack of recognition in the faculty formal reward structure presents a significant deterrent for faculty involvement in service-learning and community engagement (Morton, 1995; O'Meara, 2002; Ward, 2003), an examination of applications for promotion and tenure reveals that institutional promotion and tenure guidelines are not constricting the consideration of engagement as scholarship *if* it is deemed to show quality and have impact. Knox (2001) examined portfolios of candidates with engagement and outreach responsibilities for tenure from land-grant universities. He found that the proportion of engagement within an assistant professor's total contribution was less important for promotion consideration than convincing evidence of balanced attention to high-quality performance and accomplishments. Further, this and other studies have found that "there has been a gradual acceptance of outreach forms of teaching, research, and service as legitimate with both similarities (quality and impact) and differences (recipients, collaboration) compared with disciplinary research, resident instruction and institutional service" (p. 74).

There is a widespread perception that interdisciplinary work is likewise not rewarded in a department-based promotion and tenure process. But institutional data at the University of Wisconsin–Madison, as one example, indicate that professors involved in interdisciplinary activities achieved tenure at a rate equal to or slightly higher than that of the rest of the faculty at the same institution (Redden, 2008).

Those cases not getting positive reviews by the National Review Board for Scholarship of Engagement typically have achieved the minimal level of scholarly productivity in the scholarship of engagement necessary for tenure or promotion, whether in quantity or quality. Dossiers may tell compelling stories about applicants doing service-learning or providing leadership in expanding and deepening the practice of service-learning of others, but the narratives lack evidence to meet criteria established by the National Review Board and applicants' respective institutions with regard to documentation of impact on students, community, and the profession and of scholarship that meets the standards of peer review in any area of the scholarship of engagement. Additionally, those not getting favorable reviews have done work "in" the community, but do not provide evidence of doing scholarly work "with" communities.

Making Engagement Count for Promotion and Tenure

A number of critical issues are embedded in the brief snapshots of trends in community engagement as faculty work and in P&T systems discussed in the previous section. What follows is a discussion of three: framing, documenting, and evaluating quality community engagement.

Issue: Framing Service-Learning and Community Engagement as Scholarship

Reward systems in higher education focus on what counts as quality academic scholarship. Promotion and tenure call for more than doing good work. That is, doing good service-learning, or good community-based participatory research, or good professional service is not enough. Work promoting student civic education through service-learning or seeking the public good will be valued and rewarded within academe only if it is fundamentally scholarly and, specifically, quality community-engaged scholarship. Community-engaged scholarship can be defined in several ways, but essentially it means activity that adheres to the principles of engagement (mutually beneficial exchange of knowledge and resources in a context of partnership and reciprocity) and to the quality standards of scholarship (intellectual work that is communicated to and validated by peers).

To apply community engagement toward P&T, faculty need, first, a philosophical and conceptual understanding of community-engaged scholarship (the why) and, second, the ability to implement it by knowing how to frame their work as engaged scholarship and how to design, build, and sustain genuine democratic engaged scholarly partnerships (the how). Faculty work can be a basis for scholarship (contributing to a knowledge base) or can itself be scholarly (well-informed) (Bringle, Hatcher, & Clayton, 2006). In studying faculty-engaged scholarship, scholars have learned that engaged scholarship can occur in teaching, in research, and in professional service. However, it often takes place as boundary-crossing scholarship—that is, as integration within and across teaching, research, and service (Fear & Sandmann, 2001/2002). Many academics advocate that better documentation of service-learning and community engagement will yield recognition and rewards; rather, I believe that first and foremost, the critical element is framing the work as scholarship.

What Counts? Scholarship Counts

Scholarship, then, is the foundation or architecture by which service-learning and community engagement is conceptualized, implemented, assessed, and communicated for promotion and tenure decisions. A number of exemplary expositions discuss community engagement as scholarship under differing nomenclatures: engaged scholarship, community-engaged scholarship, public scholarship, the scholarship of engagement. Appropriately, these documents represent their context through interpretations of intellectual foundations, implementation, and assessment of community-engaged scholarship that reflect institution type and disciplinary sector. For example, the report *New Times Demand New Scholarship* (Stanton, 2007) explores community-engaged scholarship within research universities. For the health professions, Community-Campus Partnerships for Health has developed a set of tools to plan and document community-engaged scholarship and produce strong portfolios for promotion and tenure (Jordon, 2007). For those in the arts, humanities, and design, there is the resource that resulted from Imagining America: Artists and Scholars in Public Life's Tenure Team Initiative on Public Scholarship (Ellison & Eatman, 2008). In management, Van de Ven (2007) offers a model most appropriate for engaged scholarship with business practitioners.

These reports and others indicate a commonality: Community engagement "counts" when scholarship is *what* is being done, engaged scholarship is *how* it is done, and for the common or public good is *toward what end.* Rather than responding to community or curricular needs, interests, problems, and requests in a just-in-time service-oriented mode, faculty become involved by framing their response as scholarship with community constituents (Sandmann, Foster-Fishman, Lloyd, Rauhe, & Rosaen, 2000). Taking this approach to community engagement typically strengthens the work by adding important new knowledge about the issue or process and the unique value, outcome, or impact of an academic–community partnership. Ramaley observes that community-engaged scholarship " 'varies' from other kinds of scholarship in some ways but it is 'no different' in others" (Ellison & Eatman, 2008, p. 9).

Although traditional scholarship in the community is an appropriate approach for some inquiry, its procedures and findings are often limited to the academy with research as the primary paradigm, separate from other forms of scholarship. Scholarship, however, can take the form of an engaged pedagogy that is contextual and social, problem-based and collaborative, and that draws on local and cosmopolitan knowledge (Barker, 2004). The keystone is engaging *with* the community. (For detailed comparisons between traditional scholarship and community-engaged scholarship, see Sandmann, 2006.) In the co-creation of knowledge and problem solving, community stakeholders (broadly defined) and faculty members, students, and staff are collaboratively involved in framing the "driving intellectual questions," in generating and interpreting the evidence, and in using the evidence for diverse purposes.

The idea of framing service-learning as scholarly faculty work deserves close attention. In addition to being framed as scholarship (contributing to a knowledge base), service-learning can be considered faculty scholarly work, that is, well-informed teaching (Bringle et al., 2006). Using this approach, faculty (employing service-learning or other pedagogical strategies) are able to provide evidence that they designed learning opportunities that conform to good practice and provide expected student learning outcomes. Possible outcomes for students include attainment of discipline-based education objectives and increased civic awareness. Bringle, Hatcher, and Clayton (2006) note that this "type of evidence would be valued in a dossier to demonstrate excellence in teaching" and that such evidence may even raise "the bar toward aspirations that could be held for documenting all types of teaching and learning" (p. 265).

Bringle, Hatcher, and Clayton (2006) further differentiate faculty scholarly work from faculty scholarship as it relates to service-learning:

> When the faculty member's work and research on service learning provides for informing others about designing and implementing service-learning courses or increases the understanding of teaching and learning in the discipline or campus-community partnerships, then it has the potential to be viewed as scholarship (i.e., scholarship of teaching and learning). As such, scholarship on service learning contributes to scholarship on civic engagement. (p. 265)

Once academic engaged work by faculty is framed as scholarship, then attention can be paid to the issues of documenting and evaluating the work.

Issue: Documenting Integrated Community-Engaged Scholarship

Faculty are not only concerned about what counts as a basis for promotion and tenure, they are also anxious about how to make it count—that is, the process involved in achieving the awards. In his 1995 faculty guide, Diamond states that there are three basic components to a promotion and tenure review: the documentation that the candidate provides, the materials that the committee collects, and the process by which the committee reviews these materials and conducts its deliberations. He concludes that "a well-prepared faculty member can go a long way in making his or her 'case' by providing strong context and solid documentation for the committee to consider" (p. 14). Institutions typically have documentation format specifications, but they are developing guides to build on those institution-specific specifications for documenting community-engaged scholarship so that it meets both campus criteria and the criteria for scholarship, thus making it visible and available for promotion and tenure assessments. For instance, example narrative portfolios are available in *Making Outreach Visible* (Driscoll & Lynton, 1999) and online in the Community-Campus Partnerships for Health (CCPH) Community-Engaged Scholarship Toolkit (http://depts .washington.edu/ccph/toolkit-portexamples.html).

By its nature, community engagement can present challenges for faculty who wish to document integrated scholarship that doesn't fit tidily within the traditional documentation frameworks of accomplishments in teaching, research, and service. David Cooper, a senior faculty member of Writing, Rhetoric, and American Cultures at Michigan State, once said, "I, my colleagues, and my discipline did not come to know my work until I could represent it as an integrated whole" (personal communication, March 12, 1997). Faculty have nonetheless achieved academic advancement by presenting evidence of such integrated accomplishments, as the following two examples show.

Shelly Jarrett Bromberg, Miami University, Hamilton, Ohio, developed an exemplary dossier themed around building bridges for new culture relationships for which she was recently awarded both promotion and tenure in Spanish and Latin American studies. She made her case through a reflective statement and a masterfully structured set of tables that presented her accomplishments in ranked order of depth of engagement. According to the reviewers of the National Review Board for the Scholarship of Engagement, "Dr. Jarrett's scholarly work to promote bridge building via cultural exchange to address immigration issues in the local community seamlessly integrated teaching, research and service" (personal communication, September 19, 2008).

Another outstanding case was that of Gregory Lindsey, now associate dean at the Hubert H. Humphrey Institute for Public Affairs at the University of Minnesota, in his promotion to full professor in public and environmental affairs at Indiana University. As part of making his integrated case, he used a figure that illustrated the linkages among his teaching (formal and nonformal), research, and service on greenway development. He showed the resulting impact as academic refereed papers, technical publications, and contract research as well as the enactment of comprehensive planning and zoning ordinances from 44 counties and 50 municipalities for indices of smart growth and sustainable development. Additionally, impact was clear through (a) the development of new analytic measures for land-use practices; and (b) evidence of student involvement and learning in the form of instruction, community-based applied research, scholarly work, and publications and presentations. He was also able to document his leadership in conceptualizing and practice of civic engagement within his institution.

Issue: Evaluating Engaged Scholarship

Maynard Mack in *Metropolitan Universities* (1994) comments, "Quality in any area should be rewarded, but mediocrity, even if it is published, should not" (p. 89). What are criteria, standards, and evidence of "quality" engaged scholarship? Evaluation criteria provide the groundwork for closing the gap between the rhetoric and the reality of community-engaged scholarship. In the last generation, significant attention was devoted to articulating such criteria, developing standards, and suggesting appropriate evidence. Many universities have adapted the six attributes identified by Glassick, Huber, and Maeroff (1997) that collectively define scholarly excellence across Boyer's multiple scholarships, across disciplines, and across institutional types. In particular, clear goals, adequate preparation, appropriate methods, significant results, effective presentation, and reflective critique are the six attributes that have been interpreted as demonstrating scholarship in service-learning and community engagement (Calleson, Kauper-Brown, & Seifer, 2005; Committee on Institutional Cooperation, 2005; Driscoll & Lynton, 1999; *Points of Distinction*, 1996; Sandmann et al., 2000). The Appendix to this chapter is an adaptation developed and used by the National Review Board for the Scholarship of Engagement.

A related challenge is to provide credible yet appropriate evidence or artifacts of quality community-engaged scholarship. As an alternative to traditional academic publications, products might take the form of curricula, training videos, policy reports, resource guides, web sites, video documentaries, and so on. Our current lack of systematic and rigorous ways to review and disseminate such forms of nontraditional scholarship compromises their potential for recognition as scholarly work in the faculty promotion and tenure system. However, innovative methodologies are being designed to facilitate peer review and dissemination of products of community-engaged

scholarship. For example, Web-based services such as MedEdPortal (www
.aamc.org/mededportal) offer peer review of educational materials.

Given criteria, standards, and peer-reviewed evidence, a pervasive issue
still remains: P&T reviewers may view scholarship broadly but continue to
evaluate it narrowly. Optimally, disciplines, departments, and institutions
would consistently employ criteria and standards for community-engaged
scholarship, and candidates would present relevant evidence so that reviewers
could make well-informed decisions. Unfortunately, even when criteria are
clear, there can be disparate views (across ranks, across disciplines, across
individual reviewers) of standards and the quality of evidence of faculty work
that is expected, particularly for nontraditional types of academic work
involved in community engagement (Bringle et al., 2006). As Ellison and
Eatman (2008) indicate, "Criteria for excellence, in themselves, do not constitute promotion and tenure policies" (p. 10).

The Who and How of Evaluation

"For the academically engaged scholar, tenure review should mark the point
where the results of public and community-based collaborative scholarship
are accorded the full dignity of informed peer review" (Ellison & Eatman,
2008, p. xi). A critical issue is "who is counting"—that is, who are those
informed peer reviewers? For community-engaged faculty, community-
based constituencies and academic and disciplinary peers comprise two
potential sets of reviewers.

The role of community partners in the review of an academic dossier is
under consideration; there are those who argue that, consistent with the values of collaboration and mutuality and of a broader and more diverse community of peers, community-based constituencies are "informed peer
reviewers" and ought to and can best comment on a faculty-partner's work.
Others maintain that community partners can provide evidence regarding
the manner in which the work was structured, the democratic nature of its
implementation, and the impact the work had on meeting the community's
needs. But they do not need to be part of the academy's review of the scholarly natures (i.e., academic, discipline-based impact) of the work or the
scholarship that results from it (Bringle et al., 2006). In practice, it appears
that for purposes of promotion and tenure review, the academic qualities of
the work are most relevant for assessment by academic peers. For other types
of review, a broader set of reviewers may be appropriate. However, for all

community-engaged work, the academy should evaluate the academic nature of the work (its scholarship and scholarly products) and the nature of the partnership that supported the work.

Academic peer reviewers, those within a faculty member's institution and those serving as external peer evaluators, must come to know and appreciate the rigors and challenges of community-engaged scholarship. Some institutions (such as Indiana University–Purdue University Indianapolis and California State University–Monterey Bay) hold formal training sessions for faculty serving on departmental-, college-, or university-level promotion and tenure committees, with discussions about interpreting broader conceptions of scholarship and how relevant criteria and documentation fit in their institution's P&T guidelines. In the absence of these opportunities, which is more typical, such discussions take place through the initiative of departmental or disciplinary leaders. Not infrequently, initiative may occur through an individual junior engaged scholar who, in developing an agenda of engaged scholarship and in working with a mentoring committee, cultivates the understanding of and then the advocacy for engaged scholarship. In academic departments, where faculty live their lives, faculty work is done, and promotion and tenure decisions are first made. These departments need to be targeted for attention to overcome inertia and active resistance to views of scholarship that go beyond the traditional, but narrow, prescriptive presumption that if it is not empirical research published in a top-tier journal in the discipline, it does not count.

Promotion and Tenure Revisited: Red Herring or Real?

The first generation of community engagement and service-learning has established a groundwork through which community engagement is indeed proving to be valued in academe. A multifaceted and growing literature, policy revision by institutions of higher education, and faculty achievement of promotion and tenure through scholarly community engagement—all reflect the growth of practice by individual faculty and the support of the academic establishment. Issues critical in building on this groundwork, particularly in the context of achieving promotion and tenure, include better and more widespread understanding of framing, documenting, and evaluating faculty community engagement work.

Continuing Challenges

Of course, thorny issues remain. Some are philosophical: Is using peer review and disciplinary impact as means for evaluating scholarship just reifying traditional approaches? Is the criterion for community impact holding engaged scholarship to higher, more demanding standards than traditional scholarship? What is nonscholarly engagement, and should it be recognized and rewarded? Other outstanding issues are more operational or instrumental: Do promotion and tenure guidelines need to be revised as an organizational strategy to prompt deliberation about what counts as quality faculty work? What about recognition and rewards for faculty types other than those in tenure-track positions, and what about rewards at various stages in their careers? What about differential emphasis by institutional type, such as those who do not have the asymmetrical reward systems focused toward research? Advocates of community engagement also must confront strategic issues that surround institutionalizing an expanded view of scholarship, including fully embedding engaged scholarship in the culture of higher education.

By their nature, service-learning and community engagement are often interdisciplinary, process-oriented, and performed by teams; they have diffuse impact across nontraditional constituencies (i.e., beyond the discipline). These factors ensure that those who practice service-learning and community engagement will face issues and challenges in evaluation of their work as long as higher education structures are organized around disciplines rather than interdisciplinary formats, and employ reward structures focused on individuals. An outstanding question to track going forward is, Will community engagement, particularly if rewarded through promotion and tenure, accommodate academic norms and traditions, or will it be a trigger for institutional transformation? Bringle, Hatcher, and Clayton (2006) point out the risk that the traditions of higher education may be more successful in changing work done under the aegis of community engagement than community engagement might be in changing the work of the academy.

Recommendations for the Second Generation

Despite its lack of widespread institutionalization (Braxton et al., 2002; O'Meara, 2005), increasing numbers of faculty are doing engaged scholarship (Campus Compact, 2005). Building on the work of these faculty and propelled by lessons learned from the first generation, a few of many possible recommendations for the second generation are as follows:

Institutional policies:

- Use an examination of promotion and tenure systems as a metric of change to reexamine and retool what faculty work is valued and rewarded.
- Clearly define parameters of engaged scholarship as a precursor to creating clear and specific criteria for evidence that faculty need to provide to demonstrate community-engaged scholarship (Saltmarsh et al., in press).
- Construct policies that reward engaged scholarship across faculty roles so that research activities will be integrated seamlessly into teaching and service activities (Saltmarsh et al., 2009).
- Operationalize the norms of reciprocity in criteria for evaluation (Saltmarsh et al., 2009).
- Develop documentation and evaluation processes for community-engaged scholarship that are appropriate, rigorous, reliable, and understood by traditionalists.
- Model collaborative and democratic methods in these institutional change processes.

Institutional development:

- Support faculty, department heads, early-career faculty mentoring committees, and P&T committees in developing and understanding the parameters of engaged scholarship through professional development. Help them to understand how to frame service-learning and community engagement as scholarship within teaching, research, or service or as integrated scholarship across the categories of teaching, research, and service.
- Develop institutional and discipline-specific learning communities to define terms, to further develop the rationale for adopting a broader conceptualization of scholarship and rewarding practice that reflects it, and to study and adapt available models from similar institutions or disciplines.
- Utilize capacity-building programs and models now available for graduate students and early-career faculty as emerging engaged scholars (e.g., National Center for the Study of University Engagement, Michigan State University's Emerging Engagement Scholars Workshop, http://ncsue.msu.edu/eesw/default.aspx) and for midcareer and senior

faculty (e.g., University of New Hampshire's Outreach Scholars Academy, www.unh.edu/outreach-scholars).

- Encourage participation in leadership development programs for institutional administrators charged with engagement as part of the strategic direction of their institution (e.g., Virginia Tech's Engagement Academy for University Leaders, www.cpe.vt.edu/ea).

Complex and Changing

Are P&T issues for community-engaged scholars a red herring or real? As the discussion in this chapter shows, the relationship of community engagement to promotion and tenure presents enormously complex issues that are entwined in the current change in higher education, a change that education and public policy scholars Schuster and Finkelstein (2006) say "is *unprecedented* [italics original] as two powerful conditions reinforce each other: the sheer number of institution-molding forces that are in play . . . and the stunning rapidity with which these forces are shaping higher education" (p. 3). The compelling issues of rewarding service-learning and community engagement are bound to broader issues related to institutional accountability and relevancy; the context of the larger civic and community engagement movement; the nature of knowledge and how it is constructed, legitimized, and shared (and thus related to broader conceptions of scholarship); and the accelerating demands on the professoriate.

Although some argue that tenure itself is outdated, tenure and promotion decisions nonetheless remain central as high-stakes assessments of both individuals and higher education institutions. The outcome of these assessments signals what colleges and universities and their faculties do and how well they do it. Internally, tenure and promotion decisions are the focal point of tensions surrounding changes in the academic workplace and workforce (Katz, 2006). Because no other academic reward carries the weight of tenure, few institutions are willing to make bold, significant changes without powerful and persistent pressure. But as a state legislator recently stated at a conference where I was discussing this topic, "I expect you, higher education, to figure this out!"

Conclusion

As this chapter reveals, we have made significant progress in "figuring it out." Evidence from the first generation indicates that community engagement can indeed "count" if it is framed as quality engaged scholarship and thus situated in the teaching, research, and service classification scheme within which faculty work is typically evaluated. This first generation has also produced efforts to assist faculty to prepare and reviewers to evaluate dossiers that provide evidence better aligned with criteria and standards for quality engaged scholarship. The convergence of forces in this period of unprecedented change has produced a fluid milieu ripe for reexamination of and progress in disciplinary and campus organizational policies and cultures that are beginning to support the newly framed architecture of engaged scholars and their work on "real" issues for the public good.

References

Abes, E., Jackson, G., & Jones, S. (2002). Factors that motivate and deter faculty use of service-learning. *Michigan Journal of Community Service Learning, 9*(1), 5–17.

Barker, D. (2004). The scholarship of engagement: A taxonomy of five emerging practices. *Journal of Higher Education Outreach and Engagement, 9*(2),123–137.

Bloomgarden, A., & O'Meara, K. (2007). Harmony or cacophony? Faculty role integration and community engagement. *Michigan Journal of Community Service Learning, 13*(2), 5–18.

Boyer, E. L. (1990). *Scholarship reconsidered: The priorities of the professoriate.* Princeton, NJ: Carnegie Foundation for the Advancement of Teaching.

Braxton, J. M., Luckey, W., & Helland, P. (2002). Institutionalizing a broader view of scholarship through Boyer's four domains. *ASHE-ERIC Higher Education Report, 29*(2). San Francisco: Jossey-Bass.

Bringle, R., Games, R., & Malloy, E. (Eds.). (1999). *Colleges and universities as citizens.* Needham Heights, MA: Allyn & Bacon.

Bringle, R. G., Hatcher, J. A., & Clayton, P. H. (2006). The scholarship of civic engagement: Defining, documenting, and evaluating faculty work. *To Improve the Academy, 25,* 257–279.

Bringle, R. G., Hatcher, J. A., & Games, R. (1997). Engaging and supporting faculty in service learning. *Journal of Public Service and Outreach, 2*(1), 43–51.

Calleson, D., Kauper-Brown, J., & Seifer, S. D. (2005). *Community-engaged scholarship toolkit.* Seattle: Community-Campus Partnerships for Health. Retrieved December 3, 2008, from www.communityengagedscholarship.info

Campus Compact. (2005). *Seasons of service.* Providence, RI: Author.

Carnegie Foundation for the Advancement of Teaching. (n.d.). *Community engagement.* Stanford, CA: Author. Retrieved December 3, 2008, from www.carnegie foundation.org/classifications/index.asp?key = 1213

Colbeck, C. L. (1998). Merging in a seamless blend: How faculty integrate teaching and research. *Journal of Higher Education, 69*(6), 647–671.

Committee on Institutional Cooperation. (2005). *Engaged scholarship: A resource guide.* Retrieved December 3, 2008, from www.cic.net/Libraries/Technology/Engaged_Scholarship.sflb.ashx

Diamond, R. M. (1995). *Preparing for promotion and tenure review: A faculty guide.* Bolton, MA: Anker.

Driscoll, A. (2008, January–February). Carnegie's community-engagement classification: Intentions and insights. *Change,* 39–41.

Driscoll, A., & Lynton, E. A. (1999). *Making outreach visible: A guide to documenting professional service and outreach.* Washington, DC: American Association for Higher Education.

Ellison, J., & Eatman, T. K. (2008). *Scholarship in public: Knowledge creation and tenure policy in the engaged university.* Syracuse, NY: Imagining America: Artists and Scholars in Public Life, Tenure Team Initiative on Public Scholarship. Retrieved December 3, 2008, from www.imaginingamerica.org/TTI/TTI.html

Fear, F., & Sandmann, L. R. (2001/2002). The "new" scholarship of engagement: Implications for engagement and extension. *Journal of Higher Education Outreach and Engagement, 7*(1&2), 29–40.

Giles, D. E., Jr. (2008). Understanding an emerging field of scholarship: Toward a research agenda for engaged public scholarship. *Journal of Higher Education Outreach and Engagement, 12*(2), 97–108.

Glassick, C. E., Huber, M. T., & Maeroff, G. I. (1997). *Scholarship assessed: Evaluation of the professoriate.* San Francisco: Jossey-Bass.

Hammond, C. (1994). Integrating service and academic study: Faculty motivation and satisfaction in Michigan higher education. *Michigan Journal of Community Service Learning, 1*(1), 21–28.

Holland, B. (2009). Will it last? Evidence of institutionalization at Carnegie classified community engaged institutions. In L. R. Sandmann, C. H. Thornton, & A. J. Jaeger (Eds.), *Institutionalizing community engagement in higher education: The first wave of Carnegie classified institutions.* New Directions for Higher Education. Indianapolis, IN: Wiley Publishing.

Jordon, C. (Ed.). (2007). *Community-engaged scholarship review, promotion & tenure packages.* Peer Review Workgroup, Community-Engaged Scholarship for Health Collaborative, Community-Campus Partnerships for Health. Retrieved December 3, 2008, from www.communityengagedscholarship.info/

Katz, S. (2006). What has happened to the professoriate? *Chronicle of Higher Education, 53*(7), B8–B11. Retrieved December 3, 2008 from http://chronicle.com/weekly/v53/i07/07b00801.htm

Knox, A. B. (2001). Assessing university faculty outreach performance. *College Teaching, 49*(2), 71–74.

Kuntz, A. (2005). Academic citizenship: The risks and responsibility of reframing faculty work. *Journal of College and Character, 7*(5), 2–9.

Lattuca, L. R. (2005). Faculty work as learning: Insights from theories of cognition. *New Directions for Teaching and Learning, 102,* 13–21.

Mack, M. (1994). Teaching matters: Reconsidering our responsibilities. *Metropolitan Universities, 5*(1), 88–91.

Moore, T. L. (2006, November). *Whole, seamless, vital: Portraits of an integrated scholarly agenda.* Paper presented at the Annual Association for the Study of Higher Education Conference, Anaheim, CA.

Morton, K. (1995). The irony of service: Charity, project and social change in service-learning. *Michigan Journal of Community Service Learning, 2*(1), 19–32.

Neumann, A. (2006). Professing passion: Emotion in the scholarship of professors at research universities. *American Educational Research Journal, 43*(3), 381–424.

O'Meara, K. (2002). Uncovering the values in faculty evaluation of service as scholarship. *Review of Higher Education, 26*(1), 57–80.

O'Meara, K. (2003). Reframing incentives and rewards for community service-learning and academic outreach. *Journal of Higher Education Outreach and Engagement, 8*(2), 201–220.

O'Meara, K. (2005). Effects of encouraging multiple forms of scholarship nationwide and across institutional types. In K. A. O'Meara & R. E. Rice (Eds.), *Faculty priorities reconsidered: Encouraging multiple forms of scholarship* (pp. 255–289). San Francisco: Jossey-Bass.

O'Meara, K. (2008). Motivation for public scholarship and engagement: Listening to exemplars. *Journal of Higher Education Outreach and Engagement, 12*(1), 7–29.

Peters, S., & Alter, T. (2006, November). *If not for the rewards . . . Why? Theory-based research about what motivates faculty to engage in public scholarship.* Symposium presentation at the Annual Conference of the Association for the Study of Higher Education, Anaheim, CA.

Points of Distinction: A guidebook for planning and evaluating quality outreach (Rev. ed.). (1996). East Lansing: Michigan State University.

Redden, E. (2008, November 6). Encouraging interdisciplinarity. *Inside Higher Education.* Retrieved December 3, 2008, from http://insidehighered.com/news/2008/11/06/interdiscipline

Rice, R. E. (1996, January). *Making a place for the new American scholar.* Paper presented at the AAHE Conference on Faculty Roles and Rewards, Atlanta, GA.

Rice, R. E., & Sorcinelli, M. D. (2002). Can the tenure process be improved? In R. P. Chait (Ed.), *The questions of tenure* (pp. 101–124). Cambridge, MA: Harvard University Press.

Saltmarsh, J., Giles, D. E., Ward, E., & Buglione, S. M. (2009). Rewarding community-engaged scholarship. In L. R. Sandmann, C. H. Thornton, & A. J. Jaeger

(Eds.), *Institutionalizing community engagement in higher education: The first wave of Carnegie classified institutions.* New Directions for Higher Education. Indianapolis, IN: Wiley.

Sandmann, L. R. (2006). Scholarship as architecture: Framing and enhancing community engagement. *Journal of Physical Therapy Education, 20*(3), 80–84.

Sandmann, L. R. (2008). Conceptualization of the scholarship of engagement in higher education: A strategic review, 1996–2006. *Journal of Higher Education Outreach and Engagement, 12*(1), 91–104.

Sandmann, L., Foster-Fishman, P., Lloyd, J., Rauhe, W., & Rosaen, C. (2000). Managing critical tensions: How to strengthen the scholarship component of outreach. *Change, 32*(1), 44–58.

Sandmann, L. R., Saltmarsh, J., Giles, D. E., & O'Meara, K. A. (2008, November). *Studying the professional lives of faculty involved in community engagement.* Presentation at the annual meeting of the Association for the Study of Higher Education, Jacksonville, FL.

Sandmann, L. R., & Weerts, D. J. (2008). Reshaping institutional boundaries to accommodate an engagement agenda. *Innovative Higher Education, 33*(3), 181–196.

Schuster, J. H., & Finkelstein, M. J. (2006). *The American faculty: The restructuring of academic work and careers.* Baltimore, MD: Johns Hopkins University Press.

Stanton, T. K. (Ed.). (2007). *New times demand new scholarship: Research universities and civic engagement: Opportunities and challenges. A conference report.* Retrieved December 3, 2008, from www.compact.org/resources/research_universities/

Trower, C. (2006, April). *Gen X meets theory X: What new faculty want.* Presentation at 33rd National Conference of the National Center for the Study of Collective Bargaining in Higher Education and the Professions, New York, NY.

Van de Ven, A. H. (2007). *Engaged scholarship: A guide for organizational and social research.* New York: Oxford University Press.

Ward, K. (2003). *Faculty service roles and the scholarship of engagement, ASHE-ERIC Higher Education Report, 29*(5.) San Francisco, CA: Jossey-Bass.

Ward, K. (2005). Rethinking faculty roles and rewards for the public good. In A. J. Kezar, T. C. Chambers, J. C. Burkhardt, & associates (Eds.), *Higher education and the public good: Emerging voices from a national movement* (pp. 217–234). San Francisco: Jossey-Bass.

Weerts, D. J., & Sandmann, L. R. (2007, November). *Community engagement and boundary spanning roles at public research universities.* Roundtable, Association for the Study of Higher Education, Louisville, KY.

Weerts, D., & Sandmann, L. R. (2008). Building a two-way street: Challenges and opportunities for community engagement at research universities. *Review of Higher Education, 32*(1), 73–106.

Evaluation Criteria for the Scholarship of Engagement

These criteria are used by the National Review Board to assess and evaluate the Scholarship of Engagement. Drawing from the criteria presented in *Scholarship Assessed: A Special Report on Faculty Evaluation* (Glassick, Huber, & Maeroff, 1997), they have been adapted to more closely reflect the unique fit with the scholarship of engagement.

Scholarship of engagement is a term that captures scholarship in the areas of teaching, research, and/or service. It engages faculty in academically relevant work that simultaneously meets campus mission and goals as well as community needs. Engagement is a scholarly agenda that incorporates community issues and that can be within or integrative across teaching, research, and service. In this definition, *community* is broadly defined to include audiences external to the campus that are part of a collaborative process to contribute to the public good.

In applying these criteria, the National Review Board for the Scholarship of Engagement is mindful of the variation in institutional contexts, the breadth of faculty work, and individual promotion and tenure guidelines.

Goals/Questions

- Does the scholar state the basic purpose of the work and its value for public good?
- Is there an "academic fit" with the scholar's role and departmental and university mission?
- Does the scholar define objectives that are realistic and achievable?
- Does the scholar identify intellectual and significant questions in the discipline and in the community?

Context of Theory, Literature, "Best Practices"

- Does the scholar show an understanding of relevant existing scholarship?

- Does the scholar bring the necessary skills to the collaboration?
- Does the scholar make significant contributions to the work?
- Is the work intellectually compelling?

Methods

- Does the scholar use methods appropriate to the goals, questions, and context of the work?
- Does the scholar describe the rationale for election of methods in relation to context and issues?
- Does the scholar apply effectively the methods selected?
- Does the scholar modify procedures in response to changing circumstances?

Results

- Does the scholar achieve the goals?
- Does the scholar's work add consequentially to the discipline and to the community?
- Does the scholar's work open additional areas for further exploration and collaboration?
- Does the scholar's work achieve impact or change? Are those outcomes evaluated and, if so, by whom?

Communication/Dissemination

- Does the scholar use a suitable style and effective organization to present the work?
- Does the scholar communicate/disseminate to appropriate academic and public audiences consistent with the mission of the institution?
- Does the scholar use appropriate forums for communicating work to the intended audience?
- Does the scholar present information with clarity and integrity?

Reflective Critique

- Does the scholar critically evaluate the work?

- What are the sources of evidence informing the critique?
- Does the scholar bring an appropriate breadth of evidence to the critique?
- In what way has the community perspective informed the critique?
- Does the scholar use evaluation to learn from the work and to direct future work?
- Is the scholar involved in local, state, and national dialog related to the work?

National Review Board for the Scholarship of Engagement
www.scholarshipofengagement.org   **Modified 2001**

6

FACING THE UNSETTLED QUESTIONS ABOUT SERVICE-LEARNING

Barbara Jacoby

S ince I joined the ranks of service-learning practitioners and advocates in 1992, much has come clear to me about service-learning and its role in higher education and society. Service-learning has become institutionalized, as we like to say, on many campuses of all shapes and sizes. The numbers of students participating in service-learning have skyrocketed. Federal and state governments, foundations, and individuals have generously contributed financial and technical resources to its development. Thousands of community-based organizations have provided sites and opportunities for service and learning. Thanks to our colleagues who are active researchers and analysts, we now have substantial evidence of the outcomes of service-learning and numerous models and guidelines for good practice. Service-learning is located squarely at the intersection of three powerful movements in higher education: the focus on active, engaged learning; the establishment and assessment of student learning outcomes; and the call for the renewal of the civic role of higher education.

Nonetheless, many challenging questions remain, including those that get at the very essence and purpose of service-learning. As reflective educators, we must take these issues seriously, examine their dimensions, debate their merits, and conduct research that suggests answers to guide our practice. This chapter raises seven difficult, unsettled questions in the hope of stimulating such discussion and study. These questions are loosely grouped into three categories. Questions 1 and 2 address "nuts and bolts" issues. The next couple of questions focus on two of service-learning's primary stakeholders, students and community partners. The final three questions are more philosophical in nature. How we answer these questions will undoubtedly affect the future of service-learning in multiple ways.

What "Counts" as Service-Learning?

One of the earliest questions about service-learning that advocates and practitioners confronted remains with us today: Must it be part of the formal academic curriculum to "count" as service-learning rather than as volunteerism or community service? Many definitions of service-learning so stipulate. For example, noted service-learning educators Robert Bringle and Julie Hatcher (1995) define service-learning as "a credit-bearing, educational, experience in which students participate in an organized service activity that meets identified community needs and reflect on the service activity in such a way as to gain further understanding of course content, a broader appreciation of the discipline, and an enhanced sense of civic responsibility" (p. 112).

On the other hand, in *Service-Learning in Higher Education*, I take the firm stance that service-learning can be both curricular and cocurricular because all learning does not occur inside the formal curriculum. Although the structure afforded by the classroom, including class meetings, syllabi, assignments, grades, and credit, makes it easier to hold students accountable for achieving the desired outcomes of service-learning, skillfully designed and carefully implemented cocurricular experiences can yield rich results. In addition, desired learning and developmental outcomes, such as collaborative problem solving, intercultural competence, and communication skills, are not necessarily related to a discipline or a particular course. By claiming that service-learning must be integrated into the formal curriculum, one would deny that service-learning can be facilitated by student affairs professionals, campus ministers, trained student leaders, and community members (Jacoby, 1996).

Does it matter whether service-learning's advocates and practitioners agree on a single definition? Or can we agree to disagree, as long as the service and the learning are of high quality and high integrity and together achieve the outcomes desired for both the student and the community participants? Do we have evidence that one form of service-learning is more likely to achieve desired outcomes? The section titled "Can We Demonstrate the Value of Service-Learning?" later in this chapter addresses this issue further.

Discussion also continues about whether one-time or short-term experiences, such as serving in a soup kitchen or participating in an environmental cleanup, can be called service-learning. If these experiences include the fundamental concepts of reflection and reciprocity and state desired outcomes for all participants, can they rightfully "count" as service-learning, whether they are inside or outside the curriculum?

Another ongoing issue in the "what counts" conversation is whether service-learning must stay away from politics or political issues. Clearly, service-learning initiatives funded by the federal Corporation for National and Community Service must avoid politics. However, the waters become muddy in this example cited by Dan W. Butin (2006):

> Is it service-learning if Jerry Falwell's Liberty University requires as a graduation requirement that all undergraduates spend a certain amount of time helping to blockade abortion clinics and thus saving the lives of the unborn? What if this activity was linked to reflection groups and learning circles and students had to create portfolios showing how such community service was linked to their academic courses? (p. 487)

Butin goes on to suggest that few service-learning advocates would quickly or easily accept the Liberty example as service-learning, much less service-learning in the pursuit of social justice. But to refuse to accept this as service-learning is to admit that service it not a neutral, universalistic practice. Many questions related to service-learning and social justice follow in the section titled "Does Service-Learning Perpetuate the Status Quo?"

Can We Demonstrate the Value of Service-Learning?

When a group of educators, researchers, service-learning practitioners, national foundation and organization representatives, government officials, and students met at the Johnson Foundation's Wingspread Conference Center in 1991 to establish a research agenda for service-learning, they found "a scarcity of replicable qualitative and quantitative research on the effects of service-learning on student learning and development, the communities in which students serve, on educational institutions, and on society" (Giles,

Porter Honnet, & Migliore, 1991, p. 5). Since then, research on service-learning has burgeoned in quantity, depth, and quality. Launched in 2005 and incorporated in 2007, the International Association for Research on Service-Learning and Community Engagement (IARSLCE) is an international, non-profit organization devoted to promoting research and discussion about service-learning and community engagement. It sponsors an annual international conference and publishes a series of volumes of papers from the annual conferences. The *Michigan Journal of Community Service Learning* is a rigorously juried publication that features high-quality research-based articles. Journals in many disciplines also publish service-learning research. Although the lack of longitudinal data in the field is notable, a prominent exception is the excellent *Where's the Learning in Service-Learning?* (Eyler & Giles, 1999).

Nevertheless, many unanswered questions remain: "For a field that engenders so much passion in practitioners and that we believe transforms students by engaging their hearts as well as their minds, there is remarkably little evidence of strong impact and even less evidence about the kinds of practices that lead to the effects we desire" (Eyler, 2002). How do issues affecting the quality of a student's experience at the service site (e.g., type of work, supervision, connection to coursework, frequency of service, length of service) affect learning? How do the frequency, mode, and intensity of reflection affect learning? Does it matter whether the service is required or optional?

Research on the effects of service-learning is challenging. As Butin (2005) points out, "Quantifying the value-added of service-learning is methodologically impossible" (p. 14). Variables are difficult to identify and define, service-learning takes place in many different settings and involves many kinds of tasks and desired outcomes, causality is difficult to determine, and extensive longitudinal studies are necessary to measure effects over time. When I expressed the latter point in a recent presentation to faculty members, one of the participants asked wryly, "Does that mean that we have to wait to read their obituaries to see how our students might have been affected by their service-learning experiences?" In fact, we do not know service-learning's effects on lifelong learning and community problem solving (Eyler, 2000).

Although service-learning is "often heralded as a pedagogical strategy with 'transformative potential,' " we lack evidence that this is in fact true and, if true, transformative in specific ways (Jones, Gilbride-Brown, & Gasiorski, 2005, p.3). We also are short on knowledge about how service-learning affects students from different social identity groups. For example, do students of color experience service-learning as "personally empowering or as uncomfortable reminders of (un)common histories"? (Chesler & Vasques Scalera, 2000, p. 25). How do class differences among students affect their service-learning experiences? How about class differences (or similarities) between students and the individuals served?

And there remains very little research on the effects of service-learning on community participants and communities. As challenging as it is to assess individual change as a result of service-learning, assessing community or social change is even more so. Studies on the satisfaction of community members and leaders with various aspects of service-learning projects exist. However, big questions yet to be answered include: Is there a net gain in assets for communities as a result of participating in service-learning? Does service-learning increase community capacity to solve problems? Does service-learning bridge town–gown gaps?

Is Service-Learning Accessible and Appropriate for All Students?

Service-learning opportunities must be accessible and appropriate for students of all races, ethnicities, social classes, religions, ages, sexual orientations, life situations, ability levels, political views, learning styles, and interests. On many campuses, the majority of students who participate in service-learning and other civic engagement activities are white, middle class, and female. Scholars have also noted that students' motivations to participate in service-learning appear to vary according to their race, ethnicity, and class (Stanton, 2007). Practitioners worry that campus-based initiatives "may not attract, be culturally appropriate for, or effectively serve" students of color and those from working-class backgrounds (Stanton, 2007, p. 21).

Butin (2006) notes:

> Service-learning is premised on full-time, single, non-indebted, and childless students pursuing a "liberal arts education." Yet a large proportion of the postsecondary population of today, and increasingly of the future, views higher education as a part-time, instrumental, and pre-professional

endeavor that must be juggled with children, family time, and earning a living wage. Service-learning may be a luxury that many students cannot afford, whether in terms of time, finances, or job future. (p. 482)

Thus, in addition to careful program design, it is important to offer financial assistance to students who otherwise would not be able to participate in service-learning both locally and abroad. This could include service-learning scholarships that function like athletic and academic scholarships to attract and retain students recognized for past achievement and current involvement in service-learning. The Bonner Foundation endows such scholarships, and they are also being offered by individual institutions. Duke University, Brown University, and Miami University of Ohio are examples of institutions that offer campus-based financial aid to encourage and support local and global service and civic engagement. Federal Work-Study funds can also be used to support student community service (Jacoby, 2009).

The policy strategies proposed by ServiceNation include two new initiatives aimed at college students. One would create the National Service Leadership Corps, the civilian counterpart of ROTC. This program would enroll college students in an intensive 4-year program to train them to be leaders in national service programs and would provide scholarships and loan forgiveness in exchange for a year of full-time, postcollege service in a national service program, a nonprofit organization, or local, state, or federal government. Students in the corps would receive a monthly stipend of $200 for providing a minimum of 10 hours of service per week. The second strategy, Serve-Study, would allow colleges and universities that designate higher-than-required percentages of Federal Work-Study funds for students to work in community service positions to earn the designation of "Campus of Service" and receive more funding and benefits. In addition, to build upon the tradition of the military service academies, the U.S. Public Service Academy (USPSA) would be created as their civilian equivalent. Like the military academies, the USPSA would recruit the most promising young people and provide full scholarships to cover their expenses during 4 rigorous undergraduate years. In return, graduates would spend 5 years serving in health care, law enforcement, emergency management, and other essential fields at all levels of government (ServiceNation, 2008).

The challenges of engaging a broad range of students in service-learning are not limited to financial ones. For example, students who come from struggling inner-city communities may experience deep and conflicting emotions when confronted by serving in a community like the one in which they were raised. Some may feel guilt for having "succeeded," while others may not want to "go back" into such communities for service-learning because they prefer not to revisit the past or to focus on what they may perceive to be situations or people who cannot be helped (Dunlap & Webster, in press).

Susan Jones, Jen Gilbride-Brown, and Anna Gasiorski (2005) describe the challenges of working with students who exhibit both passive and active resistance to service-learning. An example of the former are "good volunteers," who may indicate that they enjoy doing the service but that they do not see how the service relates to classroom concepts and theories or their own learning (Jones et al., 2005). "Active resisters," on the other hand, can be hostile and disruptive during the entire service and classroom experiences (Jones et al., 2005). It is critical that service-learning educators respect and support students' current realities and engage them starting with where they are in their own development. Fortunately, resources exist to assist service-learning educators in addressing these challenges, including Dunlap and Webster (in press); Jones, Gilbride-Brown, and Gasiorski (2005), and O'Grady (2000).

Can Campus–Community Partnerships for Service-Learning Be Reciprocal Relationships Among Equals?

Jane Kendall began to address this question after observing that in the 1960s and 1970s, the early years of service-learning, colleges overlooked community voice, much less partnership, as fundamental. She reflects on some of the hard lessons learned in this process:

> We are learning that without an emphasis on the relationship between the server and "those served" as a reciprocal exchange between equals that relationship can easily break down. . . . Paternalism, unequal relationships between the parties involved, and a tendency to focus only on charity— "doing for" or "helping" others—rather than on supporting others to meet their own needs all became gaping pitfalls for program after well-intentioned program. (Kendall, 1990, pp. 9–10)

In the ensuing years, scholars have noted another significant side effect of the growth of service-learning, that some communities feel that they have been used as "learning laboratories" or are "being partnered to the point of exhaustion" (Ramaley, 2000, p. 241). Despite tremendous inequities in resources, colleges have attempted to establish partnerships with community organizations that, all too often, simply lacked the human, organizational, or fiscal infrastructure to be able to serve as a full partner. In addition, there has been a history of " 'partnerships in name only,' in which the partnership essentially exists in a grant application or university promotional brochure" (Jacoby, 2003, pp. xvii–xviii).

A considerable literature has developed in recent years on the principles and practices of campus–community partnerships for service-learning and beyond (see Jacoby, 2003; Ramaley, 2000; and Torres, 2000). Each set of principles references mutual goals, trust and respect, clear and regular communication, collaboration, and shared resources brought to bear to solve mutually agreed-upon problems. These principles, like my own definition of service-learning, are all based upon the concepts of reciprocity and mutuality (Jacoby, 1996, 2003). In the words of Community-Campus Partnerships for Health (2001), "The partnership balances power among partners and enables resources among partners to be shared" (p. 14). John Saltmarsh (1998) defines what he believes is "true reciprocity":

> To learn what it means to be part of a community is to participate in the life of the community in such a way that power and its relations are analyzed and critiqued in the context of a reciprocal relationship—what affects me affects the wider community, and what affects the wider community affects me. The consequences are indistinguishable. (pp. 7, 21)

In light of these principles, the question has been raised whether institutions of higher education can enter into genuinely equitable, reciprocal partnerships with community organizations or communities. Katie Hershey and Jason Chan (2007) posit that "we have not fully considered the degree to which our relative power and privilege (mis)informs how we design, structure, and implement our service-learning programs." Can campus–community partnerships ever be reciprocal partnerships among equals? Or are the disparities in resources, power, and sphere of influence on the side of higher education too striking to permit equality?

Nadinne Cruz and Dwight Giles (2000) propose an approach to assessment of service-learning from the community's perspective that focuses on community assets; uses action research; and, most significantly, involves the campus–community partnership as the unit of analysis. Sherril B. Gelmon (2003) elaborates on this approach by offering an assessment framework for understanding the process of collaboration and for assessing the level and viability of partnership. Much more research and assessment are required to determine the extent to which colleges and communities can authentically and equitably partner to meet mutual needs and to enhance the commons.

Does Service-Learning Perpetuate the Status Quo?

Service-learning scholars and practitioners have long wondered whether service-learning is—and should be—about social change or social justice. In 1995, Keith Morton proposed three paradigms for service-learning: charity, project, and social change. He argued that service represented by each of these paradigms can be done in "thick" ways that are "grounded in deeply held, internally coherent values; match means and ends; describe a primary way of interpreting and relating to the world; offer a way of defining problems and solutions; and suggest a vision of what a transformed world might look like" (p. 28). The "thin" versions of the paradigms, on the other hand, include charity that imposes services on "others" and projects that institutionalize power inequality, perpetuate dependency, raise false expectations, and magnify social divisions (Morton, 1995).

Kathleen Densmore (2000) observes that community service has historically not been directed at analyzing or eliminating the root causes of social injustice. Even today, she states that many service-learning programs

> are oriented toward helping individuals and groups accommodate themselves to current economic and political realities, rather than toward designing and constructing new possibilities for social progress. Conceived in these terms, [service-learning] tends to reinforce basic inequalities and, at best, to postpone explosive social conflict. (Densmore, 2000, p. 54)

If we fail to confront the structural inequities that create unjust and oppressive conditions, service-learning risks offering what Paolo Freire (1970/1997) calls "false generosity," acts of service that validate the status quo by perpetuating the need for service (p. 26). Margaret Himley warns that even service-learning supposedly committed to social justice may perpetuate oppressive conditions and assumptions:

The "goodness" of proximity to the "stranger" becomes transformed as a reflection of one's own "good citizen" status; the "helping" of the server masks a deeper need since "the [college] students need to meet their twenty-four hour requirement, need stories to tell about the kids, need the site and its documents to write about. . . . They also need something big to happen for their final papers." (cited in Butin, 2007, p. 3)

Another issue to consider is whether community agencies and institutions that serve as service-learning sites function in ways that seek to liberate oppressed racial and class groups, or in contrast, whether they render services to these populations without significantly challenging the status quo of power and privilege (Chesler & Vasques Scalera, 2000). The nature of the agency's or institution's approach as one of charity versus justice will affect the kinds of work that students perform and what they learn from their service. The questions that Morton (1995) raises in the conclusion of his article about the three paradigms of service are still critical ones today: "Is our concern the type of service activity that is done, or the integrity with which it is done? How do we know if we are moving toward justice?" (p. 31).

Should Service-Learning Be Globalized?

American institutions of higher education universally recognize their fundamental role in preparing students to engage responsibly and productively in a world that is becoming increasingly interconnected and interdependent. Nearly every institutional mission statement includes something to the effect of educating students to be global citizens who are prepared "to understand, live successfully within, and provide enlightened leadership to a richly diverse and increasingly complex world" (Wilson-Oyelaran, 2007).

As a result, there is no doubt that among the most rapidly growing practices in higher education are those designed to promote global citizenship. The number of American students studying abroad for credit rose from 84,000 to more than 220,000 in the past decade (Redden, 2008). As study abroad options for American students grow in number, they also grow in variety. More and more colleges are developing programs that combine study abroad with service-learning.

Although service-learning advocates have reason to be happy about the growth and proliferation of programs based on the powerful educational potential of global service-learning, the increasing importance placed on student participation in international experiences raises concomitant concerns. The same concerns that many of us have with the affordability and accessibility of study and travel abroad apply equally well to international service-learning opportunities. The issues addressed earlier under question 3 regarding whether service-learning is accessible to all students apply here and are complicated by the life situations of students who must work to attend college, who have family obligations, or who face cultural and other personal obstacles in spending time abroad in study and service.

Another challenge for international service-learning is that the obstacles that inhibit the viability of domestic campus–community partnerships affect international partnerships as well. For example, the duration and consistency of the service needed by the community often conflict with the length of academic terms. In addition, the recent trend toward shorter experiences abroad, often 1 to 3 weeks in duration, has profound effects on community partners. The duration and regularity of student participants' contributions must be sufficient to offset the time spent by members of the community or organization. Anything less amounts to exploitation of the very people that the service intends to assist (Brown, 2006). As is the case for domestic partnerships, it is critical to avoid placing students in local or international settings based solely on desired student learning outcomes or on providing services that perpetuate a state of need, rather than seeking and addressing the root causes of the need (Jacoby, 1996).

A significant issue to consider in the rush to create global service-learning opportunities for our students is whether our neighboring communities will suffer if our energy and resources turn from the local to the global. It is worth noting that there is virtually nowhere in the United States without an immigrant population. This country is itself an international culture, and there are many opportunities for students to interact with individuals of widely varying backgrounds, cultures, customs, and beliefs. Global problems—including hunger and homelessness, unequal educational opportunity, crime, and lack of accessible health care—also plague cities and communities throughout this nation. We need to ask ourselves questions such as: Could students learn about the assets and problems of indigenous populations by visiting an American Indian reservation in South Dakota instead of traveling to an Aboriginal homeland in Australia? Could they learn Spanish language skills as they engage in community enhancement projects

in Latino neighborhoods near the campus? Our domestic community partners will surely ask these questions; it would serve us well to consider them
ourselves first.

Should Service-Learning Be Institutionalized?

Service-learning educators and advocates have created a strong, comprehensive, and credible set of models for institutionalizing service-learning through
the development of a campus-wide infrastructure (Bringle & Hatcher, 1996;
Furco, 2001; Holland, 1997; Hollander, Saltmarsh, & Zlotkowski, 2001;
Pigza & Troppe, 2003). These models offer assessment tools to enable institutions to determine the degree—ranging from low relevance to full integration—to which service-learning is institutionalized. Although factors vary
from model to model, they generally include the following: presence in key
documents, such as the mission and strategic plan; whether funding is shaky
or secure; the extent to which the president and other leaders mention it in
speeches and fund-raising efforts; the breadth and intensity of cross-campus
and community partnerships; and the percentage of students, faculty, and
staff who are aware of the initiatives and are involved in them. Institutionalization of service-learning has been strongly supported through funding and
technical assistance by the federal government through the programs of the
Corporation for National and Community Service.

Although most service-learning educators believe that institutionalization is required for service-learning to survive and thrive in the long run, a
growing number question this assumption. The underlying query is: What
is the fundamental purpose of service-learning in higher education? If, in
fact, the purpose of service-learning is transformational, to challenge the
status quo of power and privilege, can this be accomplished if service-learning is part of the fabric of the institution?

The general tendency of service-learning is to avoid politicizing the
learning experience (Vogelgesang & Rhoads, 2003). However, "as a consequence, student idealism and its transformative potential may be thwarted
by the power of institutionalized norms and structures" (Vogelgesang &
Rhoads, 2003, p. 3). Contrary to the service-learning mainstream, a small but
powerful body of work conceptualizes service-learning in a way that places
issues of social justice at the center (Mendel-Reyes, 1998; Neururer &
Rhoads, 1998; Rhoads, 1997, 1998; Westheimer & Kahne, 1998). Embracing

the work of Freire, they advocate for service-learning to be a counternormative pedagogy in which "the political becomes the very center of learning" (Vogelgesang & Rhoads, 2003, p. 4). Meta Mendel-Reyes (1998) exemplifies the almost revolutionary potential of service-learning in this way: "The challenge of democratic education today is to teach students how to participate in a democracy that does not yet exist, and more, how to help bring about that democracy" (p. 34). Joseph Kahne, Joel Westheimer, and Bethany Rogers (2000) believe that

> the vast majority of large service-learning initiatives emphasize voluntarism and charity but do not teach about social movements, analysis of social and economic structures, and systemic change. Accordingly, research has concentrated on a conception of citizenship that privileges individual acts of compassion and kindness over social action and the pursuit of social justice. (p. 45)

In terms of institutionalization, Hershey and Chan (2007) wonder: "Does institutionalizing service-learning programs effectively institutionalize need for service?"

Critical questions include: Can service-learning be institutionalized in higher education and, at the same time, seek to create social justice by countering current structures of power and privilege? Would service-learning lose its power to make a difference if it lost its transformational edge and became a mainstream, neutral practice? This places service-learning squarely in a double bind: "If it attempts to be a truly radical and transformative (liberal) practice, it faces potential censure and sanction. If it attempts to be politically balanced to avoid such an attack, it risks losing any power to make a difference" (Butin, 2006, pp. 485–486). The future of service-learning will be shaped by how its proponents address this challenge.

Conclusion

Despite the complex questions that face the field of service-learning, I remain one of its strong advocates and one who believes in its potential to affect students, communities, and higher education positively. However, this optimism does not come without serious qualification. We have much challenging work to do. It is essential that educators, community partners, students, civil society and business leaders, and representatives of government and foundations come together to carefully consider the questions raised in this chapter and to act according to sound judgment, guiding principles, promising practice models, and continued research and analysis.

We must not allow our practice to become all consuming so that we fail to engage in ongoing reflection, discussion, and scholarly inquiry. We must do all we can to create and sustain institutions and environments that nurture the dynamic tension between action and reflection that is the very essence of service-learning.

References

Bringle, R. G., & Hatcher, J. A. (1995, Fall). A service learning curriculum for faculty. *Michigan Journal of Community Service Learning*.

Bringle, R. G., & Hatcher, J. A. (1996). Implementing service learning in higher education. *Journal of Higher Education, 67*(2), 221–239.

Brown, N. (2006). Embedding engagement in higher education: Preparing global citizens through international service-learning. http://www.compact.org/20th/read/preparing_global_citizens.

Butin, D. W. (Ed.). (2005). *Service-learning in higher education*. New York: Palgrave McMillan.

Butin, D. W. (2006). The limits of service-learning in higher education. *The Review of Higher Education, 29*(4), 473–498.

Butin, D. W. (2007). Justice-learning: Service-learning as justice-oriented education. *Equity & Excellence in Education, 40*, 1–7.

Chesler, M., & Vasques Scalera, C. (2000, Fall). Race and gender issues related to service-learning research. *Michigan Journal of Community Service Learning*, special issue, 18–27.

Cruz, N., & Giles, D. E., Jr. (2000, Fall). Where's the community in service-learning research? *Michigan Journal of Community Service Learning*, special issue, 28–34.

Densmore, K. (2000). Service learning and multicultural education: Suspect or transformative? In C. R. O'Grady (Ed.), *Integrating service learning and multicultural education in colleges and universities*. Mahwah, NJ: Lawrence Erlbaum Associates.

Dunlap, M. R., & Webster, N. (in press). Enhancing intercultural competence through civic engagement. In B. Jacoby (Ed.), *Civic engagement in higher education*. San Francisco: Jossey-Bass.

Eyler, J. (2000, Fall). Impact of service-learning on student learning. *Michigan Journal of Community Service Learning*, special issue, 11–17.

Eyler, J. (2002). Stretching to meet the challenge: Improving the quality of research to improve the quality of service-learning. In S. H. Billig & A. Furco (Eds.), *Service-learning through a multidisciplinary lens.* Advances in Service-Learning series. Greenwich, CT: Information Age Publishing.

Eyler, J., & Giles, D. E. (1999). *Where's the learning in service-learning?* San Francisco: Jossey-Bass.

Freire, P. (1997). *Pedagogy of the oppressed.* New York: Continuum Publishing. (Original work published 1970).

Furco, A. (2001, June). *Institutionalizing service-learning in higher education: Findings from a three-year study (1997–2000).* Paper presented at The Forum on Volunteerism, Service, and Learning in Higher Education, College Park, MD.

Gelmon, S. (2003). Assessment as a means of building service-learning partnerships. In B. Jacoby (Ed.), *Building partnerships for service-learning.* San Francisco: Jossey-Bass.

Giles, D., Porter Honnet, E., and Migliore, S. (1991). *Research agenda for combining service and learning in the 1990s.* Raleigh, NC: National Society for Experiential Education.

Hershey, K., & Chan, J. (2007, February 9). Perpetuating systems of power and privilege? A critical approach to service-learning. Presentation at Maryland Student Affairs Conference, College Park, MD.

Holland, B. (1997). Analyzing institutional commitment to service: A model of key organizational factors. *Michigan Journal of Community Service Learning, 4*, 30–41.

Hollander, E., Saltmarsh, J., & Zlotkowski, E. (2001). Indicators of engagement. In L. A. Simon, M. Kenny, K. Brabeck, & R M. Lerner (Eds.), *Learning to serve: Promoting civil society through service-learning.* Norwell, MA: Kluwer.

Jacoby, B. (Ed.). (1996). *Service-learning in higher education: Concepts and practices.* San Francisco: Jossey-Bass.

Jacoby, B. (Ed.). (2003). *Building partnerships for service-learning.* San Francisco: Jossey-Bass.

Jacoby, B. (Ed.). (2009). *Civic engagement in higher education: Concepts and practices.* San Francisco: Jossey-Bass.

Jones, S., Gilbride-Brown, J., & Gasiorski, A. (2005). Getting inside the "underside" of service-learning: Student resistance and possibilities. In D. W. Butin (Ed.), *Service-learning in higher education.* New York: Palgrave McMillan.

Kahne, J., Westheimer, J., & Rogers, B. (2000). Service-learning and citizenship: directions for research. *Michigan Journal of Community Service Learning.* Special issue.

Kendall, J. (1990). *Combining service and learning: A resource book for community and public service* (Vol. 1). Raleigh, NC: National Society for Internships and Experiential Education.

Mendel-Reyes, M. (1998). Academic service-learning: A pedagogy of action and reflection. *New Directions for Teaching and Learning, 73*, 31–38.

Morton, K. (1995, Fall). The irony of service: Charity, project and social change in service-learning. *Michigan Journal of Community Service Learning*, 19–32.

Neururer, J., & Rhoads, R. A. (1998). Community service: Panacea, paradox, or potentiation. *Journal of College Student Development, 39*(4), 321–330.

O'Grady, C. R. (2000). *Integrating service learning and multicultural education in colleges and universities.* Mahwah, NJ: Erlbaum.

Pigza, J. M., & Troppe, M. L. (2003). Developing an infrastructure for service-learning and community engagement. In B. Jacoby (Ed.), *Building partnerships for service-learning.* San Francisco: Jossey-Bass.

Ramaley, J. A. (2000). The perspective of a comprehensive university. In T. Ehrlich (Ed.), *Civic responsibility in higher education.* Phoenix: Oryx.

Redden, E. (2008). Managing study abroad. *Inside Higher Ed.* www.inside highered.com/news/2008/01/16/nafsa]

Rhoads, R. A. (1997). Interpreting identity politics: The educational challenge of contemporary student activism. *Journal of College Student Development, 38*(5), 508–519.

Rhoads, R. A. (1998). In the service of citizenship: A study of student involvement in community service. *Journal of Higher Education, 69*, 277–297.

Saltmarsh, J. (1998, Summer). Exploring the meanings of community/university partnerships. *National Society for Experiential Education Quarterly*, 6–22.

ServiceNation. (2008). *ServiceNation: Strategies for becoming a nation of service.* Cambridge, MA: Author.

Stanton, T. K. (2007). *New times demand new scholarship II.* Los Angeles, CA: University of California–Los Angeles.

Torres, J. (Ed.). (2000). *Benchmarks for campus-community partnerships.* Providence, RI: Campus Compact.

Vogelgesang, L. J., & Rhoads, R. A. (2003). Advancing a broad notion of public engagement: The limitations of contemporary service learning. *Journal of College and Character.* Retrieved October 8, 2008, from www.collegevalues.org/seere view.cfm?id = 1017

Westheimer, J., & Kahne, J. (1998). Education for action: Preparing youth for participatory democracy. In W. Ayers & T. Quinn (Eds.), *Democracy and education: A teaching for social justice reader.* New York: New Press and Teachers College Press.

Wilson-Oyelaran, E. (2007). Blending local and global experiences in service of civic engagement. http://www.compact.org/20th/read/blending_local_and_global_ex periences

7

SERVICE-LEARNING'S IMPACT ON ATTITUDES AND BEHAVIOR

A Review and Update

Joseph A. Erickson

I n this chapter, I reexamine and update the ongoing discussion regarding service-learning's impact on learners' attitudes and beliefs. For many years, advocates have promoted service-learning's capacity to influence student attitudes and beliefs, especially toward diversity, social justice, and other pro-social attitudes (Delve, Mintz, & Stewart, 1990; Dunlap, 1998). At the same time, many researchers have cautioned service-learning practitioners about the potential risks involved in using service-learning to affect these attitudes and beliefs. In particular, researchers have cautioned about the potential for unintended consequences of service-learning—the potential for increased prejudice, stereotyping, and victim blaming in service-learning participants (Erickson & O'Connor, 2000; Hollis, 2004; Jones, 2002; Kendall & Associates, 1990).

The goals for using service-learning have always included an array of intended and expected outcomes such as cognitive, behavioral, and social outcomes (Batchelder & Root, 1994; Billig, Root, & Jesse, 2005; Eyler & Giles, 1994, Eyler & Giles, 1999; Hurd, 2006). More recently, advocates have attempted to redirect and expand the service-learning community mission toward the goals of using service-learning as a means to promote civic and political engagement (e.g., Berman, 2008; Boyte & Hollander, 1999; Checkoway, 2001; Colby, Beaumont, Ehrlich, & Corngold, 2007; Glickman, 2008; Haynes & Pickeral, 2008; Leighninger & Levine, 2008; Mendel-Reyes, 1998). The particular reasons for this shift could (and perhaps should) be a topic for an entirely different essay, but I believe this switch is an attempt by members of the education community to place civic engagement and democratic values in a more central place in the mission of K–16 education in the United States during a period of higher expectations and accountability.

My primary purpose in this chapter is to tease out what difference it makes to emphasize civic engagement versus other pro-social attitudes and discover whether the same caveats that applied earlier still apply to our pursuit of civically engaged learners. I also review the latest research in the social psychology of attitude change to see what impacts refinements in this field have for those employing service-learning.

Personal and Social Outcomes and Service-Learning

I have argued previously that service-learning practice has a strong basis in psychological theory and practice and that service-learning has a tremendous potential to affect learners in ways other forms of teaching may not (Erickson & Santmire, 2001). But this previous research also raised some red flags: unanticipated outcomes such as increased prejudice and bias on the part of learners toward the very groups with whom they are doing service. The concern expressed in my earlier writings was that to be ignorant of these red flags may lead to counterintuitive outcomes that are the *opposite* of that which most service-learning practitioners would have anticipated. In 2000 and 2001 (Erickson & O'Connor, 2000; Erickson & Santmire, 2001), I argued that it may very well be the case that those attempting to implement service-learning in their classrooms may do more harm than good if they engage in service-learning that doesn't fulfill certain minimum necessary requirements suggested by the learning of social psychologists.

At least two issues need to be addressed to better understand what's changed and what's the same in regard to the critical question of how effective service-learning is on changing learners' attitudes: (a) the emerging emphasis in the service-learning community on civic engagement as a primary attitudinal and behavioral goal (rather than the earlier goal of reducing antisocial attitudes) and (b) to draw upon the very latest research on attitude change to see what updating may be necessary in our approaches to be successful in engaging students in the democratic process.

Changing Attitudes and Intentions

Although civic engagement and democratic values have appeared among the intended goals for service-learning for probably all of its history, recently many advocates have urged service-learning practitioners to renew and reframe their efforts primarily around these goals. These efforts have been tied to broader institutional goal setting at the college and university levels (Boyte & Hollander, 1999; Checkoway, 2001; Colby et al., 2007; Ehrlich, 2000; Rhodes, 2003). At the K–12 level, the civic mission of schools has been touted as a highly desirable goal for schools to seek and is perhaps even the preferred option (Berman, 2008; Boston, Pearson, & Halperin, 2005; DeCesare, 2006; Education Commission of the States, 2000; Glickman, 2008; Gomez, 1999; Haynes & Pickeral, 2008; Leighninger & Levine, 2008), although this goal may struggle for acceptance in K–12 schools in light of greater emphasis on accountability and testing in public schools.

What is meant by civic engagement? Erhlich (2000) proposes "civic engagement means working to make a difference in the civic life of our communities and developing the combination of knowledge, skills, values, and motivation to make that difference" (p. vi). Others write in terms of "citizenship skills" (Mendel-Reyes, 1998), "political engagement" (Colby et al., 2007), or "political-moral identity" (Youniss & Yates, 1997); each involves "students learning the skills of democracy—critical thinking, public deliberation, community building, and collaborative action—by practicing them" (Mendel-Reyes, 1998, p. 36).

Although not abandoning other pro-social attitude benefits, the main focus of service-learning's attitude-change intentions appear to have shifted during the past 10 years away from the reduction of prejudice, empathy with disadvantaged communities, and so forth, to the goal of civic engagement. Again, the reasons for this shift may be the topic for a completely different paper, but I believe it is safe to assert that the core institutional goal of many service-learning advocates and administrators has dramatically shifted. This is understandable given the tremendous pressures American schools face in the early 21st century. Schools are wedged between the enormous forces of learner and community needs on one side and government and community expectations on the other. Positioning schools in this pressure-packed environment demands a set of social and political skills that can be described at the very least as demanding. Reminding community members of the schools' historic place in educating its citizens in democratic values captures for schools a place at the table as the United States continues to struggle with building a nation out of divergent peoples and their different cultural experiences.

Advocates promote service-learning as a tool for affecting the entire array of learning outcomes, including knowledge, skills, and attitudes (Billig et al., 2005; Hurd, 2006). To effect attitude change, social psychologists suggest a need for learner engagement that involves cognitive and affective components and promotes reflecting on personal identity, reducing anxiety, and developing new affiliations and attitudes (Dovidio, Glick, & Rudman, 2005). Changing attitudes and beliefs, whether they are pro-social (i.e., attitudes such as the reduction of prejudice or the enhancement of empathy for the disadvantaged) or civil (i.e., enhancing civic engagement and commitment to democratic and community values), involves substantial reflection and reintegration of personal identity and beliefs as well as the acquisition of new knowledge and skills. Both pursuits involve substantially similar cognitive and affective change processes. Both tasks are very difficult to achieve and involve the possibility (even high probability) that even if the necessary conditions are present, change still may not occur.

Therefore, is the pursuit of civic engagement substantially different in character and intentions to suggest that the same cautions that applied previously would not continue to apply? I believe the answer is no. In essence, it appears that the goal of changing attitudes toward civic and political engagement is strikingly similar to changing attitudes toward out-groups, stereotypes, and prejudice. Although resetting the attitudinal goals for service-learning toward civic engagement and away from other pro-social goals such as reducing prejudice and appreciating diversity may represent a significant shift for the service-learning field, it appears this change doesn't substantially alter the need for certain types of social and personal engagement and reflection. Whether we aim to change personal prejudices or promote civic engagement, the general road map for how we affect these attitudes remains the same. If the pedagogical tasks are substantially similar, then the same caveats to which the earlier critics pointed still apply.

What were those caveats? In the next section, I briefly review those classic concerns and also discuss the changes to these concerns as a result of the latest findings in social psychology.

Social-Psychological Factors in Attitude Change: A Review and an Update

Claims for service-learning's effectiveness as an attitude change agent comes from practitioners and participants who have observed attitude change among service-learning participants. The theoretical basis for claims of service-learning's efficacy as a social change tool go all the way back to Dewey (1938). Dewey's theories of experience and learning have formed the foundation for experiential education's claim that learning through experience is superior to less engaging forms of learning. Others extended Dewey's thinking to the practice of service-learning (e.g., Giles, 1991; Kolb, 1975, 1984). These theories form the core of service-learning's basic formulation and are the basis for evaluating what is appropriate service-learning practice.

Many have promoted service-learning practice as having the capacity to change negative social attitudes toward out-groups (i.e., target groups of people about which one has a stereotypic, biased, or prejudiced set of attitudes and/or beliefs). For example, Delve, Mintz, and Stewart (1990) draw on frequent examples illustrating ways in which service-learning creates the necessary conditions for positive attitude and value change.

Alternately, a number of critics (e.g., Erickson & O'Connor, 2000; Hollis, 2004; Jones, 2002; Kendall & Associates, 1990) have suggested that service-learning may do more harm than good if the experience is too short or the community is given too little attention by participants. Negative and stereotypical attitudes will be strengthened if crucial and little-known minimum standards for effective practice are not followed. As Allport (1954) pointed out, "Casual contact has left matters worse than before" (p. 264). These critics suggest that too little attention is paid to a precise understanding of the theoretical assumptions and pedagogical activities necessary for service-learning to be effective at changing attitudes in its participants.

So, what are the precise conditions in which real attitude change can occur according to social psychologists and others engaged in studying personality and social cognition? Classically, that question was often answered by looking at the Contact Theory (Allport, 1954; Amir, 1969; Cook, 1985).

More recently, refinements in Contact Theory have deepened our understanding of the necessary (conditions that must be present for change to occur) but not sufficient (even when present, do not always guarantee change) conditions for authentic attitude change to occur. Presently, I discuss these conditions to ascertain whether any changes are necessary in our formulations of service-learning practice for our renewed effort at forming civically engaged learners.

Contact Theory: Minimum Conditions to Reduce Prejudice

Contact Theory (CT), also called the *contact hypothesis,* was introduced and developed by social psychologists as a way to understand and evaluate the various conditions under which face-to-face contact would promote greater personal and social understanding between members of different groups (Allport, 1954; Amir, 1969; Cook, 1985). In this section, I review CT as a theoretical framework from which I can evaluate the potential effectiveness of service-learning as an attitude-change tool. CT traces the minimum necessary conditions through which favorable experiences with individual members of an out-group may be transmitted or generalized to one's group-related attitudes (Pettigrew, 1988; Rothbart, 1996). Recent research has outlined important clarifications to CT, although much of the basic core of CT remains consistent (Dovidio et al., 2005). Many of these concerns focus on the specific context(s) in which varied social identities (i.e., the relevant aspects of the self that are tapped in different social contexts) are aroused (e.g., to engage in active reflection on our opinions about our own or another's culture, we must have our own cultural identity in conscious awareness) (Dovidio et al., 2005; Gaertner, Dovidio, & Bachman, 1996).

At its core, CT describes the necessary conditions under which contact inhibits or reduces prejudice. The four main factors as outlined by Allport (1954) in his classic book, *The Nature of Prejudice,* are as follows:

1. Equal status contact
2. Pursuit of common goals
3. Intergroup cooperation
4. Support of authorities, custom, or law

Let's briefly review these conditions, and then identify two new concerns raised by more recent research developments. (For a more thorough discussion of CT and its application to service-learning, see Erickson & O'Connor, 2000.)

Equal status contact refers to the extent to which both the service provider and recipient of service have a comparatively equal amount of social status. In practice, this is very difficult to obtain in many community service interactions because of the lower status implied by being in need of service in some way.

The pursuit of common goals refers to the character of the task on which both service provider and recipient are working. Perhaps the best example of a social situation in which the common goal factor is met is the sports team—different people from different social groups performing differentiated tasks in pursuit of a unified goal. When the affiliation between provider and recipient is authentically in pursuit of common goals, real attitude change may occur.

Intergroup cooperation refers to the manner in which the service participant first identifies as a member of a special group such as ethnicity, political affiliation, or nationality. Once one's in-group identity is salient, the service participant must then recognize others' group (or "out-group") identity and perceive a constructive cooperative relationship between in-group and out-group. In civic engagement, I wonder whether service participants, once their political identity has been activated, will tend to see pursuit of their goals as involving the cooperation of the "opposition" (or out-group) forces or entities.

Finally, the prevailing social norms of a community, that is, the support of authorities, social custom, or laws, must promote positive contact with out-group members. This support could be in the form of special outreach programs such as structured diversity training; laws prohibiting discrimination; or other organizational efforts such as a special initiative from a business, religious, or fraternal organization (e.g., a "Get Out the Vote" drive).

Another condition long associated with classic CT is long-term contact. Quick, casual, and/or superficial interactions generally promote entrenched attitudes. Social psychologists, especially those focused on the cognitive aspects of attitude change, say that it is for this purpose (i.e., making quick judgments) that we form generalizations in our attitudes in the first place (Allport, 1954; Dovidio et al., 2005).

Because of the practical logistics of doing service-learning in educational settings (academic terms, transportation issues, student turnover via matriculation and graduation, etc.), many service activities are short in duration and may violate this condition. Without long-term contact (long-term either in intensity or duration, or both), service relationships can actually increase the degree and severity of attitude entrenchment.

Long-term status may be difficult to achieve as long as schools define service placements solely within the context of a course or academic term. One way to move beyond these limits and potentially expand the time frame in which the contact occurs is to create service placements that extend over two or more academic terms or over several years in more than one course. This would require coordination among two or more instructors and involve a more comprehensive and careful integration of the service activities with the school's curriculum, but the benefits would be a greater likelihood of authentic attitude change on the part of students.

These five conditions form the core of classic CT. Recent developments have extended our understanding of the facilitating conditions that promote attitude change.

New Developments in Contact Theory

To commemorate the 50th anniversary of the release of Allport's classic book, Dovidio, Glick, and Rudman (2005) released *On the Nature of Prejudice: Fifty Years After Allport*. In this book, more than 40 social psychologists attempt to review and renew Allport's classic theory based on the latest research developments. Although many new details have emerged over the past 50 years, a consistent theme among these authors and others in this field is the degree to which most of Allport's original formulations have held up. The conditions we have just reviewed (equal status, common goals, intergroup cooperation, and community support, along with the fifth condition of long-term contact) all remain important to the attitude change process.

Several new issues have emerged in recent research that have extended and elaborated Allport's original formulation, whereas other aspects of Allport's work have been dropped or deemphasized. Some of these issues do not apply to the question at hand, but two issues emerge as potentially expanding our understanding of attitude change in the classroom and community: the important role of affect, particularly anxiety, in facilitating or inhibiting attitude change (Pettigrew & Tropp, 2000, 2005), and the importance of rousing a sense of identity among participants (Gaertner & Dovidio, 2000; Kenworthy, Turner, Hewstone, & Voci, 2005).

Much of the emphasis among advocates of using service-learning as a means to increase civic engagement focuses on developing not only the necessary cognitive skills, but also the personal and social attitudes required of full civic participation. Recent research indicates that the affective state of the learner may play a critical facilitating role in the process of attitude change, possibly even more important than cognition (Pettigrew & Tropp, 2000, 2005). When learners experience higher levels of anxiety, they cognitively shut down and are not open to unfamiliar thoughts. It appears that those attempting to engage learners in the civic life of the community would be well advised to attend carefully to reducing as much as possible elevated levels of anxiety in their participants.

Advocates also often point to personal and political identity factors as being crucial to developing civic engagement in learners (e.g., Colby et al., 2007; Youniss & Yates, 1997). Identity formation has also been recognized as an important factor in attitude change research. When attempting to engage learners in attitude change, learners' ability to rouse a sense of identity, in terms of their uniqueness and differences, needs to be addressed (Dunlap, 1993; Kenworthy et al., 2005). Individuals cannot begin to reflect on and reassess their identities without first placing themselves in the relevant social contexts in which their identity is situated. For example, one cannot reflect on what it means to be an American unless one can first rouse a cognitive vision of "American-ness," and then differentiate that awareness from what it means to *not* be an American. This finding suggests that learning activities aimed at developing a civic identity must first provoke a sense of group affiliation. Only after this requisite first step is accomplished ("I am an American") can we assist learners in reevaluating or activating their role in that group ("I intend to be an engaged American citizen").

Conclusion

How should these civic virtues be taught? What are good models of the engaged campus? There are no easy answers to these pressing questions.

—T. Ehrlich, *Civic Responsibility*
and Higher Education

Service-learning pedagogy *must* meet certain necessary but not sufficient conditions as described to have any hope of successfully changing learner attitudes and behavior. Researchers have looked at these mechanisms for more than 70 years and have identified these conditions, and how, if followed, we can be successful in changing learners' attitudes and behavior. Although there are no simple answers or recipes to follow, if we are serious about promoting authentic civic engagement, we should not be satisfied accepting service-learning practice that is vague or inattentive to these necessary conditions. The ultimate value or worth of the service-learning experiences we provide depends on the quality of these experiences (Eyler & Giles, 1999). Rigorous understanding and application of theories of development, cognition, and attitude change suggest that service-learning, designed and implemented in such a way as to meet these conditions, should be expected to enhance academic learning and attitude change over instruction that does not involve these components.

If these conditions are not met, the intended results (enhancing civic engagement) could be diminished or, even more problematic, could make students' attitudes worse than they were before; that is, students may be turned off to civic engagement. Studies of service-learning's effectiveness should include assessments of the extent to which these conditions are met. Such assessments would allow a much richer and rigorous examination of the effects of service-learning on learner attitudes.

As I have argued previously (Erickson & O'Connor, 2000; Erickson & Santmire, 2001), service-learning can be expected to enhance knowledge and change attitudes as long as it is conducted in the context of an academic discipline and in a manner that applies the powerful social and cognitive psychological principles noted here. I believe many of the concerns highlighted in previous research regarding service-learning and attitude change continue to be relevant. In general, service-learning teaching activities aimed at attitude change continue to lack the necessary conditions proposed by social psychologists. As a result, we can expect poor outcomes with respect to students' attitude change, and we will also see a *worsening* of student attitudes in the very domains in which we want to have impact. As Allport and others have observed, if we don't meet the minimum necessary conditions laid out in Contact Theory, we risk making matters worse rather than better. The new findings in social psychological research extend our understanding of the necessary conditions through which successful attitude change might occur, and we would be wise to consider these conditions when designing service-learning activities aimed at promoting civic engagement.

References

Allport, G. (1954). *The nature of prejudice.* Cambridge, MA: Addison-Wesley.

Amir, Y. (1969). Contact hypothesis in ethnic relations. *Psychological Bulletin, 106,* 74–106.

Amir, Y. (1976). The role of intergroup contact in change of prejudice and ethnic relations. In P. Katz (Ed.), *Toward the elimination of racism* (pp. 245–308). New York: Pergamon Press.

Batchelder, T. H., & Root, S. (1994). Effects of an undergraduate program to integrate academic learning and service: Cognitive, prosocial cognitive, and identity outcomes. *Journal of Adolescence, 17,* 341–355.

Berman, S. (2008). A superintendent's systemic notion of civics. *School Administrator, 65*(9), 29–31.

Billig, S., Root, S., & Jesse, D. (2005). The relationship between quality indicators of service-learning and student outcomes: Testing professional wisdom. In S. Billig, S. Root, & D. Jesse (Eds.), *Advances in service-learning research: Vol. 5. Improving service-learning practice: Research models to enhance impacts* (pp. 97–115). Greenwich, CT: Information Age.

Boston, B., Pearson, S., & Halperin, S. (2005). *Restoring the balance between academics and civic engagement in public schools.* Washington, DC: American Youth Policy Forum.

Boyte, H., & Hollander, E. (1999). *Wingspread declaration on renewing the civic mission of the American research university.* Wingspread Conference Report. Racine, WI: Johnson Foundation.

Checkoway, B. (2001). Renewing the civic mission of the American research university. *Journal of Higher Education, 72,* 125–147.

Colby, A., Beaumont, E., Ehrlich, T., & Corngold, J. (2007). *Educating for democracy.* San Francisco: Jossey-Bass.

Cook, S. (1985). Experimenting on social issues: The case of social desegregation. *American Psychologist, 40,* 452–460.

DeCesare, D. (2006). Transforming students into active stewards of democracy. Retrieved October 31, 2008, from www.ecs.org/clearinghouse/67/71/6771.pdf

Delve, C., Mintz, S., & Stewart, G. (1990*). Community service as value education.* San Francisco: Jossey-Bass.

Dewey, J. (1938). *Experience as education.* New York: Collier Books.

Dovidio, J., Glick, P., & Rudman, L. (2005). *On the nature of prejudice: Fifty years after Allport.* Malden, MA: Blackwell.

Dunlap, M. (1993). *New methods for examining prejudice.* Ann Arbor, MI: UMI Dissertations Services.

Dunlap, M. (1998). Methods of supporting students' critical reflection in courses incorporating service learning. *Teaching of Psychology, 25*(3), 208–210.

Education Commission of the States. (2000). Every student a citizen: Creating the democratic self. Retrieved October 31, 2008, from www.ecs.org/clearinghouse/16/77/1677.pdf

Ehrlich, T. (2000). *Civic responsibility and higher education.* Westport, CT: American Council on Education.

Erickson, J., & O'Connor, S. (2000). Service-learning's effect on prejudice: Does it reduce or promote it? In C. O'Grady (Ed.), *Transforming education, transforming the world: The integration of service-learning and multicultural education into higher education.* Mahwah, NJ: Erlbaum.

Erickson, J., & Santmire, T. (2001). Psychological bases of effective service-learning. In J. Anderson, K. Swick, & J. Yff (Eds.), *Strengthening service and learning in teacher education.* Washington, DC: American Association of Colleges for Teacher Education and the ERIC Clearinghouse for Teaching and Teacher Education.

Eyler, J., & Giles, D. (1999). *Where's the learning in service-learning?* San Francisco: Jossey-Bass.

Gaertner, S. L., & Dovidio, J. F. (2000). *Reducing intergroup bias: The Common Ingroup Identity Model.* Philadelphia, PA: Psychology Press.

Gaertner, S. Dovidio, J., & Bachman, B. (1996). Revisiting the contact hypothesis: The induction of a common ingroup identity. *International Journal of Intercultural Relations, 20*(3/4), 271–290.

Giles, D., Jr. (1991, Winter). Dewey's theory of experience: Implications for service learning. *Journal of Cooperative Education, 27*(2), 87–90.

Giles, D. E., & Eyler, J. (1994). The impact of a college community service laboratory on students' personal, social, and cognitive outcomes. *Journal of Adolescence, 17,* 327–339.

Glickman, C. (2008). Educating for citizenship. *School Administrator, 65*(9), 18–23.

Gomez, B. (1999). Service-learning: Every child a citizen. Education Commission of the States Issue Paper. Retrieved October 31, 2008, from eric.ed.gov:80/ERIC-Docs/data/ericdocs2sql/content_storage_01/0000019b/80/16/89/af.pdf

Haynes, C. & Pickerel, T. (2008). Renewing the Civic Mission of Schools, *School Administrator, 65*(9), 10–12.

Hollis, S. (2004). Blaming me, blaming you: Assessing service learning and participants' tendency to blame the victim. *Sociological Spectrum, 24,* 575–600.

Hurd, C. (2006). Is service-learning effective? A look at current research. Retrieved October 31, 2008, from tilt.colostate.edu/sl/faculty/Is_Service-Learning_Effective.p df

Jones, S. (2002). The underside of service learning. *About Campus, 7*(4), 10–15.

Kendall, J., & Associates. (1990). *Combining service and learning: A resource book for community and public service.* Raleigh, NC: National Society for Internships and Experiential Education.

Kenworthy, J., Turner, R., Hewstone, M., & Voci, A. (2005). Intergroup contact: When does it work, and why? In J. Dovidio, P. Glick, & L. Rudman (Eds.), *On the nature of prejudice: Fifty years after Allport* (pp. 278–292). Malden, MA: Blackwell.

Kolb, D. (1975). Toward an applied theory of experiential learning. In C. Cooper (Ed.), *Theories of group processes* (pp. 33–57). New York: Wiley.

Kolb, D. (1984). *Experiential learning: Experience as the source of learning and development.* Englewood Cliffs, NJ: Prentice Hall.

Leighninger, M., & Levine, P. (2008). Education in a rapidly changing democracy. *School Administrator, 65*(9), 25–28.

Mendel-Reyes, M. (1998). A pedagogy for citizenship: Service learning and democratic education. In R. Rhoads & J. Howard (Eds.), *Academic service learning: A pedagogy of action and reflection* (pp. 31–38). San Francisco: Jossey-Bass.

Pettigrew, T. (1988). The intergroup contact hypothesis reconsidered. In M. Hewstone & R. Brown (Eds.), *Contact and conflict in intergroup encounters* (pp. 169–195). Oxford: Basil Blackwell.

Pettigrew, T., & Tropp, L. (2000). Does intergroup contact reduce prejudice? Recent meta-analytic findings. In S. Oskamp (Ed.), *Reducing prejudice and discrimination* (pp. 93–114). Mahwah, NJ: Erlbaum.

Pettigrew, T., & Tropp, L. (2005). Allport's intergroup contact hypothesis: Its history and influence. In J. Dovidio, P. Glick, & L. Rudman (Eds.), *On the nature of prejudice: Fifty years after Allport* (pp. 262–277). Malden, MA: Blackwell.

Rhodes, R. (2003, Spring). How civic engagement is reframing liberal education. *Peer Review,* 25–28.

Rothbart, M. (1996). Category-exemplar dynamics and stereotype change. *International Journal of Intercultural Relations, 20*(3/4), 305–321.

Youniss, J., & Yates, M. (1997). *Community service and social responsibility.* Chicago: University of Chicago Press.

8

FUNDING SERVICE-LEARNING PROGRAMS

Marybeth Lima

The impetus for this chapter comes from practical experience and unfortunate reality. Service-learning programs cost money to run, and although many of us are accustomed to getting work done on a shoestring, the truth is that our work won't be done as well or at all without adequate funding. I facilitated two workshops on funding service-learning programs at the Gulf South Summit on Service-Learning and Civic Engagement in 2006 and 2007; there were overflow audiences both times, which leads me to believe that funding is an important topic for many of us. I have a capital-intensive service-learning program, and as a result, I spend more time chasing money than any other single activity. I have noticed that many organizations are willing to fund a program once, or to fund start-up of a project, but funds to maintain programs can be elusive. These factors require creativity and flexibility on the part of anyone raising funds for service-learning. I've also been turned down for funding—a lot. My successes, failures, trials, and tribulations have led to this chapter.

Although geared toward faculty and community partners, this chapter also contains information intended for service-learning directors. This chapter contains four major parts:

- How to determine whether you need funding, and if so, how much
- Overview of funding agencies and options
- Developing a fund-raising plan
- Writing successful proposals

Before we start, I'd like to share a quick note with respect to your philosophy on money. Money is one of the most charged issues we face in Western society. We all have a relationship with money, and some of our thoughts about it (for example, that it's a necessary evil) may not be conducive to making us feel excited about fund-raising or grant writing. Remember that money in and of itself is not evil; give yourself permission to go after it. There are many organizations and people who are eager to support a cause like yours. Your work has value, and if you don't determine its value and report it in ways that others will recognize, someone besides you and your service-learning team will. My suggestion is to focus on your service-learning goals, to execute a well-designed fund-raising plan to meet your goals, and to come to peace with the nuances of living in a capitalistic society.

How to Determine Whether You Need Funding and, If So, How Much

To determine whether you need funding (and if so, how much), you need to answer two questions:

- What is the objective of your service-learning project or program?
- What kind of budget is necessary to run this program (which items cost money in your program)?

For example, the objective of my service-learning program is to design and construct a safe, fun, accessible playground at every public elementary school in my city using a community-based design approach. We require approximately $2M to complete this task, a figure which we determined through a detailed needs assessment of every public elementary school playground.

Once you articulate the goals and objectives of your service-learning program, determining the budget is the next step. Typical budgetary items that you may need to execute a service-learning program are contained in Table 8.1. Keep in mind that you may not be asking for money for every item on this list, and that you may be matching a budget with some of these items (matching is discussed in Table 8.2).

When you figure out how much funding you need, you then have to figure out what kind of funding you need. There are hundreds of spending rules depending on the source of funding and the university's, agency's, and/

TABLE 8.1
Common Budget Components for a Service-Learning Project

Item	Description
Personnel	Salary for faculty, staff, student workers, community partners, volunteers, stipends for participants, etc.
Fringe benefits	For professional staff, usually a percentage of the salary requested, for example, 32%.
Operating costs	Phone, copier, office supplies.
Travel	Participant travel to service site, travel to conferences to share/learn about service-learning.
Materials and supplies	Physical items needed for the execution of your service-learning project (for me, pipes, platforms, timbers, mulch, fence, etc.).
Entertainment	Meals, T-shirts, etc., for volunteers at site.
Equipment	Equipment necessary to execute project.
Consulting	You may need a separate consultant to help execute aspects of your project such as assessment and evaluation.
Overhead (indirect costs)	A percentage of the grant funds requested to support your institution (maintenance of buildings, labs, streets, landscaping, and janitorial services, etc.).

or funder's rules regarding budgets. Two basic types of funding include grants, which you typically secure by writing a successful proposal, and donations, which you typically get from fund-raising. The next section provides a basic overview of funding agencies and an overview of options that you can pursue to raise necessary funds.

Overview of Funding Agencies and Options

Funding agencies fall into two broad categories, public and private. There are also two ways to pursue funding from these categories: solicited (the funder asks for proposals or requests for funding) and unsolicited (you approach the funder when it has not requested solicitations). Most funding opportunities are solicited. This section is not intended to be comprehensive, but it should provide you with the information you need to be familiar with major public and private funding agencies and to get started on researching funding opportunities through solicited and unsolicited channels.

Public funders include federal, state, and local governments, whereas private funders include corporations, faith-based organizations, foundations, service organizations and clubs, and other groups with a specific mission (for example, professional societies, fraternities, and sororities).

Other options include fund-raising events (silent auctions, pancake breakfasts, etc.), approaching individuals such as politicians and members of your community, and operating auxiliary programs in which you perform services for which you receive revenue. Examples of auxiliary programs include training, executive style or distance learning programs, forums, workshops/conferences, discussion communities, certification programs, and service programs.

The following sections provide more details about funding agencies and options as they relate to developing a fund-raising plan, and then more specifically to developing proposals for funding.

Developing a Fund-Raising Plan

A fund-raising plan is a comprehensive document that describes your short- and long-term funding needs and desires. All fund-raising plans should have (a) clear, measurable objectives; (b) a summary of descriptive and contact information of the public and private avenues that you plan to pursue for funding; (c) a list of the people who can help you (directly or indirectly) with your plan; and (d) a timeline and description of how you will proceed. Supporting documentation for your plan is also necessary, including a continuously updated database that describes the status of the agencies and people you've contacted and where you are in the process with each prospect, and targeted promotional materials that will help to promote your project. The following tips are intended to help you develop your fund-raising plan:

> *Work in a team setting.* As with every aspect of service-learning, when the community partner and university work together to pool their collective talents, contacts, and resources, the fund-raising plan will be as strong as possible. Even with this approach, many people involved in service-learning have little background in fund-raising

and public relations. These skill sets are critical if your service-learning program is capital intensive. If at all possible, recruit a team of people to assist with developing and executing your fund-raising plan. A strong public relations and/or marketing campaign goes hand-in-hand with fund-raising because people are more likely to support service-learning programs that have communicable, documented, significant success from a community standpoint and from a financial standpoint. A public relations expert can help to develop promotional materials for your program, for example, a one-page proposal/pitch with sample budget and illustrations of your project accomplishments; newspaper, newsletter, radio, or TV segments; short movies of your project; and various oral presentations for prospective funders (30-second elevator conversation, 5-minute sales pitch, full-blown presentation, etc.). Look for social entrepreneurs in your community and make use of their expertise. Once you have your team in place, make sure that everyone has the same "talking points" and divide the prospects accordingly.

Do research locally. Many times it is easy to get a start with funding from local charitable groups and expand to state, regional, national, and international venues as you are successfully funded. University and community partner members will have some overlapping but also some different ideas about funding prospects. Develop these ideas and tap your local service-learning and volunteer directors, state campus compacts, local association of nonprofit organizations, and state and local government (mayor's office, etc.) to brainstorm prospects.

Develop knowledge of budgets and accounting. Although your organization will have a financial professional(s), it is critical that you understand the components of a budget and restrictions on money that you have to spend. You should have a strong relationship with budget and accounting professionals and should seek out their advice and input often. You may need honest but creative accounting approaches because service-learning funding may not be similar to other types of grants and funding that your organization is accustomed to administering. Having a supportive budget person in place is critical for helping you navigate accounting issues with respect to your service-learning program.

Develop strategies for the overall approach for funding. Try to maximize your impact. For example, make sure that there is a match between your mission and the mission of the funding agency. Prioritize prospects that you believe have a high probability of funding your service-learning program. Look for "low hanging fruit," which are low-effort, high-payoff funding programs that may not be well publicized.

Critique the fund-raising plan. Once the fund-raising plan is developed, knowledgeable people outside your team should critique it to ensure that it is complete.

Assess your progress. You should take time to assess your progress periodically and make sure that you reassess your priorities, goals, or approach to ensure that you stay timely, responsive, and competitive for funding. In terms of my service-learning program, I meet with the college fund-raising team two or three times a year to assess and review progress, and with university fund-raising once a year.

Following are some common agencies that may be strong candidates for service-learning funding:

- Campus Compact (www.compact.org) is the premier national organization for service-learning in higher education. Additionally, 34 states have state Campus Compacts. State Compacts are often a great place to start to apply for funding and to identify other funding sources for your service-learning program.
- Corporation for National and Community Service (www.nationalser vice.org) is the largest grantmaking organization in the country in terms of service and volunteering programs. This organization administers AmeriCorps, Learn and Serve America, and Senior Corps.
- National and international service organizations (Kiwanis, Rotary, and Lions Clubs) have a local presence in most places. These are great organizations to approach for funding; additionally, most have expertise in fund-raising for service projects and may be able to serve on your fund-raising team or critique your fund-raising plan.

Advice on Funding for Service-Learning Directors

I asked two directors of service-learning, Jan Shoemaker (LSU) and Vincent Ilustre (Tulane), to share advice and experience with funding university-wide service-learning efforts. Their comments are as follows:

- Federal funding opportunities are becoming increasingly collaborative in nature. I suggest that you work with other universities at the state or regional level to establish consortiums of universities. Although this creates logistical issues, it enables universities to better compete for federal funding.
- Explore private funding. Work with your university foundation if at all possible; there are fewer strings attached to the money (in terms of allocation and spending) and less paperwork. Also, the overhead rate (amount that you have to pay the university to administer your grant) is much lower with the foundation than with the office of sponsored programs. The key is finding the right person to fund projects.
- Try to secure undesignated funds to allow for long-range planning; it is useful to have a cushion to help plan ahead for things like incentive grants and dynamic response to community issues. For example, the academic calendar sometimes requires soliciting faculty incentive grant proposals before funds are secured. With a backup fund, you can solicit proposals with confidence while you are securing funding for the specific proposals.
- Service-learning directors need to be entrepreneurial and proactive to locate funding sources. Work closely with your university's development officers; make sure that the service-learning program is at the forefront of what development officers are doing. Also make sure that the development and president's offices know that you are ready at any time with a presentation to prospective donors.
- Touch base with your university's advisory committees and councils and with alumni affairs. Multiple presentations to these groups provide great visibility and recognition and generate donors.
- Public relations goes hand in hand with fund-raising. I keep an updated development packet that describes different programs in the service-learning center, a list of things I need for the center, and the approximate budget it takes to run each program on an annual basis. I distribute this packet to all development officers and meet with the vice president of development every 6 weeks.
- Visibility in the community (inside the university and outside the university) is key. Working with the president and head of development is critical—these offices get the big gifts and set the agenda for

the rest of the development officers; your service-learning center needs to be on that agenda.

Writing Successful Proposals

Proposals are written requests for funding that you submit to a funding agency. The proposals that you write are usually in response to a request for proposals (RFP), which is published by the company or organization; this organization has a pot of money available, and it's looking to spend it on projects whose objectives and goals match its mission. When you write a proposal in response to an RFP, your proposal will be sent to the granting organization and will typically go to the program officer. This person is in charge of administrative aspects of the proposal program. Your proposal will be critiqued, and a decision to fund your proposal will be made. The following sections are intended to provide more detail on proposal preparation, submission, and critique. Table 8.2 defines terms commonly used in proposal writing.

Preparing a Proposal

Preparing a successful proposal can be a daunting task. This section is intended to provide you with general tips for preparing a proposal that has a strong chance of being funded. If you have the opportunity to attend a workshop on writing proposals, I suggest that you participate; detailed information on proposal writing is beyond the scope of this chapter, but such information can be very useful for your future success. Reference books such as *Getting Funded: The Complete Guide to Writing Grant Proposals* can also be useful. The following list of proposal writing tips is intended to help you submit the best possible proposal.

> *Develop your idea.* Having a well-researched and concisely presented idea is critical for a successful proposal. Make sure that your idea matches the mission of the organization from which you are requesting funding. Most funding agencies can fund a small fraction of the proposals submitted; proposals that do not directly match the mission of the funding agency are not considered for funding. Your idea must stand out compared to other submitted proposal ideas—don't be average!

TABLE 8.2
Commonly Used Terms for Proposal Writing

Term	Definition
Contract	Most granting agencies require you to sign a contract, a legally binding agreement that you will complete the objectives in the project using the money provided by the agency.
Co-PI	The persons responsible for the administration of the project. If there are two or more people primarily in charge or with significant duties for a project, then they are co-PIs.
Grant	The money that you receive if you've written a successful project.
In-kind donation	An item or service that is worth money to your proposed project but that is not actual cash. For example, a company donates playground safety surfacing to a playground design, and the materials, supplies, and labor for the company to install the surfacing is worth ~$10,000 to the project. This is a $10,000 in-kind donation.
Match	Money (or in-kind donations) that you already have in hand for your proposed project. Funding agencies like to see matching funds because they believe that your project has a better chance of success with more resources.
Overhead (indirect costs)	A percentage of your project budget (usually minus equipment costs) that goes directly to the university for items such as maintaining buildings, labs, and roads; providing electricity; and paying support staff. Overhead is usually charged as a percentage of the funds requested, for example, 45–50%. Many funders limit this percentage. For small grants (<$10,000), you are usually not charged overhead.
PI	Principal investigator; the person responsible for the administration of the project.
Program officer	The primary contact person at the agency that is sponsoring the RFP. Any questions that you might have about your project would be addressed to the program officer. This person can often give you extra information that may not be contained in the RFP!
Proposal (grant application)	The document that you prepare to request funds for a project.

TABLE 8.2 (Continued)

Term	Definition
Proposal reviewer	A person who reads the proposal and critically reviews it. Reviewers check to make sure that the project is important and meaningful, the objectives are measurable, the proposed plan of work is excellent, the proposal is well written, and the budget is reasonable.
Resubmission	Grant funds are hard to get! Usually there are many more potential projects to fund than money to go around. Many federal granting agencies fund only about 10% of the projects submitted! This means that some excellent ideas and projects will not receive funding. If your project is not funded, look at the comments from proposal reviewers (these are usually included with a letter telling you that you didn't receive funding). If you do a good job addressing these comments and resubmit your proposal during the next funding cycle, your chances for funding on this resubmission are much better!
RFP or rfp (or rfa)	Request for proposals (or request for applications).

Source: Partially excerpted from Carson & Lima, 2008.

Have a "hook"; highlight the uniqueness of your project or community. Focus on the need for your project and the positive impacts that will occur if it is completed.

Follow the rules described in the RFP. Your proposal should follow the same headings in the same order as those presented in the RFP. Follow the instructions in an RFP exactly. You should carefully read the RFP and follow it to the letter. Many proposals are not considered if they have even one small preparation error! General rules apply to your entire proposal, for example, page limit, budget limit, allowable fonts, font sizes, margins on text, whether or not you can include supplemental information in an appendix, the deadline for receiving proposals, the method for submitting proposals, the number of copies required, and so forth. Additional rules pertain to individual sections of your written proposal. Typical sections contained in a proposal include a summary of the project, a background and justification for the project, objectives, the project plan, an evaluation plan, a budget and written budget justification, and a conclusion. If you are in doubt in terms of whether you are properly following the instructions in the RFP, contact the program officer and ask. Keep in mind that answering questions from prospective applicants is one part of the program officer's job. Many program officers wish that more people would contact them with questions about potential projects. They really do wish to help and are a great resource that you should use.

Include graphics. Remember the adage "a picture is worth 1,000 words?" Because proposals involve concise writing, it is often useful to include diagrams, flow charts, pictures, or other graphics to illustrate the parts of your project that take a lot of words to explain. One successful proposal writer said, "Always put a graphic on page 2 of your proposal. It breaks up the monotony for proposal reviewers!"

Review your proposal after you have completed it and critique the proposal from the perspective of a reviewer. (See the section titled "What Are Proposal Reviewers Looking For?" later in this chapter for details.) You should wait at least 2 days after finishing the proposal before you go back and look at it again so that you can "see" the proposal with fresh eyes. Also, give your proposal to a friend who knows nothing about your project. If this person can't understand your proposal, then you should change the text until your friend understands it. Another way to check your proposal is to read the proposal out loud to another person—this approach is an effective way to catch errors or text that doesn't make sense. One of the major ways to improve a proposal at this stage is to eliminate extraneous words. Most editors will tell you that your final document can have approximately 25% of the words removed without losing any meaning. Read your finished proposal one more time with this editorial suggestion in mind to see if you can eliminate unnecessary words and phrases, for example, "in order to," "very," or "both." Proposal reviewers are busy and usually have a number of projects to review in a short time frame. Thus, you should make your case as concisely as possible.

Submitting a Proposal

To submit a proposal, typically two steps are involved. First is getting internal approval from the institution that you work for (the process is sometimes called routing), and second is actually submitting the proposal. In my experience, routing a proposal is often more painful than writing one because in higher education, service-learning projects do not always fit easily into the policies and procedures that were developed for traditional proposals. This means that people checking your proposals may refuse to give approval to various aspects of your project, or they may require that you have cooperative agreements in place that release your agency from liability before they approve the proposal.

I have almost always been successful in routing service-learning proposals through my university using a combination of relentless pleasantry and dogged tenacity. If the answer to approval on some or all of your proposal is no, ask the proposal checker why the answer is no. If you can suggest an alternative or ask about other ways to get approval, almost all checkers are willing to work with you to find an alternative. If you hear the statement, "No one's ever done this before," question how it can be done or why it can't be done. Enlist the support of your unit's budget folks; most have numerous ideas and a lot of wisdom when it comes to creative ways to make your proposal acceptable. Also enlist the support of the other members of your service-learning team; if a university is unwilling to approve a proposal for submission, the community agency may be able to submit it, or vice versa. If you work for a university, I strongly suggest that you contact your service-learning office if you have one. Chances are that the director and/or staff have already had significant experience dealing with proposal routing issues.

At a large university, usually an office of sponsored programs (or similar name) checks and administers grants and contracts; also a university foundation office (or similar name) manages gifts and prospective donors. You need to determine which office (sponsored programs or foundation) to route your proposal through. Sponsored programs offices usually handle proposals, but foundations often handle proposals to be submitted to private funders (family foundations, etc.). If you have a choice in the matter, consider the indirect cost rate (see Table 8.2 for details) for the foundation and for your sponsored program office. Most times, the foundation rate is much lower than the sponsored program rate (3–5% vs. 45–50%). Also check whether your university's sponsored programs office has a lower rate for service-learning proposals. At Louisiana State University, there is a public service proposal designation with an overhead rate of 36% instead of the regular 49%.

To submit your proposal to a funding agency, follow the rules for submission as described in the RFP. If your proposal is unsolicited, call the agency to find out the way to submit your document properly. Increasingly, submission is completed online; if your submission is to be submitted by mail or in person, usually you will submit multiple copies of your proposal so that the agency can send each copy to a reviewer for critique. After submitting your proposal, wait until you hear a response from the funding agency; you may get a response directly from the funding agency, or you may be directed to an online site in which you can view a list of funded proposals.

What Are Proposal Reviewers Looking For?

Grant proposal reviewers look for specific information in proposals. By including this information, you can increase the likelihood that your proposal will be funded.

- *Did you follow the directions set forth in the RFP?* Some proposals may be eliminated from consideration if the directions were not followed exactly. Your proposal may not be eliminated, but proposal reviewers are likely to be more critical when you don't follow the proposal rules. You do not want to present yourself as someone who will not follow rules; proposal reviewers may decide that you are not organized or committed enough to complete the project.
- *Are the objectives measurable?* Proposal reviewers want to know what your project objectives are. If the objectives contain something measurable, then they (and you) will be able to figure out when the project is completed and whether or not it was successful.
- *Do you have an evaluation plan in place?* Proposal reviewers want to make sure that your project contains a component that involves evaluating your project activities. Projects that have evaluation built into them have a higher probability of being successful.
- *Is the budget reasonable?* It takes some experience to match a reasonable budget with a project plan. Inexperienced proposal writers often make the mistake of promising that they will do a lot while getting very little money. Proposal reviewers worry about this situation because if you are overloaded, you may not be able to complete the project or complete it well. Ask for exactly what you need (not more), completely justify every dollar that you request, and don't promise too much in your project. If you do not have a good sense of budget,

visit with your departmental or agency grants and contracts or accounting person. You can get a lot of insight from these experts— take them out for coffee and listen to their ideas and wisdom.

- *What is the impact of the project?* Proposal reviewers are looking for the potential impact that the service-learning project will have on your community. You should have a succinct statement that describes the positive impacts of your project on the participants and on the community.

- *Do you have special features that make your project stand out?* Proposal reviewers are always looking for aspects of a project that make it exceptional. Any former or current successes with your project will make it stand out. For example, if you have previous successes in similar projects, you should briefly discuss them. If you already have some funding in hand and are looking for more funding to complete the project, include these details—projects that already have funding tend to get more funding. Include anything in your proposal that will make your project stand out compared to others; you can consult the program officer for ideas on what these features are.

Getting the Answer From the Funding Agency

If your proposal is funded (at which point it becomes a grant), congratulations! Get with your service-learning team and celebrate big! If you are not funded, do not stop trying to secure funding. It is difficult to get funding; only about 10% of federal grants are funded, and most are not funded the first time they are submitted. Take the critical review comments from your proposal, revise your proposal accordingly, and resubmit it during the next eligible funding cycle. Some proposals, particularly those submitted to foundations, may not provide you with review comments. If this is the case, follow up with the program officer and try to get informal feedback. Use this feedback to resubmit your proposal.

It may be that the review comments say that your proposal simply does not fit the mission of the organization or, for whatever reason, the funding agency does not recommend resubmission. If this is the case and you believe that even with revision the proposal does not have a strong chance of funding (check your opinion with the program officer), look for another funding agency for your proposal.

I cannot overemphasize the importance of tenacity when your proposal has been rejected. I have written many more unsuccessful proposals than successful ones—I once wrote nine successive unsuccessful proposals to put a playground at a specific elementary school. I was successful on the 10th try. Remember that "no" means "no at this time." Don't let a no stop you until you hear the Texas version of a no, which is "HELL NO, and don't ask me again!" I always try to remember that failure is not about how many times you've been turned down; it's about not submitting at all.

Conclusion

Funding service-learning projects is becoming increasingly necessary as nonprofit agency and university budgets are getting tighter. A well-researched, developed, and executed fund-raising plan is critical for garnering the funds you need for your service-learning program. This chapter is organized into four major sections to target your funding efforts: (a) how to determine whether you need funding, and if so, how much; (b) overview of funding agencies and options; (c) developing a fund-raising plan; and (d) tips for writing successful proposals. If you are steadfast, team-oriented, and comprehensive in your approach, and if you are able to continue trying for funding in the face of many rejections, you should be successful in funding your service-learning program. Good luck and please contact me at mlima1@lsu.edu with your successes (and your failures if you feel so inclined). Good luck!

Acknowledgments

I would like to acknowledge Jan Shoemaker and Donna Elisar for critically reviewing this chapter.

References

Carson, R., & Lima, M. (2008). *Play on! Program for learning activities for youth.* Reston, VA: AAPAR.

Hall, M., & Howlett, S. (2003). *Getting funded: The complete guide to writing grant proposals* (4th ed.) Portland, OR: Continuing Education Press.

PART THREE

EMERGING MODELS IN SERVICE-LEARNING PARTNERSHIPS

9

SERVICE-LEARNING AND THE DEVELOPMENT OF CRITICAL REFLEXIVITY IN TEACHER EDUCATION IN THE UNITED KINGDOM AND REPUBLIC OF IRELAND

Emerging Paradigms

Timothy Murphy, Jon Tan, and Christine Allan

Preface

Jean Strait

As we work to become a more global community, through technology we are more easily able to share best practices in service-learning. What might have taken weeks to share by post between countries 20 years ago now can be exchanged instantly via phone or Internet. We can access resources and models online and print them in moments. Although these tools are handy, conflict arises when cultural distinctions confound terms, definitions, and pedagogical differences. For example, *service-learning* is a term used primarily in the United States to depict a mutually beneficial partnership in which students provide service and through the experience gain valuable learning. The word *service* means "to help"; however, in different international contexts, *service* can have a more complex or negative connotation.

For the last decade, *international service-learning* is a term that has been used to explain the work U.S. students do in international contexts with international organizations. Students have been in South Africa (Bender, 2008), East Africa (Johnson-Pynn & Johnson, 2005), Ireland (Murphy 2008), and Hong Kong (Ngai, 2006). Social justice, intercultural competence, environmental education, and the impact of service-learning on life careers have been studied. Today, the definition of *international service-learning* has evolved. Instead of viewing it as something U.S. students do in other countries, it now embodies many different models and methods used by international students and practitioners in international settings. The questions become:

What, then, is international service-learning?
How is it configured?
What is the purpose?
What models exist and how can those models be replicated?

As a result of social complexities, service-learning models look different in different countries. By remembering that there are essential elements of service-learning, such as reciprocity and reflection, we can begin to create international models that follow common themes. Once we identify the themes, we can begin a more systematic process of creating international models that can be compared and analyzed.

This chapter offers two such models that focus on the critical need for reflection. The first model is the Irish Educationalist and Open Spaces for Dialogue and Enquiry (OSDE) model. The second is English Pre-Service Teachers and Internationalization. Both take a service-learning component, reflection, and use critical reflexivity to create models that can be used for international comparison. This represents an innovative approach. In the next 10 years, we expect common terms will be adopted by international associations and that these associations will also call for the essential components of service-learning in all contexts to be identified and used. Jon Tan, Timothy Murphy, and Christine Allan are pioneering this research in Ireland and the United Kingdom. What follows is their accounts, which will no doubt lead us to implement and analyze service-learning in global contexts in a more systematic fashion.

This chapter provides evidence for the strong association that can exist between engagement with service-learning-related activities and the fostering of skills related to critical reflexivity. We provide examples from the English and Republic of Ireland contexts to illustrate paradigms in international service-learning. Service-learning is being interpreted as a reciprocal reflective transactional learning process that involves teachers, teacher–educators, learners, and a teaching context. The reciprocal nature of the process is a critical component that is being developed here.

In this chapter, we interpret the orientation to service-learning as a directed experiential learning (DEL) encounter or project. The project is framed in a manner similar to that described by Green (1995a) as the ongoing sculpturing of our identities as educators in response to engagements. In her view, such encounters can jolt us out of our familiar, taken-for-granted ways of interpreting reality and thereby open us to "new avenues for choosing and for action" (Greene, 1995b, p. 123).

The researchers from England (Tan and Allan) illustrate the ways in which the directed experiential learning projects they engaged in affected their identities as teacher–educators, the identities of their students, as well as the identities of the teachers and teacher–educators with whom they collaborated. This is especially evident in their international work. The case study from Ireland (Murphy) focuses on the impact that an international service-learning approach had on the roles of teacher–educators.

Service-Learning and Directed Experiential Learning

Before describing the case studies in more detail, we explore the connection between directed experiential learning and service-learning. We draw another useful parallel with the work of Greene: She suggests that our self-identity as educators is always in a process of becoming. In her view, such an orientation allows for the educator to draw a distinction between treating the world as predefined and given and, alternatively, "applying an initiating, constructing mind or consciousness" to it (Greene, 1995b, p. 23). The capacity for reflection, in her view, is pivotal for the coming-into-being of teacher identities-in-the-making. In that connection, she makes reference to Schön (1983) and his work on "reflective practice" (Greene, 1995a, p. 70). The significance for reflective practice is clearly articulated by McLean and Bullard (2000) when they suggest:

> Professional education has taken a wrong turn in seeing the role of the
> practitioner as interpreter, translator, and implementer of theory produced
> by academic thinkers and researchers . . . instead . . . practitioners, includ-
> ing teachers, must read their own work sites. This involves their recogniz-
> ing and generating their own contextually sensitive theories of practice.
> (p. 94)

The separation of practice and teaching, we argue, requires a reconcep-
tualization of practitioners in schools and those involved in initial teacher
and professional education. The directed experiential learning encounters in
the studies presented in this chapter provide a favorable context for the
grounding of theories of practice. Furthermore, the evidence suggests that
such activities allow for spaces to be created that invite participants to reflect
in dialogue with others, with a view to further extending or reframing their
perspectives. Participants are exposed "to proper intellectual challenge, of the
kind one would apply to any proposition in the field of research or theory in
one's discipline" (Andresen 2000, p. 143). It is here, in this act of connecting
intellectual challenge with dialogic pedagogies, that we see value in partnerships among academics, practitioners, and research.

We use the term *meaning frame* in a manner similar to Mezirow's concept of "meaning scheme," which he describes as "the particular knowledge,
value judgments, and feelings that become articulated in an interpretation"
(Mezirow, 1991, p. 44). Such schemes constitute for him "the concrete mani-
festations of our habitual orientation and expectations" (Mezirow, 1991, p.
44). This habitual orientation in turn manifests in "meaning perspectives,"
which provide us with an "orienting frame of reference . . . for interpreting
and evaluating the meaning of experience" (Mezirow, 1991, p. 42).

Mezirow describes an "articulated, theory-based, collectively held meaning perspective" as a paradigm (Mezirow, 1991, p. 46). It is here, in the inter-
rogation of existing meaning frames, that the close coupling of learning and
experience—as represented by service-learning—presents us with complex
challenges regarding the engendering of critical reflection that supports
transformative knowledge building. The following case studies from Ireland
and England provide insight into how two programs centralized critical
reflection at their pedagogical core to enable students to interrogate their
practice experiences and to make sense of these learning opportunities in
terms of their professional and personal development.

Directed Experiential Learning and Meaning Schemes

Directed experiential learning (DEL) projects provide open spaces for dialogue and enquiry that encourage the critical examination of existing paradigms. They are underpinned by the existentialist belief that "I am what I am not yet." Such uncertainty, however, can be very disconcerting, and several of the case study respondents acknowledge that their initial engagement with the directed experiential learning encounters was a little unnerving.

Mezirow (1991) identifies this as a state of "disequilibrium," when there is a misfit between our "meaning schemes" and our "meaning perspectives." He contends, however, that such a state is often a transitionary phase on the road to "perspective transformation," which he describes as the process of becoming critically aware of

> how and why our assumptions have come to constrain the way we perceive,
> understand, and feel about our world; changing these structures of habitual
> expectation to make possible a more inclusive, discriminating, and integra-
> tive perspective; and, finally, making choices or otherwise acting upon
> these new understandings. (Mezirow, 1991, p. 167)

The examples that follow provide strong evidence for the transformative potential inherent in DEL projects. Participants critically reflect on their emerging educational identities, especially on the manner in which they have been influenced by the particular contexts in which they work. As the American Association of Colleges for Teacher Education (AACTE, 2002) acknowledges, such considerations can have personal growth, academic learning, and civic responsibility offshoots. It is evident that the English and Irish participants encountered a number of significant milestones, each of which provided openings for critical reflexivity. Those openings also triggered the initiation of engaged reflective processes that ultimately led to transformed understandings of their identities as educators, in a manner similar to that described by Mezirow (1991).

The reflective processes occurred in the context of engaged cofacilitated experiential learning encounters with co-educators. They were underpinned by a process of mutual consultation. As previously mentioned, such a process was pivotal for enabling the enactment of Open Spaces for Dialogue and Enquiry (OSDE) referred to later. The DEL encounters, which we equate with service-learning, occurred in these spaces, and it was essential that they were based on mutual trust. Without trust, the participants' willingness to engage in real dialogue was undermined, and such dialogue is an essential building block of the DEL process.

Irish Educationalists and Open Spaces for Dialogue and Enquiry (OSDE) Model

In 2005–2006, we initiated a research project with practicing first-, second-, and third-level educators in the Republic of Ireland that corresponds to the directed experiential learning initiative and its associated service-learning characteristics. As part of their course requirements for the degree of Masters in Education (M.Ed.) at Mary Immaculate College, University of Limerick, students undertook a core module, Theory and Practice of Education. The research findings for this project are based on the results of this module, which invited teacher–learners to reflect on their teaching contexts and to share those reflections with their co-learners. In particular, they were invited to assess the impact of policy and practice on their professional identities as educators, especially in the context of challenging teaching and learning environments.

The educators conducted their reflections using OSDE developed by Vanessa Andreotti and colleagues at the Centre for the Study of Social and Global Justice at the University of Nottingham (see www.osdemethodology .org.uk). The approach offers a set of procedures and ground rules to structure safe spaces for dialogue and enquiry about global issues and perspectives focusing on interdependence.

The OSDE model was adapted to meet specific learning outcomes of the Theory and Practice module and to align with the intended research. The module structure was negotiated with the learners. The extent to which this was possible was circumscribed by the module requirements. Nevertheless, it was still important to dialogue with the participating educators to underscore the reciprocal nature of the learning process for the module leader (researchers) and the participating educators. They fully subscribed to the principles of the Open Spaces for Dialogue and Enquiry approach:

1. Every individual brings to the space valid and legitimate knowledge constructed in their own contexts.

2. All knowledge is partial and incomplete.
3. All knowledge can be questioned.

The participants' reflections were supported with input from the researcher. It could reasonably be suggested that the apparent dual role of the researcher and module leader could adversely affect the conduct of the research. However, such concerns are easily assuaged when the reciprocal nature of the research process is taken into account. Both the researcher and the participating educators adopted the role of co-investigators and co-learners for the duration of the module.

The module encouraged participants to draw on multiple perspectives to investigate and characterize aspects of their professional practice, build on their professional experience, and bring critical insight to their work. Additionally, they were invited, with the researcher, to reflect on the opportunities and challenges presented by teaching contexts characterized by increasing diversity. This is also a central aspect of the research that was conducted in England and France, which is discussed later in this chapter.

Research Findings: Republic of Ireland

A semistructured questionnaire was designed and forwarded to each participant. The OSDE approach underpinned the process. In acknowledging this approach, for example, one participant commented:

> We certainly recognized that we're all coming from different experiences and backgrounds within the one education system but that this added to the group—listening to and hearing other angles widened our perspective and therefore our understanding of our context and the influencing factors that resulted in how we experienced and viewed the education system.

This educator also recognized the limits of her situated knowing: "Our own knowledge was certainly partial also in the sense that we only experienced certain parts of the education system. Our own attitudes and experiences colored our views on the theories we discussed."

In both these comments is evidence to suggest that this educator is beginning to acknowledge the limits of her own meaning scheme. Such an acknowledgment may very well initiate feelings of disquiet and uncertainty that, as previously noted, Mezirow (1991) identifies as a state of disequilibrium. This state is an important transitionary phase on the road to perspective transformation.

Perspective transformations can trigger paradigm shifts in understanding that can result in a move away from fixed, limited, and circumscribed worldviews toward conceptions of reality that are more open and permeable. The following comment from another participating educator intimates a transformed understanding:

> The overbidding memory of the module was that it opened up the senses to view education from a positive critical manner and not a blear eyed "educationalist." . . . It helped to develop a lighthouse effect on all aspects of education and its possible implications whether good or bad.

Significance of the Findings: Republic of Ireland

The DEL approach adopted for this study, with its associated service-learning characteristics and underlying principles from the OSDE methodology, provides spaces and opportunities for engagement with processes for critical reflexivity.

Such processes of enquiry are not a common feature of the Irish educational landscape. This is partly a result of the fact that the schooling system in the Republic of Ireland is beholden to an overarching economic agenda. The *OECD Review of Higher Education in Ireland* in 2004, for example, acknowledges that the primary purpose of higher education is linked to prioritizing national prosperity. In his article, Collins (2005) makes reference to the Review and points out those wider concepts of higher education as a critical presence in society merit hardly a mention. In *Proposals for the Future of Senior Cycle Education in Ireland*, the National Council for Curriculum and Assessment (NCCA, 2004, p. 18) underscored the significance of education for recognizing such a critical presence in society.

The researchers from England also identified the skills of critical reflexivity as being of pivotal importance. The dispositional transformations that occurred in the pre-service teachers who participated in this research resonated with the experiences of the Irish educators.

English Pre-Service Teachers and Internationalization

In the English context, the importance of an international component in the education of children and young people has gained impetus in recent years

(Department for Education and Skills, 2004, 2005). Although governmental expectations have been clearly voiced, they represent complex educational challenges for teachers, their schools, and those engaged in initial teacher education (ITE).

In the interests of extending research knowledge and informing future development, we considered it timely to examine student experiences of a bilateral exchange program between France and England. We focused on the development of students' intercultural awareness and on the ways in which international placement changed them personally and professionally. The following case study details experientially based learning strategies with critical reflective pedagogies centrally positioned. It offers insight into the value of such approaches for similar activities that connect learning and experience in service-based settings.

Byram's conceptualization of intercultural and communicative competence has been widely reported in academic spheres (Driscoll & Frost, 1999; Guillerme, 2002) and has been influential in the framing of key strategic policy documents such as the Common European Framework for language teaching, learning, and assessment (Council of Europe, 2001). Byram and Doyé (1999) developed five *savoirs* (see Driscoll & Frost, 1999), and their work provided an overarching framework for engaging with this research. Because this chapter focuses attention on the issue of critical reflection and experiential-based learning, it is not our intention to examine the conceptualization of these *savoirs* in detail. However, drawing from Byram and Doyé (1999, p. 142), it is useful to summarize them here:

- *Savoir être*—relating to attitudes about difference. Byram and Doyé give the example of "the kind of learner who notices and asks questions, who expresses wonder and interest in other people's behaviors and beliefs, rather than rejection and disgust."
- *Savoirs*—relating to knowledge. Here Byram and Doyé offer the example of having "knowledge of different eating habits or work practices and how the differences can lead to misunderstandings and rejection."
- *Savoir comprendre*—relating to interpretive skills. Important here is the definition of *interpretation* that is not simply used in the sense of *interpreter* (i.e., translator). Rather, Byram and Doyé make clear that this is more about the learner being able to recognize contextual significance and how something relates to other aspects of the cultural

context, for example, the learner's ability to locate the significance of a particular teaching approach (e.g., the use of synthetic phonics in reading to a wider national policy emphasis on skills-centered training, and notions of literacy in crisis).

- *Savoir apprendre/faire*—referring to skills of discovery and interaction. Here Byram and Doyé stress the individual's ability to ask questions that enable deeper insight to be gained and that perhaps constitute implicit cultural knowledge.
- *Savoir s'engager*—relating to a critical cultural awareness. Byram and Doyé's descriptions suggest that this layer of competence is greatly significant in educational terms in that it involves a critical, evaluative, and perhaps reflective engagement.

In our study of students' placement experiences and their professional and personal development, we drew on their depiction of *savoir s'engager,* particularly as it relates to critical cultural awareness. This *savoir* provided us with a lens through which we could interrogate student experiences of placement abroad that are illustrative of the dispositional changes reflected in their discussions and reflective writing.

Methodological and Pedagogical Approaches

At the core of the study's approach, both methodologically and pedagogically, were opportunities for students to reflect on and interrogate practice. As part of their preparations for their placements abroad, students were thus encouraged to focus their attention on *their* understanding of the key components and concepts contained within policy documentation and to provide a critical examination. Further, activities that encouraged dialogue (e.g., class discussions around intercultural and pedagogical themes) were built into the program. As an ongoing program, an average of 10 students per year has been involved in this work over 5 years (i.e., approximately 50 students all together).

For three of these years, the program has been able to introduce systematic qualitative research involving three cohorts of students (approximately 30 students). The rationale for taking this research approach is that, in focusing on the experiences of student teachers undertaking placements in France, we want to capture their own frames of reference through which they assess value and challenge. From the outset, the study was designed to yield a richness of data, beyond descriptive accounts through quantitative means, such as the use of survey-based attitudinal scales. In accordance with Bryman (1993) and Walker (1988), we thus considered a qualitative approach that would allow us to examine students' experiences with this rich contextual data intact.

A range of methods for obtaining data have been implemented, again providing opportunities for students to consider their experiences through dialogue and reflection. These have included, in sequence, the use of pre-placement focus group discussions, classroom observations of their placements, and semistructured postplacement group interviews. Perhaps of great significance in the ongoing connection between research and critical reflective pedagogy has been the embedding within their coursework a set piece of reflective writing based upon their placement. This latter component provides another source of data, much of which is drawn upon in the following analysis.

Adopting such a range of data collection methods was important in a number of ways: First, the combination of focus groups, interviews, and observations enabled the researchers to probe student answers to questions concerning classroom experiences with reference to specific examples. This was useful in establishing a level of shared contextual knowledge about their schools, their classrooms, and significant others (such as host teachers). Second, this combination further supported our interpretation of students' responses and the subsequent understanding of their experiences in context. Finally, by using a combination of methods, we could establish trustworthiness in our data analysis through a process of triangulation (Flick, von Kardorff, & Steinke, 2004, pp. 180–181; Bryman, 1993, p. 131). This analysis was conducted using established processes of data reduction and thematic identification as described by Miles and Huberman (1994).

Findings

The data obtained from three cohorts of trainee teachers from England teaching in France provide a rich account of their experiences, their assessment of the value of international exchanges, and comments on how such placements enriched professional learning in teacher education. Clearly evident is that these international directed experiential learning opportunities extended and developed participants' understanding of their emerging identities as professional educators in a manner similar to the experiences of the Irish educators outlined earlier. It is also important to emphasize that, although it is possible to identify themes within the following analysis (e.g., cultural shock, professional and personal reorientation, and acting as a cultural mediator), students did not experience these in an identifiably linear way. Indeed, the interrelatedness of their experiences has a dialogic quality. Organizationally, then, the following themes are helpful, but their interactional and interconnected qualities must be recognized to understand how these exist in reality.

Culture Shock and Reorientation

All participants referred to the experience of culture shock. For the purposes of this chapter, we report only the U.K. students' placement experiences in France; however, it is worthy to note how such experiences were also common to French students teaching in U.K. primary schools.* A further facet of their experiences was evident in the ways in which they talked about getting to know and respect cultural difference. As one U.K. student reflected:

> Immediately I entered my school [in France] I sensed the cultural differences that surrounded me. Every face was different and I knew that the children knew I wasn't someone who had the same cultural background. Approaching the classroom I was extremely nervous . . . scanning the classroom, I could see and feel the immediate similarities and differences between a classroom in England and [one] in France.

Participants' reflections suggest that part of the whole international teaching experience for them required a great degree of reorientation—moving from a position of identifying difference to *understanding* its significance. Such a movement was often expressed in terms of how they, as future educators, would encourage this progression in their classes and work to balance "a celebration of [children's] own cultures and enlightenment about others [that makes] certain that children accept differences as normal examples of the diversity that is present in human beings" (U.K. student, reflective writing, 2008).

In such ways we could argue that, through engaging in critical reflection, students' experiences were deeply complex, shifting through the different layers of Byram's *savoirs*. Although a number of their reflections exhibited

---

* Tan and Allan will report on the experiences of French students on U.K.-based teaching placements in subsequent publications.

recognition of difference and exhibited curiosity, others indicated that students were decoding the meaning of these experiences, situating them, and making sense of their wider meaning. What was also interesting was the significant degree to which participants, through their reflection, projected a sense of becoming, a vision of their professional and personal identities and intentions. Such expression can be found in the following example alongside a real sense of how such experiential opportunities in learning stimulate participants:

> I feel excited at the prospect of bringing an intercultural dimension into my future teaching and I hope that I can be an enthusiastic and stimulating teacher who can help develop the children's appetite for learning through teaching in a creative and stimulating way. By using my experiences, I hope I can be an "inspirational catalyst" to future learners.

There is a resonance here with the Boud, Keogh, & Walker (1985) view of reflection as being "a generic term for those intellectual and affective activities in which individuals engage to explore their experiences in order to lead to a new understanding and appreciation" (p. 19).

As we have stated, such reflection is a prerequisite for the effective integration of the learning potential offered by associated directed experiential learning, or service-learning approaches. Of further significance in our consideration of critical reflection and its role in experientially oriented learning is the sense of participants' repositioning of the self.

Professional and Personal Repositioning: Becoming
Cultural Interlocutors

Interestingly, in concert with the work of Byram and Doyé (1999), students also expressed a sense that they were sitting between cultures and that, in their professional capacity, this transcending of cultural boundaries was important.

> [In] sharpening children's curiosity while making cultural comparisons, I began to achieve this by becoming a sort of mediator between two cultures, through the use of a scrapbook about myself, my family and where I live and through discovery about the children's cultures and backgrounds in comparison. (U.K. student, reflective writing, 2008)

Students talked about "mediating" and about "finding bridges," echoing Driscoll and Frost's (1999) work. Others visualized their futures as practicing teachers and the techniques they would take into the learning environment of their classrooms. They talked practically about creating "language corners where there would be books available for the children to read about different countries, languages, traditions and ways of life" (U.K. student, reflective writing, 2008). There was also a real sense of these future opportunities being experiences felt on many levels, for example, "arousing children's interest" through dedicated cultural days that use role-play and artifacts to stimulate. In such ways, the students' sense of themselves as future practitioners and what they would do to promote intercultural understanding mirrored their own experiences as individuals abroad.

Perhaps most significant in their responses was the sense of professional and personal change, as well as an expressed feeling of mutual exchange. And maybe the best example of these dispositional changes that occurred on professional and deeply personal levels was that of a student who likened her growth to that of a sunflower:

> During my intercultural experience in France, I feel that I have grown as a person and professionally. My confidence and linguistic skills have improved as a result and I am thoroughly proud of my achievement because it is something that I felt was totally unachievable. Metaphorically thinking, before my experience in France, I felt like a sunflower seed. I was extremely nervous and lacked confidence. However, by the end of my [placement] I could sincerely relate myself to a sunflower, because I felt so confident and proud of myself. . . . After considering the value of my experience in France, I feel that I have developed as a professional.

Most notable in this student's reflection was that these changes were personal changes. She goes on to say:

> My intercultural experience has given me so many happy memorable memories that I will keep with me forever. The outcomes of the international exchange for me are unreal because I am quite a timid person but I was given strength and confidence by my [host] tutor and I achieved everything that I thought was unachievable. Furthermore, the experience has taught me to believe in yourself and always take life-changing opportunities because you may never get a second chance.

Arguably, in terms of intercultural awareness the significance of the international teaching placement is profound for all involved. Although perhaps these reflections have immediacy and thus may contain some residuum of cultural shock and amplified value, there is some indication that the dispositional nature of these experiences may have longer reaching currency in empathic terms. Many of the interview responses from students, such as the following, make this point:

> I've broadened my own knowledge to teach about difference in cultures. As well the fact that we've been and seen it as an outsider and we've been that different person. Like when you're teaching about the kind of [cultural] differences and stuff, it's the fact that we . . . I can't seem to explain it properly: You can't understand what it's like to be completely different until you've done it. It helps you in that way because at least you understand in a very small way how they [children coming from other cultures] must be feeling. I suppose in a way you've gained from that as well because we've very much been an outsider. (student, interview response, 2007)

> As an educator, I feel more confident in the way that I could teach, not just French, just having a more rounded view of things . . . seeing differences and similarities and bringing them back over to England . . . I'm a little bit more open to ideas . . . spending four weeks in France will undoubtedly make you a better teacher because of all the experiences . . . you can read and look at research, but you need first-hand experiences. (student, interview response, 2007)

Interestingly, in the reflections of this group of student educators was the parallel between their own dispositional change and their envisioning of themselves as mediators and catalysts of similar changes in their learners. For us as professional educators engaged in teacher education, it is significant that this international placement provided an opportunity for students, as nascent professionals, to develop a range of critical, reflective lenses—both culturally and pedagogically. Drawing conceptually from Loughran (2006), we suggest that the encouragement of such critical dialogue lies at the heart of real, productive partnership, professional learning, and the co-construction of knowledge. The value of connecting such critical dialogic and reflective approaches with opportunities for experiential learning such as those akin to service-learning, we suggest, is profound. As one student intimates, perhaps they also recognize their role in this co-construction of knowledge beyond "their" classroom:

> But coming back I can see what they are trying to get across. Like my views, now I suppose I'm kind of thinking and talking more positively

about France, about a different country . . . so in some respect, I could talk to students who are going next year about my experiences, my attitudes, things like that. So in some respect they may see me as a bit of a student ambassador. (student, interview response, 2007)

Conclusion

Drawing on research findings from both the English and Republic of Ireland contexts, this chapter provides evidence for the strong links that can exist between engagement with directed experiential learning activities and the fostering of skills of critical reflexivity in future professional educators. Such skills are recognized as being of critical importance for their ongoing professional development. In this way, the pedagogies represented here may be seen as rich in their sense of interconnecting pre-service, in-service, and academic communities in the co-construction of knowledge.

It is also evident that reflection can lead to feelings of unease for the emerging educators. But, as Mezirow (1991) points out, such feelings are part and parcel of the journey that culminates in transformed understandings and perspectives. We recognize that the approach being developed here extends the parameters of what typically comes under the rubric of service-learning. Certainly, it is not unusual for the exclusive focus to be on the impact that this approach has on the learner. We, too, have centered on learner voices in our exploration of experiential learning opportunities.

However, in our consideration of experiential-based learning, the focus shifted to the professional educator in-the-making. Typically with service-learning programs, participants engage with and reflect on extension activities. In the model that we discuss here, the professional practice site becomes both the context and opportunity for critical reflexivity.

At the same time, this shift in emphasis leads us to reflect on our contributions as teacher educators in this teaching–learning relationship. At a pedagogical level, perhaps we should also consider the ways in which we act as facilitators of learning and professional and personal development, and how we, in ourselves, accommodate modifications to our understandings of the world and our professional knowing. In this sense, entering into dialogue and critical conversations can equally effect dispositional change in all those engaged in the learning activity. Where such activities involve intersections of pedagogy, culture, and collaborative knowledge building, perhaps the magnitude of this dispositional effect is amplified. It follows, then, that in close coupling teacher education with experiential learning and critical, dialogic pedagogies, the implications for service-learning may be significant and may anticipate a broader conceptualization of the field.

We suggest that the approaches discussed in this chapter have the potential to transform understandings for everyone involved—the educator along with the learners. Moreover, we emphasize the value of research in both understanding experiences and interrogating the pedagogies we enact. Although the case studies illuminate many aspects of critical reflective approaches in two national settings, the centrality of culture, partnership, and co-learning suggests a place for collaborative, international inquiry for the future. We look forward to such work offering deepened insights and new perspectives on the role of the professional educator in the 21st century and similar consideration of the pedagogies and learning experiences that are employed in its support.

References

American Association of Colleges for Teacher Education. (2002). Service-learning issue brief. Retrieved April 30, 2009, from http://usm.maine.edu/servicelearning/pdf/sl%20know.pdf

Andresen, L. W. (2000) A usable, trans-disciplinary conception of scholarship, *Education Research and Development, 19*(2), 137–153.

Bender, G. (2008). Exploring conceptual models for community engagement at higher education institutions in South Africa. *Perspectives in Education, 26*(1), 81–95.

Boud, D., Keogh, R., & Walker, D. (1985). *Reflection: Turning experience into learning.* London: Kogan Page.

Bryman, A. (1993). *Quantity and quality in social research.* London: Routledge.

Byram, M., & Doyé, P. (1999). Intercultural competence and foreign language learning in the primary school. In P. Driscoll & D. Frost (Eds.), *The teaching of modern foreign languages in the primary school* (pp. 138–151). London: Routledge.

Collins, T. (2005, November 15). The trouble with boys: Why schools can't solve everything. *Irish Times,* 12–15.

Council of Europe. (2001). Home page. Retrieved June 20, 2006, from www.coe.int/t/e/human_rights/equality/

Department for Education and Skills. (2004) *Every child matters: Change for children.* London: HMSO, DfES Publications.

Department for Education and Skills. (2005). *Developing the global dimension in the school curriculum*. London: HMSO, DfES Publications.

Driscoll, P, & Frost, D. (1999). *The teaching of modern foreign languages in the primary school*. London: Routledge.

Flick, U., von Kardorff, E., & Steinke, I. (Eds.). (2004). *A companion to qualitative research*. London: Sage.

Greene, M. (1995a). Choosing a past and inventing a future: The becoming of a teacher. In W. Ayers (Ed.), *To become a teacher: Making a difference in children's lives* (pp. 65–77). New York: Teachers College Press.

Greene, M. (1995b). *Releasing the imagination: Essays on education, the arts, and social change*. San Francisco: Jossey-Bass.

Guillerme, M. (2002). *Critical citizens for an intercultural world: Foreign language education as cultural politics*. Clevedon, England: Multilingual Matters.

Johnson-Pynn, J. S., & Johnson, L. (2005). Successes and challenges in East African conservation education. *Journal of Environmental Education, 36*(12), 25.

Loughran, J. (2006). *Developing a pedagogy of teacher education: Understanding teaching and learning about teaching*. London: Routledge.

McLean, M., & Bullard, J. E. (2000). Becoming a university teacher: Evidence from teaching portfolios (how academics learn to teach). *Teacher Development, 4*(1), 79–101.

Mezirow, J. (1991). *Transformative dimensions of adult learning*. San Francisco: Jossey-Bass.

Miles, M. B., & Huberman, A. M. (1994). *Qualitative data analysis: An expanded sourcebook* (2nd ed.). Thousand Oaks, CA: Sage.

Murphy, T. (2008). Democratic schooling practices in the Republic of Ireland: The gaps between the rhetoric and reality. *Irish Educational Studies, 27*(1), 29–39.

National Council for Curriculum and Assessment. (2004). *Proposals for the future of senior cycle education in Ireland*. Dublin, Ireland: NCCA.

Ngai, S. S. (2006). Service-learning, personal development, and social commitment: A case study of university students in Hong Kong. *Adolescence, 41*(16), 165.

Schön, D. A. (1983). *The reflective practitioner: How professionals think in action*. Aldershot, England: Ashgate.

Walker, R. (Ed.). (1988). *Applied qualitative research*. Aldershot, England: Gower.

10

SERVICE-eLEARNING

What Happens When Service-Learning and Online Education Unite?

Jean Strait

For the past 7 years, the Sloan Center for Online Education has conducted a survey about changes and growth in online education (see www.scole.olin-babson.org). Highlights of the most recent survey are as follows:

- More than 3.9 million students were taking at least one online course during the fall 2007 term, a 12% increase over the number reported the previous year. More than 1.6 million students took at least one course online in 2002, showing that this number has doubled in 5 years.
- The 12.9% growth rate for online enrollments far exceeds the 1.2% growth of the overall higher education student population.
- More than 20% of all U.S. higher education students were taking at least one online course in the fall of 2007. This number was 11% in 2002.
- There is widespread agreement that higher fuel costs will lead to more students selecting online courses.
- Institutions that offer programs to serve working adults are the most positive about the potential for overall enrollment growth being driven by rising unemployment.
- Close to 70% of institutions agree that there is now competition for students in online courses and programs.

There is no doubt that higher education is utilizing online learning at progressively expeditious rates. As faculty members teach more online courses, they grapple with the complexities of integrating experiential learning in different delivery formats.

Six years ago, across the country small research pockets of faculty and staff who were avid service-learning practitioners began experimenting with service-learning online. Having the benefit of first teaching courses face to face using service-learning, these practitioners wanted to translate best practices to online learning. They were also armed with 20 years of research documenting the fact that experiential learning enhances student retention of content materials (Eyler, Giles, & Schmide, 1996; Stanton, Giles, & Cruz, 1999; Bringle & Hatcher, 1996). They began recruiting colleagues to discuss how best to incorporate online content and multiple experiential encounters for online students. The blending of these two elements is called *service-eLearning.*

Some faculty resist teaching online because they feel it is inferior teaching. However, good and bad teaching can be achieved in online, traditional, and hybrid classes. Even so, the pedagogical and technological issues surrounding online teaching tend to hamper participation in and understanding about service-eLearning. Before the best practice of using service-learning in classrooms can become the next practice of using service-eLearning in multiple formats, we need to educate practitioners about those issues, use existing examples to teach them how to use service-eLearning, and provide some items to consider when implementing service-eLearning. We need to acknowledge that faculty have set ideas about how best to deliver course content and that sometimes faculty and administration differ on what they think may be the best delivery methods for the institution.

The Rise of Electronic Delivery in Higher Education

Classroom spaces are provided by an institution for face-to-face (f2f) instruction. As college enrollments rise, real space becomes more costly, limited, and difficult to schedule. Although f2f enrollments are increasing nationwide, there is an explosion of enrollment in online courses. The average growth rate for online enrollment was about 21% per year from 2001 to 2007 (Allen & Seaman, 2007). The current population of online learners is approximately 3.5 million students. Why the large growth? For many full-time workers, online education is the most accessible and affordable type of education. As employers recognize the retention benefits of additional training, many are adding educational allowances to their employee benefit packages.

Institutions are also being called upon to train students for complex workplace issues. Thomas Friedman, in *The World Is Flat* (2005), offers four new workplace skills for future employment: learning how to learn, having passion and curiosity, playing well with others, and nurturing the right brain. All of these skills can be developed through service-eLearning. Howard Gardner, in *Five Minds for the Future* (2006), argues that future educators will look to develop five distinct minds: the disciplined mind, the synthesizing mind, the creating mind, the respectful mind, and the ethical mind. He further argues that as the world shrinks through technology, global society will demand capacities that in the past were options. Electronic delivery, including service-eLearning, is a vehicle that is already being used to develop Gardner's five minds skills.

Key Features in Service-eLearning

More and more, workers are telecommuting, interacting online, and working with global citizens. At the time of this writing, changes in the U.S. economy have caused the unemployment rate to rise to a national average of 7.2% after the biggest yearly job loss since 1945. When unemployment rates rise, enrollment in higher education institutions also increases. To meet these changes, institutions offer a blend of f2f and online instruction that is called a hybrid class. Imagine a continuum from pure f2f to pure online instruction. Every possible configuration in between is a variation of a hybrid model. The challenge, with so many possible configurations, is that service-eLearning can look very different in each delivery format. Even so, consistent features integral to each variation remain:

- Community partners
- Institutional resources
- Course content
- Service-learning to service eLearning
- Student interaction and ownership of course content

- Technology issues
- Reflection
- Faculty guidance in learning process

The following sections look at the possible barriers to and assets for each feature and potential considerations to examine while creating a service-eLearning environment.

Community Partners

One of the most essential components of a service-learning partnership is the relationship among the community partner, the institution, and the course participants. Traditional models of service-learning tend to identify needs of community partners and try to find ways that students could provide service to meet these needs. Many community partners have been working with sister institutions for more than a decade. Feedback from community partners is now starting to include requests for institutions not only to consider partner needs (some of which no longer exist because of a long-term successful partnership) but to focus on community partner assets and what partners can offer the educational community.

This needs versus assets switch is something that will be prevalent in the next practices model. When considering service-eLearning, community partners may have greater capacity to offer students workplace skills through online learning formats and by partnering with institutions to create community solutions than either could have previously provided independently. Service-eLearning offers a generic framework that can then be transported and even transplanted to other areas of the country or world to address similar situations. It also affords the opportunity for collaboration to take place in infinite time configurations.

Institutional Resources

In traditional service-learning, we often see faculty and students working with an office of service-learning and/or state, national, and professional organization(s) to create and manage a project. For service-eLearning, a different and, in some cases, new set of institutional resources needs to be accessed and examined. Because the environment is different, faculty need to ask the institution what technology is currently in use, what kinds of online or hybrid courses are being offered, and what types of interface technology are available or could be made available through funding streams aimed at technology.

Where traditional service-learning may be connected to teaching and learning centers, service-eLearning will also need to be connected to instructional technology resources. Items such as networks, operating systems, web servers, Internet access, and liability issues will take the forefront in planning and developing a service-eLearning project. In addition, students are coming to institutions more equipped with technological skills. Current modes of communication for college students consist of text messages, YouTube, and Facebook dialogues. Faculty who understand this new generation of students and their use of technology will best be able to use service-eLearning variations. Online instructors should be encouraged to experiment with these modes of communication.

Course Content

Traditionally, faculty maintain jurisdiction over the content and delivery of their assigned courses. When teaching online or in a hybrid form, course content does not change; the delivery changes. At first, it can be intimidating to have community partners and administrators be able to log on to a site and view one's class sessions and content. One of the ways to move beyond this fear is to plan the course with the community partner. This helps institutions move into the community partner as asset model. However, faculty also have to be mindful of time limits community partners may have, so it may be best to start out with one or two areas that the community partner can highlight for the class.

When first starting with service-eLearning, begin with low-tech options in a hybrid format. For example, while working on a particular subject where the community partner is the expert, design discussion board areas where, for a set time, students could access the community partner online and ask questions and give comments. Not only does this allow access to partner assets and build community, it also builds essential relational trust that is vital for partnership success. It can be difficult for a faculty member to let go of the "I am the expert" model and share knowledge with the community partner. Once a working relationship is built, it is easier to trust the community partner. Faculty will also enhance their own learning through the community partner experience.

With continued practice over several semesters, faculty may move into more high-tech options and offer choices such as live streaming feeds so that the community partner could join a "live" class. Recording these interactions and then using them is another way to honor time constraints of a community partner. Another benefit is the ability to connect with other experts recommended by the community partner to give students immediate access to voices that otherwise would not be heard. This technology encourages deep analysis of course content and can make the subject come alive for many participants.

Practitioners are able to stay connected with classes through online interaction while traveling and engaging in conferences and other professional activities; in some cases, faculty can bring additional experts into classes from the conference that they are attending. Students would have the opportunity to learn about the latest work that was happening in the field and ask questions of the experts.

A potential barrier to service-eLearning is the technology itself. Faculty need to investigate the technology that community partners have available. As many of us know, we work with nonprofit groups and corporations, so the level of technology ranges from having minimal to moderate equipment that was donated (and no one knows how to use it) to having the latest technology. Although it may seem daunting, this is a prime opportunity to send technology-savvy students into the field to help train partner staff in the uses of the technology and, in some cases, to have students serve as coordinators for partner technology. The best way to understand these variations is to examine a model. I share my own personal journey in the next section.

Service-Learning to Service-eLearning: My Personal Story

The first time I attempted to use service-learning with an online course was in 2001 when I was teaching in an entirely online program for Bemidji State University (BSU), a public 4-year institution. I had already been using service-learning in my teacher education courses for about 6 years at Augsburg College and knew the benefits that the experiential learning brought. In this particular program, my students lived throughout the state of Minnesota. We had three f2f meetings a semester, but the majority of our interactions were online.

The struggle was how to transfer traditional service-learning, in which a course group was working with one or two community partners, to having individual students connect with community partners in their local communities. A class of 25 students could potentially have 25 community partners. It would not be possible for one instructor to keep track of all those partnerships. This made me rethink how the service-learning would be set up.

I created a service-learning planning sheet for the students (see Figure 10.1). Here, each week students chose one or two items from class to investigate, identified a community partner or partners they thought would benefit

FIGURE 10.1
Service-Learning Planning Sheet

Service-Learning Project

Student Example
Student: 12-year-old 7th-grader (two additional students were involved in tour and
    project)
Subject: History of Utensils

Content Areas	History, Geography, Anthropology, Art
Materials/Preparation	Reference librarian, reference books, art exhibit tour(s), tests, articles, books, plastic silverware
Schedule	Week 1: Assess student needs, discuss content area reading options and service-learning ideas, set scheduled times for working together.
	Week 2: Research Internet sites. Compare and contrast findings. Trip to library, discussion with reference librarian and research of reference materials (photocopy), followed by discussion of findings. Prepare outline of reading materials.
	Week 3: Reading session.
	Week 4: Administer pretest, tour Minneapolis Institute of Art (MIA; possible interview with volunteer), administer Cloze test, and discuss results of tests and knowledge gained from field trip experience.
	Week 5: Silverware art project.
Resources	East Lake Library, MIA, www.calacademy.org/research/anthropology, www.cuisinet.com
Reflections	

from the semester of service, and created a way for the instructor to connect periodically with their community partner. Each week, the individual students had a group discussion online about their service-learning project, their challenges and struggles, and what impact the project was having on their community.

Students were creative with project design. One literacy education student created a children's book display each week for her local library and increased circulation by 500%. Partners who had the technology were able to join special discussions with other community partners around the state, sharing issues and resources. It was a win-win for everyone. Again, the biggest change was the preplanning required by the faculty member. Once initial contacts and relationships were created with community partners, students participating in other BSU courses who lived in the same communities could connect again with that partner, creating long-term relationships and sustainability.

In 2004, I moved to Hamline University, a traditional private 4-year institution. My position required I teach f2f, but I wanted to maintain the level of interaction I had reached through the online engagement. I began using hybrid models of service-learning, where I met with students f2f but held service-learning discussions online. Through continued connection with community partners in discussion rooms, I began to think of other ways to use this technology.

In 2007, my students and I created Each One, Teach One (EOTO). We had been doing recovery service in New Orleans since 2005 when Hurricane Katrina devastated the area. We traveled to the Ninth Ward, worked 7 to 10 days cleaning and repairing local parks in the mornings and tutoring students at Martin Luther King Science and Technology Magnet in the afternoons. In the evenings, we repaired the Depot House, a national landmark. We returned to St. Paul, continuing our tutoring and mentoring with the students online. Over this 3-year period, students witnessed our collective efforts to create change. We cleaned the school building and rebuilt it, gathered materials and supplies for teachers, and tutored students online. We are currently seeking funding to do a joint project with Tulane University in which Tulane students will serve as technology coordinators in the New Orleans schools and Hamline students will serve as online mentors to the New Orleans students. It is our hope that EOTO could be replicated as a disaster response model to serve in any area.

Student Interaction and Ownership of Content

As mentioned, students' level and type of interaction change with each variation of service-eLearning. Many educators argue that different students prefer different formats for learning and that a certain type of student will opt to take online courses. For example, many professors believe that more nontraditional students take online courses. Although that may have been true with initial online course offerings, 86% of the growth in online course enrollment over the last 5 years is attributed to the traditional undergraduate (Allen & Seaman, 2006, 2007).

One of the other ways student interaction has changed with service-eLearning is the practice of creating teams to implement projects. As Lou, Abrami, and d'Apollonia found in 2001, small group learning had significantly more positive effects on student achievement than individual learning did. Hoover, Casile, and Hanke (2008) argue that "learning teams operating in an eLearning environment are better able to engage in service-learning by encouraging students to work in a more reflective fashion, listen better, open up, share their perspectives, and invite feedback" (p.60). I have found this to be the case in the EOTO teams that work with New Orleans students. These skills match the skills Friedman (2005) asserts our future students will need to be successful. Students learn from each other and not just from the instructor. They are able to investigate projects in more depth and breadth by working with each other, which leads students to take more ownership of course content.

Technology Issues

There is no doubt that technology use has changed dramatically in service-learning. For example, when I started using service-learning in 1993, I was working on a Mac classic computer, the Internet was new, and my students were showing me how to use devices. In 15 years, practitioners have gone from using e-mail to using Skype to collaborate with fellow professors in other countries. Because technology supports long-distance communication, service-eLearning can connect to a global network, offering limitless possibilities for partnerships and projects. If you are a non-tech-savvy teacher but want to try service-eLearning, the first thing you should do is contact your information technology (IT) department. If your institution doesn't have IT, consider talking to whoever manages the technology in your unit or department.

You need to discuss several issues with your institutional contact. First, are there any policies for users of the technology (including teachers, students, staff, parents, and community)? Hamline University uses an online site to assist users (see Figure 10.2). Remember to consider parent permission for access with K–12 students and privacy issues (Family Educational Rights and Privacy Act, or FERPA) with college students. Next, find out which course platform(s) your institution uses and supports. Many universities have contracts with course platform providers such as Desire to Learn (D2L) or Blackboard, which provide instructors a framework with which to create and manage a course. Many free online open source platforms exist such as Moodle or Bluenog ICE. Textbook publishers also offer premade online course packages that accompany textbooks. Many of these course platforms are housed outside of your institution and may be on servers located in other states. You may want to consider using a format that your community partner is able to access easily so that they can best participate in the course.

Another issue to inquire about is security. Is your site password protected? Can students access other students' work? Can outsiders access course materials? Make sure you understand the security of your site so that you can also explain it to the community partner and students. Each institution has its own network that connects the university internally. Your institution's technology professionals know about the security of that network. Be sure to ask whether there are any concerns or special considerations when partners are outside the state or country in which you teach. Firewalls are used to block unwanted access to networks. Be careful that you are not accidentally blocking out your community partner. There may be rules about transporting student information across state, county, or country borders. When working with multiple partners, a project may have three or four different networks talking to each other. It will be important to have technology professionals from each partner in communication with the others to prevent any breeches and assist with smooth communication between partners.

Types of technology interactions are changing as well. Wikis and blogs are communication tools that are quickly becoming common in online and hybrid classes. One of the big issues with postings is that student work is public and open. Be sure to talk with your students about this public forum and encourage professional behavior and language. You can link your courses to several online "netiquette" guides and encourage this same level of behavior in discussion room interactions (Ko, 2002). Too often, when students are

FIGURE 10.2
Screen Shot for Technology Resources for Learning

Technology for Learning

GET STARTED!

Follow the steps below to begin using Hamline University's technology resources for learning.

1. **Knowing Your Piperline PIN**
   Piperline is the system that provides you access to your Hamline records. Newly admitted students receive their PIN and information on how to use Piperline. The Office of Student Administrative Service can help you reset your Piperline PIN.

2. **Obtaining Your Hamline Identification Card**
   Hamline student identification cards (ID cards) are required for all students. ID cards may be obtained at the Safety and Security Office. The ID card includes your Hamline ID Number and Library Code.

3. **Using the Piperline System**
   Piperline is the system that provides students access to their records. To access Piperline, you need to know your Hamline ID number (or your Social Security number) and Piperline PIN. You can contact the Office of Student Administrative Service if you need help on how to use Piperline.

4. **Learning about Hamline University's Computer Requirements**
   Hamline minimum computer requirements are intended to ensure that the equipment you bring to campus meets any software requirements placed on it for the current academic year. Computer equipment recommendations represent what we consider to be the ideal system configuration for a computer that is expected to support you through your academic program.

FIGURE 10.2 (Continued)

5. **Using Your Hamline E-mail Account**

   Hamline University provides an e-mail account for students. All degree-seeking students are required to use the official Hamline e-mail account for Hamline-related correspondence. The ITS Help Desk provides support in the use of the Hamline e-mail account.

6. **Using the Blackboard Course Management System**

   Blackboard is the Hamline University course management (e-learning) system, which allows for learning to extend to the online environment. You may use Blackboard in the courses you take at Hamline University.

7. **Using the NetStorage System**

   NetStorage is a web-based file storage system available to students. You have a 30-MB private space assigned in the NetStorage server.

8. **Accessing Library Databases**

   Bush Library offers students free access to diverse databases. Access to library databases is available through the Bush Library web site. Accessing library databases from off-campus requires authentication in the Hamline Proxy Server.

9. **Learning about the Campus Wireless Network**

   All Hamline University buildings that directly affect students, teaching, and learning are served by secure wireless connectivity. To access the campus wireless network, you need to authenticate using your Hamline (NetMail/GroupWise/Novell) username and password.

10. **Learning about Computer Labs on Campus**

    Over 150 microcomputers are housed in public computer labs across the campus. The main computer lab is located in the lower level of Bush Library.

FIGURE 10.2 (Continued)

11. **Learning about Printing/Copying Equipment on Campus**
    Hamline University uses a billing-code-based printing/copying solution for all students. All of Hamline University's computer labs and public printer/copiers are under this billing code system. You need to know your Printing/Billing Code in order to use printing/copying equipment on campus.

12. **Knowing Where to Find Help**
    Technology-related support for students is available through different university offices. Make sure you know the right office/staff member to contact to help you solve your specific issues.

not in the same area physically and interact only online, it is easy for them to be blunt or confrontational. It is helpful to have discussion guidelines for your courses and use these guidelines for all interactions. This helps to bring a level of accountability and ensures that all participants experience quality interactions.

Another need expressed by practitioners of service-eLearning is the desire to share/talk/discuss with others around the world who are doing similar work. Many are looking to move beyond the networks and tools of their institution to create forums, cafés, and blogs on open sites. One idea may be for some of the service-learning professional organizations to offer such tools on their websites, which in turn will foster greater communication and collaboration within their organizations and between global practitioners. In the future, technology growth and development will add an additional dimension to learning. Imagine having a student attending a class through virtual hologram or having virtual glasses to "see into" multiple learning environments around the world.

Reflection

The key ingredient for any service-learning project is reflection. Students use reflection to assess and integrate experiences into their learning. Traditionally, journaling has been the most used form to capture student reflection in service-learning (Dailey-Heibert, Donnelli-Sallee, & DiPadova-Stocks, 2008). In service-eLearning, technology can offer different vehicles for reflection. Some practitioners begin by using electronic dialogue journals, where students write the journal online to the professor and then the professor responds to the students online. Discussion boards, interactive journals, video journaling, and online interviewing are excellent ways to get students to delve into personal learning examination. Technology allows for easy access and storage of reflection products, so students and community partners can refer back to them with relative ease. Students and partners can see, in visual terms, the growth in learning through these tools.

In the future, the challenge may be for instructors to find new ways to assign grades for these projects. Course-generated rubrics are wonderful tools to use for focus, accountability, and grading. Students help select the criteria and then use it to develop their product. Because they are involved in the creation of the rubric, they are better able to explain it to each other and the community partners, as well as to evaluate each other's products.

Individual reflection in service-eLearning contexts can be accompanied by social reflection when groups, individuals, and community partners continue dialogue through technology formats (chat rooms, MySpace, Facebook). This past summer, I had a team of students communicating by text messaging each other on their cell phones. They even included me in the discussion. Perhaps where traditional classrooms have a set amount of time in a physical space, students are more likely to "turn off" content when they leave the room. With service-eLearning, the conversation can and does move beyond previous limitations of space and time, encouraging metacognitive growth in all participants.

Faculty Guidance in the Learning Process

When teaching online, the instructor delivers course content in a visually decentered way. A great deal of work is front-loaded for online and hybrid classes because the work needs to be preplanned and completed before the students begin. Relationships with community partners start long before meeting some of the students. In the past, this extra preplanning was perceived as a function of online learning. Now we realize that it is a pedagogical shift and that our role as guide, negotiator, resource dispenser, and community liaison has us interacting with students, community, and content in a richer, deeper conversation, even more so than in traditional service-learning.

General Suggestions for Using Service-eLearning

When colleagues ask me how to get started with service-eLearning, my number one recommendation is to *start small*. These projects have the ability to be huge; you don't want to be overwhelmed. Start with one class section, one community partner, and one content goal. Next, *train participants*. You need to have clearly stated expectations, and you need to guide students and community partners through each of the technology tools you plan to use. You will need more than one training session, and it helps if you have students working in small groups so that they can learn from each other. Once the training has begun, *plan for unexpected surprises*. More than once, we have had a glitch in our server; our Blackboard site has gone down; or for some unknown reason, technology didn't want to cooperate with us, and this has taught me to always have a backup plan.

Always have at least one space where students can have *confidential reflection* that stays between you and them. Although students are much more active with all forms of dialogue in technology, there still is and will always remain a need to discuss personal concerns and private issues. Some things you don't want on a public discussion board. Consider creating a space that can be used as an instructor "office" where students can drop by at set times and share privately. Have a *water cooler* area where students can take a break and have a space where they can interact with each other.

Students love having a second space where they can talk to each other without having to worry about instructors looking in. Finally, when structuring service-eLearning, it is essential to create a structure that has team leadership. As practitioners found in working with partner schools, if a contact leaves unexpectedly, it is vital to have a team that can train a new member and pick up the slack so that nothing falls between the cracks. A team usually consists of two leaders from the institution, two from the community partner, and two students who serve as leaders of the learning community. Two from each group works best, especially if you hold leadership meetings and not everyone can attend. The partner leader from each area is then responsible for bringing the missing leader up to speed.

Conclusion

What does the future look like for service-eLearning? The sky truly is the limit, and as technology evolves, so will our imaginations to use it. When service-learning and online education unite, the fusion can engage this tech-savvy generation on multiple levels, providing the best possible learning environment. I strongly recommend using service-eLearning. It is relatively easy to implement and it will deepen your knowledge of the dimensions of service-learning.

References

Allen, I. E., & Seaman, J. (2006). *Making the grade: Online Education in the United States.* Needham, MA: T. S. Consortium.

Allen, I. E., & Seaman, J. (2007). *Online nation: Five years of growth in online learning.* Needham, England: T. S. Consortium.

Bourne, J., & Moore, J. C. (2005). *Elements of quality online education into the mainstream.* Needham, England: T. S. Consortium.

Bringle, R. G., & Hatcher, J. A. (1996). Implementing service-learning in higher education. *Journal of Higher Education, 69*(2), 221–239.

Collison, G., Elbaum, B., Haavind, S., & Tinker, R. (2000). *Facilitating online learning: Effective strategies for moderators.* New York: Atwood.

Dailey-Herbert, A. D., Donnelli-Sallee, E., & DiPadova-Stocks, L. (Eds.). (2008). *Service-eLearning: Educating for citizenship.* Charlotte, NC: Information Age Publishing.

Eyler, J., Giles, D. E., & Schmide, A. (1996). *A practitioner's guide to reflection in service-learning: Student voices and reflections.* Nashville, TN: Vanderbilt University.

Friedman, T. (2005). *The world is flat.* New York: Farrar, Straus, and Giroux.

Gardner, H. (2006). *Five minds for the future.* Cambridge, MA: Harvard University Press.

Gould, T. (2007). Crossing bridges with rural communities: Building and maintaining multilingual websites to support immigrant populations in the Great Plains. *International Journal of Technology, Knowledge and Society, 3*(4), 89–101.

Hoover, K. F., Casile, M., & Hanke, R. (2008). How discussion boards drive course concept mastery in service-elearning. In A. D. Dailey-Heibert, E. Donnelli-Sallee, & L. DiPadova-Stocks (Eds.), *Service-eLearning: Educating for citizenship* (pp. 59–73). Charlotte, NC: Information Age Publishing.

Ko, S. (2002). *Teaching online: A practical guide.* Boston: Houghton Mifflin.

Lou, Y., Abrami, P. C., & d'Apollonia, S. (2001). Small group and individual learning with technology: A meta-analysis. *Review of Educational Research, 71*(3), 449–521.

Moore, J. C. (2005). *Quality framework and the five pillars.* Needham, England: T. S. Consortium.

Noromele, S. (2006). Service-learning in the online classroom. *International Journal of Technology, Knowledge and Society, 1*(3), 79–85.

Saulnier, B. (2006). Service learning as an eLearning paradigm for technology higher education. *International Journal of Technology, Knowledge and Society, 1*(2), 81–88.

Stanton, T., Giles, D. E., & Cruz, N. (1999). *Service-learning: A movements' pioneers reflect on its origins, practice, and future.* San Francisco: Jossey-Bass.

Stephenson, J. E. (2001). *Teaching and learning online: Pedagogies for new technologies.* Sterling, VA: Stylus Publishing.

"I DO MORE SERVICE IN THIS CLASS THAN I EVER DO AT MY SITE"

Paying Attention to the Reflections of Students of Color in Service-Learning

Tania D. Mitchell and David M. Donahue

" I do more service in this class than I ever do at my site."

This reflection, shared by a student in a short paper, was an unexpected outburst prompted by several weeks of frustration in his service-learning class. This young Latino from the local community was struggling with a community experience that he found incredibly rewarding while partnered with a classroom experience that depressed and frequently angered him.

This response is not one usually reported in the service-learning literature. Much of the literature touts the transformational nature of the pedagogy, stressing the benefits students gain: improved grades, strengthened communication, leadership skills, and appreciation for diversity, among many others (Astin & Sax, 1998; Densmore, 2000; Eyler & Giles, 1999; Kezar, 2002; Markus, Howard, & King, 1993). On occasion the literature warns against the possibilities of service-learning reinforcing deficit notions and prejudicial attitudes (Boyle-Baise, 1998; Butin, 2005; Chesler & Vasques Scalera, 2000; Green, 2001). The deficits that service-learning reinforces are frequently race-based and place blame on the identity of the people or communities where students serve. And those who walk away from service-learning experiences harboring deficit attitudes are either named or assumed to be White.

This student's reaction to the experiences of the classroom—to questions, to arguments, to unsolicited disparaging comments about his community—led to a host of questions about how service-learning is different for students of color. Literature speaks to working with children of color in service (Dunlap, 2000) and to creating service-learning experiences on college and university campuses that serve underrepresented populations (e.g., historically Black colleges and universities and tribal colleges) (Boyer, 1995; Brotherton, 2002; Ward & Wolf-Wendel, 2000), but speaks less to the experiences of students of color in the service-learning classroom, particularly how those students' experiences contrast to those of White students.

One of the unspoken truths about service-learning is that it is a pedagogy that has traditionally targeted privileged students. The frameworks that guide how we shape and teach service-learning courses have often been about crossing borders and connecting across difference, with that "difference" mostly embodied by the community served (Mitchell, 2008). The reality of service-learning, especially as college and university classrooms become more diverse, is that the differences explored through service-learning are more often the lived experiences of students in our classrooms. Students who are participating in service-learning may often be from privileged backgrounds, but they may also have experienced the very concerns that we ask students to address through community service. How do we structure the curriculum of service-learning classrooms to address these perspectives?

Our understanding is that, in any classroom with diverse students making sense of service, understanding of service (those processes of engaging and acting with others in community-based work) is shaped by different kinds of consciousness. Although consciousness may be shaped by many dimensions of identity, this chapter focuses on race consciousness—or perhaps more descriptively, consciousness about racism. Two different types of consciousness affect the classroom and then manifest as several tensions in service-learning that affect White students and students of color differently.

This chapter aims to illuminate the experiences of students of color in service-learning classes by presenting challenges and concerns of traditionally underrepresented students in dealing and working with their White peers.

The chapter incorporates interviews with 10 students of color enrolled in a required service-learning course at a small public university. Our analysis is guided by a conceptual framework that employs DuBois's (1903/1982) double consciousness alongside King's (1991) dysconsciousness as a way of uncovering how a person's understanding of racism may in turn guide and shape his or her approach to making sense of service-learning. What results are three tensions that affect the classroom and how students respond to the service-learning experience.

Double Consciousness and Dysconsciousness

This chapter draws on an understanding of two different types of consciousness—double consciousness (DuBois, 1903/1982), an understanding of self including race through the eyes of others, and dysconsciousness (King, 1991), a lack of awareness about race and racism, to make sense of the experiences of students of color and White students reflecting together on service. Although not all students of color bring a double consciousness and not all White students are dysconscious of racism—these differences in consciousness and understanding generally characterize different worldviews based on race, and they lie at the core of the tensions in learning from service explored in this chapter. These two types of consciousness generally inform different understandings about personal identity and beliefs about the social world and in particular about racism, privilege, and inequity.

DuBois (1903/1982) describes double consciousness as a "sense of always looking at one's self through the eyes of others, of measuring one's soul by the tape of a world that looks on in amused contempt and pity." He continues, "One ever feels his twoness,—an American, a Negro; two souls, two thoughts, two unreconciled strivings, two warring ideals in one dark body, whose dogged strength alone keeps it from being torn asunder" (p. 45).

In classrooms with students from diverse racial and ethnic backgrounds, students of color are constantly reminded of how they are viewed by others when they hear White students' comments (Solórzano, Ceja, & Yosso, 2000). Such comments, especially in service-learning, frequently reflect unexamined privilege and cast persons and communities of color as "problems." In fact, service-learning is often defined in part as meeting the needs or problems of a community (Kretzman & McKnight, 1993). Because service-learning often sends White students who are unfamiliar with persons from backgrounds other than their own into communities of color defined as having problems, it is no surprise that White students reflect the contempt or pity described by DuBois. For students of color in such classrooms, DuBois's (1903/1982) words ring true more than 100 years after he first wrote them: "Being a problem is a strange experience,—peculiar even for one who has never been anything else" (p. 44).

Awareness of being defined as a problem by White supremacist thinking (hooks, 2003) while recognizing that the problem is White supremacist thinking is a mark of double consciousness. This double consciousness, when shared in classrooms with White classmates, presents opportunities for those classmates to develop critical understanding of racism, privilege, and how they benefit from both. Sharing such understanding of the world viewed through the lens of double consciousness, in effect, becomes a "service" for students of color who are responsible for addressing the "miseducation" (Dewey, 1938/1997) of their White classmates. Miseducation results in students who unquestioningly accept unjust norms, which include racism and White supremacist thinking, of larger society (Woodson, 1933).

Uncritical acceptance of racism is "dysconscious racism." King (1991) defines dysconcsious racism as "a form of racism that tacitly accepts dominant White norms and privileges. It is not the absence of consciousness (that is, not unconsciousness) but an impaired consciousness or distorted way of thinking about race as compared to, for example, critical consciousness" (p. 135). Dysconscious White students are aware of racial prejudice and discrimination, but lack critical understanding of why such phenomena exist. For example, when presented with statistics on racial gaps in infant mortality, income, or educational achievement, dysconscious students see such problems "as a historically inevitable consequence of slavery or as a result of prejudice and discrimination" (p. 138). They locate the root of the problem in negative psychological or cultural characteristics of African Americans. They do not see "structural inequity built into the social order" and "fail to account for White people's beliefs and attitudes that have long justified societal oppression and inequity in the form of racial slavery or discrimination" (p. 138).

Dysconsciousness is characteristic of many White students' reflection on their service-learning experiences. By defining social problems in terms of those marginalized and oppressed and assigning responsibility for remedying such problems to the same population, White students shift problems and responsibility away from themselves. As King (1991) notes, "The ability to imagine society reorganized without racial privilege requires a fundamental shift in the way White people think about their status and self-identities and their conceptions of Black people" (p. 136). The job of those facilitating reflection on service is not to prove to White students that they are racist, but to highlight how their thinking is impaired by dysconscious racism. As King points out, "Uncritical and limited ways of thinking must be identified, understood, and brought to their conscious awareness" (p. 140). This is where students of color, seeing the world through a double consciousness, provide a typically unrecognized service by helping White students gain such awareness.

In the following sections, we describe the resulting tensions—going home versus serving the other, responsibility versus privilege, and teaching to versus learning about—that emerge as students with double consciousness and dysconsciousness reflect together on service. Implications for service-learning and ways practitioners can capitalize on experiences and perspectives brought by students of color conclude this chapter.

Going Home Versus Serving the Other

As educators design service-learning experiences, the selection of community partners is an important part of the process. Students' community experiences will often shape their understanding of course material and impart new understandings of the communities and populations experienced through service. Students' prior experience with communities served can either be a source of empowerment or resistance. White students or privileged students who have limited experience with community service may be excited about the opportunities of working with a new or different population or be afraid of what they will see and experience. For students of color and students who have lived or grown up in the communities (or communities similar to those) identified as recipients of service, the opportunity to serve can similarly engender feelings of empowerment or resistance.

These feelings that emerge are just a piece of a tension that can result in a service-learning classroom. What does it mean when students are going home (to their own or similar communities) for the service experience? What does it mean when students entering those same communities for the first time bring their questions and concerns, often steeped with deficit notions and prejudice, back to the classroom?

The experience of going home for a student in service-learning may breed excitement and empowerment with the possibility of giving back to a community that nurtured and provided, as reflected in the comments of a Latina serving in a place very similar to her home community:

> When I'm at [my service site] and I'm working in the Spanish class [helping women achieve literacy in their first language], I know that I'm doing it for my *family*. Like my mom who didn't get to go to school past third grade or my grandmother who still draws pictures and takes empty packages to the grocery store cause she can't write. [The service site] is like my kitchen table. (Interview, April 19, 2006)

The opportunity to participate in a community service experience where she could recognize and understand the people she was serving—believing that her work at the service site could be useful to members of her own family—encouraged her and gave her great pride in her service and in the community that provided this service for them. This excitement can be quickly tempered when a peer returns this enthusiasm with disdain, negative stereotypes, or fear.

The experience of going home may also trigger resistance for students in service. For students for whom the college experience is an escape or a step toward "getting out" of a difficult home situation, being asked or required to go back in the name of service may be a challenging experience that neither the student, course facilitator, or community partner is prepared to handle.

Students of color from economically privileged backgrounds may feel empowered or excited by the opportunity to work with people who share their racial identity but who have very different life experiences. However, these students may also show resistance, especially if they have class bias or unexamined stereotypes about inner cities and "urban communities," if they are concerned about being in communities where they fear community members may make assumptions about their abilities to interact that will be quickly disproved (i.e., they will be "found out"), if they carry fears about the community members they will serve, or if they worry that their peers will view them as "like" the community members they are serving. These are pressures of identity that frequently are ignored or underestimated in service-learning experiences.

Typical in the framing of service-learning courses is an assumption that the community is an unfamiliar "other" to our students. When educators frame reflections on service as if everyone is new to the community served and the issues encountered, students of color may feel their lives and experiences are being analyzed and criticized (they become objectified and/or exploited) or may feel a responsibility to defend their communities, to educate and correct misconceptions. At the service site, students who have experienced circumstances similar to those affecting the community may be troubled by actions and statements made onsite that negatively affect community members or make students from the campus look bad in the eyes of the community. Similarly, they may question the effectiveness of their peers at the service site—either those who look negatively on the community, those who purport to know everything about the issues encountered in service (because they've read about it), or those who are too afraid to truly engage with the community their service is aimed to address. An African American woman in service-learning suggests:

> I know that not everyone grew up with addicts on their corners. But people like to pretend like it's something that only happens in movies. People are so surprised when they see someone on [the street next to the service site] shooting up or coming down and they just freak out, but I'm like, "This is real. If you can't face this part of your service what good can you really do down here?" (Interview, May 4, 2006)

The very dichotomy of server–served often positions college students as the altruistic heroes entering communities to help and fix them. Service-learning automatically privileges students as those with the knowledge, position, and power to respond to community problems and sometimes permits them to deny the problems that exist outside the communities they serve. In these kinds of situations, the community served becomes the site of difficulty, inadequacy, and concern, and the community *not* served is viewed as a point of aspiration (Donahue, Bowyer, & Rosenberg, 2003). These observations can lead to an opportunity to discuss differences between communities and to explore structural inequalities that create difference. The responsibility in these discussions is to ensure that conversations do not degenerate into stereotypes and blanket statements about wealth and poverty.

The idea of safety is another issue that illuminates this tension of going home. Service-learning positions the community where students serve as a place of "risk" where students need to be trained before they enter. The framing of service-learning experiences rarely frames the community served as a familiar place and certainly doesn't recognize the places where students of color are unsafe, such as their own campuses or in the predominantly White and economically privileged college towns where they may be targeted by police, and the contradictions that may be produced for students of color. Students are trained to feel uncomfortable, unsafe, or on guard when entering the communities they will serve, so students who grew up in environments similar to the service site may feel that their upbringing is being disparaged. This is reflected in this comment from a Latina in service-learning:

> Ugh! Sometimes the kids in our class just get on my nerves. They talk about how bad my neighborhood is—how dangerous—they don't even know. It's like because people around them don't speak English and wear blue they are all of a sudden in the middle of a gang shootout. It's fucked up, you know? 'Cause a lot of us live there and our families are there and we know how the community looks out for each other. (Interview, March 17, 2006)

The questions raised about student safety and risk in service-learning are important conversations, but they must be tempered with recognition that no place is "safe for all" and that all communities have assets to be leveraged.

Responsibility Versus Privilege

Another phenomenon playing out in classrooms of students from diverse backgrounds reflecting on service is the tension between responsibility and privilege. Responsibility, on two levels, is a characteristic of many students of color in the service-learning classroom.

On the first level, responsibility refers to the sense of moral accountability for serving in the community, especially when students identify with a community or have roots in that community. The same moral accountability is evident in the classroom when students are reflecting on their service. When students of color hear comments by White students rooted in racism and stereotypes, many shut down or otherwise intellectually withdraw from the classroom. But others feel a responsibility to challenge such misinformation. In that sense, these students become responsible for the education of their White classmates about race and racism. Similarly, when students of color hear comments that draw on unexamined assumptions and limited life experiences, they feel responsible for pointing out those assumptions and sharing stories about their own life experiences to counter those assumptions. Often students feel this responsibility because their instructors share the same assumptions and limitations as White and middle-class students and do not have the capacity to challenge racist and class-biased comments.

On the second level, responsibility refers not only to the accountability that students of color initiate, it also refers to a burden placed on them by instructors and classmates. In this sense, students of color are called to be accountable for explaining actions and values of communities about which White and middle-class students have little knowledge. This burden carries the danger of essentializing, or oversimplifying and narrowing, questions of race and making students of color spokespersons for explaining an entire group.

This second level of responsibility is a product of other students' privilege, particularly the privilege that comes with being White. Privilege refers to benefits or advantages that accrue to a particular group. Being privileged means operating without being subject to the usual rules because of one's special characteristics. White students are often unaware of the privilege that comes with their color and take whiteness as the norm. Students operating from such privilege may not, for example, understand that communities of color have experiences with police, teachers, and store owners different from their own. They may assume that anyone can travel, shop, or vote with the same ease they enjoy. Operating from a position of privilege, White students may ask other classmates to explain racial differences and then be upset or feel "unsafe" when those classmates point out their privilege or shift responsibility to White students for their own learning.

One comment by a student of color illustrates the idea of responsibility as a sense of moral accountability for serving in the community, especially the students' own community:

> I took this class because we have to, but I was excited at the same time because I knew I could have an impact. I knew that I would have the chance to help people see what was possible. Not everybody from neighborhoods like mine gets to college, not everybody from my high school

graduated, you know? It's like here's my chance to show kids like me what it takes to make it. (Interview, December 7, 2005)

This student's comment speaks to feeling responsibility for young people in a neighborhood like his own, a responsibility to make sure that young people like him also graduate from college. He does not see the young people he serves as "other" or "underprivileged." He understands that his own life as a college student can provide a model for young people. He defines service-learning with an emphasis on making changes in the lives of young people. By contrast, students operating from a position of privilege might focus less on making a difference and more on fulfilling the requirements of service, tutoring for a set number of hours, for example. They might approach service as something from which they can learn much but not necessarily as a compelling part of making long-lasting change in the world.

Students operating from privilege see service-learning as an opportunity to learn from vicarious experiences of poverty or marginalization, not as opportunities to revisit their own lived experiences. As another student of color noted about her privileged classmates, "I get so frustrated. I mean where do these stereotypes about people on welfare come from? None of them has had to be on welfare. I bet none of them knows how hard it is to be on welfare" (Interview, November 10, 2005). This student points out how classroom discussions can often be forums where privileged students voice unexamined assumptions. In such contexts, students of color and poor and working-class students face the choice of remaining silent and mentally withdrawing from the class or teaching their classmates by sharing their own stories in an effort to challenge notions about the experiences of "others." Both choices are unattractive: the first because it alienates students from the classroom, the second because sharing one's life with others who may not have the capacity to understand it can feel exploitive, depleting, or even futile.

One student who chose not to share his life story reflected on his frustration with privileged classmates and his desire to see them reframe how they viewed problems in the community:

I don't talk about being homeless because it's my past and I want it to stay there. But I go down there [to the soup kitchen] and it comes back hard. . . . And when we're talking in class people are like, "It's so sad to see people like that," but you know that they drive right past the homeless

guy who stands on that corner asking for food. It just feels hypocritical—
like the people at [the soup kitchen] are the "good homeless people." They
need to get that homelessness is bad for everybody who has to sleep on the
streets or in their cars. I want them to see it as *our* problem not just *their*
[meaning the homeless people's] problem. (Interview, November 16, 2005)

This student's comment raises questions about whether service-learning
transforms privileged students' thinking or actions. He notes that, although
privileged classmates might feel sympathy or pity for persons who are homeless, they are not necessarily moved to feel empathy or act outside a course's
service-learning requirements. This student also points out how poor and
working-class students see social ills such as homelessness as something that
is not separate from them. They define such problems as "ours" rather than
"theirs." Students from racially or class privileged backgrounds are more
likely to see such problems as separate from them, as something that they
might help alleviate, but ultimately as something that other communities,
not the ones with which they identify, need to solve.

As students of color observe, White students experience discomfort
when they move out of their circle of privilege. They note that, although
their White and middle- and upper-class classmates might talk about feeling
unsafe in some contexts, what they are really experiencing is discomfort. One
student of color said:

There's a big difference between being safe and being comfortable. I feel
like most of the time when people in class are talking about being "unsafe"
when they go into [town] it's more about being uncomfortable. I mean
you can hear it when they complain about how they were "the *only* person
speaking English" or that "no one else looked like them." I wanna say
". . . and?!" [*laughs*]. (Interview, November 11, 2005)

This student's comment sums up two aspects of the tension between responsibility and privilege: the lack of identification and empathy that White students feel with those they serve, and the frustration felt by students of color
when they hear unexamined stereotypes. In addition, this comment illustrates how students of color operate with a double consciousness, understanding that the communities where they serve are safe while also knowing
that White students will define them as unsafe when in fact White students
feel uncomfortable moving out of their privileged spheres. It also illustrates

the dysconsciousness of White students who do not understand their own privilege, who take their own backgrounds as the norm, and who feel threatened in a context that departs from that norm.

Teaching To Versus Learning About

Another tension we've identified emerging from race consciousness in the service-learning classroom is a phenomenon of teaching and learning. The literature about teaching in diverse classrooms frequently names the dysconsciousness of White students as evidenced by their "raceless" or "colorblind" discourse (Frankenberg, 1993) in the classroom. As a result of not seeing or not admitting to race and racism, students use language that evades racial difference and inequity based on race. Because such discourse fails to observe and question racism, it perpetuates racism (Bonilla-Silva, 2003; Helms, 1990; Marx, 2006; Tatum, 2007). Service-learning is designed to enhance students' understanding of academic concepts through applied community work, so there is some (though undesired) expectation that students learn at the expense of the communities where they serve. Our concern, uncovered in this tension, is that White and economically privileged students also learn at the expense of their peers—students of color and those from communities that reflect the service sites. Students of color then bear the burden of redirecting colorblind classroom discourse.

The students interviewed in this research talked about feeling like their work—their *real* service—was in the classroom more so than in the community. Most plainly felt, in the words of the Latino student whose writing opened this chapter, "I do more service in this class than I ever do at my site" (Student narrative, collected in short response paper, October 17, 2005). Students of color often felt that their time in the classroom required them to teach their peers about what they were experiencing in the community— about the people in the community and about the realities of privilege and oppression as they affect real people in the world.

Students frequently named the classroom component of their service-learning course as the most difficult aspect of their experience. Feeling forced to fight or defend their communities, feeling silenced by the continuous voicing of unexamined stereotypes and negative labeling, feeling hurt by their peers' lack of awareness and understanding—the classroom for these students of color became the space where they crossed boundaries and borders. The classroom became the service site over the communities, which were often more comfortable and more familiar. Instead of experiencing the classroom as a site for learning, students of color were too often teaching their White and economically privileged peers.

An African American man in a service-learning experience shared:

> When I'm at the site, it's like I'm hanging out with my cousins. I see people who look like me, who dress like me, who know where I come from. In the class, man, I feel like I'm at a job. I just work all class long. I'm over it! You can only challenge someone's stereotypes about poor people or black people or whatever, so many times before it gets old. And then, when I ask people questions, trying to understand where they're coming from, they get defensive and shut down. It's like they know that the way they feel is wrong—like it's from misinformation or ignorance or media stereotypes or whatever—but they don't want to have their opinions challenged. They just want to keep on believing what they believe. In some ways, I'm like, "Fine." Because at least I know who they are and what I need to do to protect myself, but at the same time I wanna see some change and know that I haven't wasted all that energy. (Interview, April 18, 2006)

This quote is reflective of an earlier tension of going home and expresses this student's experience of the familiar in community tempered by a classroom environment filled with frustration and tension. He expresses a sense of exasperation with his peers and the process, but also a desire to see change—to know that his actions have not been in vain. For students of color in service-learning experiences, the classroom where their peers are learning about the community creates a site that requires them to be on guard, prepared to defend, and situated to forfeit their learning and process for the benefit of peers.

A young woman revealed her experience of feeling silenced in the classroom as students present perspectives that praise and demean simultaneously. "They just keep saying, 'They're so cute but they're *so* loud!' or 'They're *so* bad!' And I want to shout out how racist that is, but I know they won't get it" (Interview, March 16, 2006). Referring to her classmates' comments about children they worked with in an after-school program, the student could not figure out how to explain to her peers how their comments troubled her. But revealing the tension more deeply is the student's feeling or desire to "shout out," which speaks to a responsibility to teach others but also to a silence on the parts of peers and instructors to challenge her fellow students on their comments.

Another reality of this tension is the understanding that students of color and students from troubled communities develop about the differences in their life experiences from many of their classmates. Students of color come to view their peers as unprepared for experiences in the community and question the effectiveness of their peers to work alongside community members. A Latina offers:

> I feel like everyone chose [the after-school program] because they think that working with kids will be easy, but I know these kids and their lives aren't easy. They go to the [program] for a reason, because it's how they know they'll eat today or because it's too dangerous to walk home alone, or because it keeps them away from a mom or dad who beats them for a few more hours. People don't even try to understand what's really going on with the kids we work with. They just think they'll get to play pool or basketball for an hour. (Interview, December 2, 2005)

This student's comment speaks to the knowledge she brings of the community where she serves and what she sees as the gaps in knowledge of some of her classmates. By referring to students who "play pool or basketball," she is questioning the commitment to social justice and to learning about the community by some of her White and middle-class peers. She sees these students as not taking their service seriously because of assumptions that all children's lives are "easy." The student is situated to teach her White classmates, but this involves additional "service" in the classroom that is often not recognized as equal to the service in the community.

Implications for Teaching

Teachers working in classrooms with students from diverse backgrounds can address these tensions in several ways. First, they can identify and name the tension and point out to students how White and middle-class experiences are taken as norms in classrooms, particularly at predominantly White institutions. They can help students develop empathy by asking them to have experiences in the community that are only about learning before they begin serving. These experiences may also be framed in ways that allow students to become more comfortable in the community where they will be serving so that concerns about safety are appropriately shifted. For example, students can spend time in cafés, grocery stores, and reading rooms of public libraries. They can explore art and local history through community centers, museums, or parks and public spaces so that they can learn about the community, its culture, and its history.

Educators utilizing service-learning pedagogy must challenge their assumptions about the communities where students are asked to serve and the students in the classrooms they teach. They can challenge unexamined assumptions and stereotypes when they are aired in the classroom by asking questions such as "what do you mean?" and "how do you know that?" When instructors take this responsibility, they remove this burden from students of color and students from poor and working-class backgrounds. This requires that we know who our students are and recognize that, although some may be unfamiliar with service or the issues encountered in specific service experiences, there will also be students who know very well the situations we ask them to experience through service.

In facilitating discussions about the service experience, educators should frame conversations about the experience from an assets rather than a deficits perspective and include community members speaking about their neighborhoods (in addition to city officials or law enforcement) to give a more complete picture of the community. The inclusion of statistics and personal narratives to educate students about the areas where they will serve will illuminate the stories of institutional and structural injustice (or privilege) that perpetuate social and community concerns.

As students share their experiences in communities, it is imperative that facilitators challenge unexamined stereotypes and refute distorted claims as they are voiced. Taking every opportunity to speak to root causes so that blame is not placed on community members allows students to understand how issues, resources, and concerns that affect communities can oftentimes be traced to policies, traditions, and history that privileges some at the expense of others.

An alternative to large-group discussion, which often results in anger, frustration, or silence for students of color facing deficit notions about their (or similar) communities, is one-on-one conversations with students where they can confidently and confidentially voice their experiences, perspectives, and questions without fear. These individual conversations can also create a space for educators to challenge, correct, or question students and for students to express frustrations, challenge the pedagogy, and interrogate situations and circumstances in the classroom and community. Similarly, affinity group discussions (i.e., same race groups) can create an important space to recognize and reflect on double consciousness and challenge dysconsciousness. These dialogues require skilled facilitators who can represent the identities of White students and students of color (Zúñiga, 1998).

To mitigate these tensions, it is important to emphasize the opportunity, resources, and the lessons accessible to *all* students in the service environment. We should not prepare students for service experiences from a place of fear or risk, but instead showcase the assets and strengths of the communities where students will fulfill the service component of their experience.

As service experiences are developed, educators should seek different kinds of opportunities that permit students to see their previous experiences as assets. This means that service experiences in troubled communities and neighborhoods can be tremendous learning experiences for students familiar and unfamiliar with those communities. At the same time, we can explore service opportunities in communities traditionally viewed as privileged or "well-off" as another learning opportunity for students. For example, a service-learning course that wanted students to work in sites with people struggling with addiction placed students in a methadone clinic in an impoverished community and a private recovery center in a wealthy area of town. Although the experiences were very different for students, these experiences provided great learning opportunities in both sites. Students noted differences in police presence, race, class, parental involvement, and location (not just the community but where in the community) that allowed them to think more deeply about the story of addiction and how various factors shape the (de)criminalization of drug use in our society.

Conclusion

We raise these tensions because the demographics of our institutions are changing. Service and service-learning can no longer be framed as an experience of "giving back" or "giving to" people less fortunate than ourselves. Increasingly, our service-learning classrooms include students whose life experiences mirror those of the community members they encounter in service. We can no longer pretend that the community experience will be new or different or unfamiliar to all our students.

This chapter gives voice to students of color whose experiences are often missing from service-learning, both in scholarly literature and in classroom discussions typically dominated by White middle-class voices. The students quoted in this chapter offer an important critique of the way service-learning is traditionally framed and help us understand the ways in which service-learning is very different for students of color. We believe these students eloquently reframe for scholars and practitioners what is considered "service" to students of color.

Finally, we appreciate how these students complicate the distinction between service and learning. These students understand that service is not just something that happens when they leave the campus. Service, for students of color, can also be helping White classmates learn about the communities where they serve and challenging their peers to understand that White and middle class are not normative perspectives. Service-learning practitioners should honor the contributions students of color bring to the classroom but not expect that they will carry the responsibility alone.

References

Astin, A. W., & Sax, L. J. (1998). How undergraduates are affected by service participation. *Journal of College Student Development, 39*(3), 251–263.

Bonilla-Silva, E. (2003). *Racism without racists: Colorblind racism and the persistence of racial inequality in the United States.* Lanham, NY: Rowman & Littlefield.

Boyer, P. (1995). Tribal college of the future. *Tribal College, 7*(1), 8–17.

Boyle-Baise, M. (1998). Community service learning for multicultural education: An exploratory study with preservice teachers. *Equity & Excellence in Education, 31*(2), 52–60.

Brotherton, P. (2002). Connecting the classroom and the community. *Black Issues in Higher Education, 19*(5), 20–24.

Butin, D. W. (2005). Preface: Disturbing normalizations of service-learning. In D. W. Butin (Ed.), *Service-learning in higher education: Critical issues and directions* (pp. vii–xx). New York: Palgrave Macmillan.

Chesler, M., & Vasques Scalera, C. (2000). Race and gender issues related to service-learning research. *Michigan Journal of Community Service Learning, Special Issue,* 18–27.

Densmore, K. (2000). Service learning and multicultural education: Suspect or transformative? In C. R. O'Grady (Ed.), *Integrating service learning and multicultural education in colleges and universities* (pp. 45–58). Mahwah, NJ: Erlbaum.

Dewey, J. (1997). *Experience and education.* New York: Simon & Schuster. (Original work published 1938)

Donahue, D., Bowyer, B., & Rosenberg, D. (2003). Learning with and learning from: Reciprocity in service learning in teacher education. *Equity and Excellence in Teacher Education, 36*(1), 15–27.

DuBois, W. E. B. (1982). *The souls of black folk.* New York: Signet Classics. (Original work published 1903)

Dunlap, M. (2000). *Reaching out to children and families: Students model effective community service.* Lanham, MD: Rowman & Littlefield.

Eyler, J., & Giles, D. E. (1999). *Where's the learning in service-learning?* San Francisco: Jossey-Bass.

Frankenberg, R. (1993). *White women, race matters: The social construction of Whiteness.* Minneapolis: University of Minnesota Press.

Green, A. E. (2001). "But you aren't white": Racial perceptions and service-learning. *Michigan Journal of Community Service Learning, 8*(1), 18–26.

Helms, J. (1990). *Black and White racial identity: Theory, research, and practice.* New York: Greenwood Press.

hooks, b. (2003). *Teaching community: A pedagogy of hope.* New York: Routledge.

Kezar, A. (2002, May–June). Assessing community service learning: Are we identifying the right outcomes? *About Campus, 7,* 14–20.

King, J. (1991). Dysconscious racism: Ideology, identity, and the miseducation of teachers. *Journal of Negro Education, 60*(2), 133–146.

Kretzman, J., & McKnight, J. (1993). *Building communities from the inside out.* Evanston, IL: Asset Based Community Development Institute.

Markus, G. B., Howard, J. P. F., & King, D. C. (1993). Integrating community service and classroom instruction enhances learning: Results from an experiment. *Educational Evaluation and Policy Analysis, 15*(4), 410–419.

Marx, S. (2006). *Revealing the invisible: Confronting passive racism in teacher education.* New York: Routledge.

Mitchell, T. D. (2008). Traditional vs. critical service-learning: Engaging the literature to differentiate two models. *Michigan Journal of Community Service Learning, 14*(2), 50–65.

Solórzano, D., Ceja, M., & Yosso, T. (2000). Critical race theory, racial microaggressions, and campus racial climate: The experiences of African American college students. *Journal of Negro Education, 69*(1/2), 60–73.

Tatum, B. (2007). *Can we talk about race? And other conversations in an era of school resegregation.* Boston: Beacon Press.

Ward, K., & Wolf-Wendel, L. (2000). Community-centered service learning: Moving from doing for to doing with. *American Behavioral Scientist, 43*(5), 767–780.

Woodson, C. (1933). *The miseducation of the Negro.* Washington, DC: Associated Publishers.

Zúñiga, X. (1998, Winter). Fostering intergroup dialogue on campus: Essential ingredients. *Diversity Digest.* Retrieved January 7, 2008, from www.diversity web.org/Digest/W98/fostering.html

12

NEW DIRECTIONS IN RESEARCH AND EVALUATION

Participation and Use Are Key

Robert Shumer

L ong ago the conduct of research was reserved for university-type experts. Only they had the knowledge and expertise to conduct studies that investigated a variety of issues, including service-learning and other forms of community-based education. It was generally accepted that mathematically based, scientific studies were the best approach to prove causality and predict future behavior. In many circles of research and evaluation, that notion of rigorous, quantitative work still rules the roost and is considered the best form of investigation (Furco & Billig, 2002; Shavelson & Towne, 2002).

But as that approach has been dominant, other methods and ideologies about research and evaluation have emerged to challenge it. From Kurt Lewin's work in the 1940s, to Michael Patton (2008), Guba and Lincoln (1989), and a host of others (Fetterman & Wandersman, 2005; Stake, 2006; Strand, Murillo, Cutforth, Stoecker, & Donohue, 2003), the focus has turned to inclusion of program participants, to utilization of research and evaluation, and to empowerment of community participants as equally important measures of research and evaluation effectiveness. Even studies of schools, out-of-school time programs, and other youth cultures have embraced the notion of participatory evaluation and research and turned the tides on the dominant paradigm of positivism. Youth themselves are becoming partners in research efforts and contributing to the research enterprise as active members of the assessment community (Sabo, 2003; Flores, 2008).

Why such a change? As Guba and Lincoln (1989) explain, there has been a slow and steady critique of positivistic, scientific approaches to social science research, with inroads made that demonstrate that there are ethical and political challenges to the quantitative methods required of such investigation. Positivism is not as "value free" as proponents claim, and there is selectivity practiced by researchers in what they choose to research and what they choose to exclude. Thus, there is a political dimension to positivistic inquiries that investigate only those elements that can be controlled, primarily by simplifying human interaction to scenarios that belie the true complexity of the human condition. There are also ethical issues to positivistic research, including all the problems raised by placing individuals in control groups that deprive them of educational opportunities simply to carry out the demands of quantitative comparison designs.

In their book *Fourth Generation Evaluation* (1989), Guba and Lincoln describe the transition periods in education for research and evaluation that preceded our current state of affairs. The first generation refers to studies that were concerned with measurement, with a focus on testing and mathematical representations of data; this was referred to as the "measurement generation." The second generation focused more on description. Citing the 8 Year Study conducted by Ralph Tyler at Ohio State, the authors discuss how the efforts to measure change led to the development of formative evaluation and research, where there was a focus on the process as well as the outcomes. The third generation added the elements of judgment, where evaluators and researchers had to judge how the standards and outcomes expected (theories included) were to be assessed and how explanations about a study's value and worth were to be presented.

These three generations all moved the evaluation and research process forward, but they left some issues unanswered. One specific area of concern is the independence of the evaluator/researcher. The new generation of researchers believed knowledge was a constructed phenomenon. In the old "measurement" generation, the researcher/evaluator assumed a managerial role that failed to involve stakeholders and others with an interest in the study in the design and measurement of the investigation. To be inclusive, all participants have to be involved in the construction of the design and measures of the study. This clearly is of concern to many in the service-learning field, where inclusion of stakeholders is an important component of high-quality service-learning work. Thus, the emergence of the fourth-generation evaluation, as

Stake (1975) describes it: Fourth-generation evaluation is "preordinate evaluation" where the focus is on interactive, negotiated studies that have participants and others engaged in the investigative process.

Guba and Lincoln (1989) admit that there are also issues with fourth-generation evaluation, such as concerns for confidentiality and violation of trust. Clearly, obtaining data using face-to-face methods does put participants at risk for abuses of trust when researchers know their identity and specific information details. However, the authors defend the new "constructivism" as a potentially superior approach in many situations because participants can be protected, and more important, social reality is "constructed" through social interaction (p. 137). This belief is supported by many constructivist theorists (Bruner, 1986, 1990; Dewey, 1938/1997; Vygotsky, 1978), who argue that all knowledge is constructed by individuals through human interaction. Knowledge is built and developed as individuals interact with their environments to construct new meaning and new understanding from new experiences.

Constructivist approaches are consistent with service-learning principles when they suggest that personal engagement through social interaction is necessary for understanding and for acknowledging the already accumulated knowledge of the people participating in the service experiences. Some in the service world have defined service-learning as an interactive process that helps participants construct new situations where they have more control over and understanding of their own community issues. Robert Sigmon (1979), developer of the term *service-learning*, defines the outcomes of service-learning programs as these:

1. Those being served control the services provided.
2. Those being served become better able to serve and be served by their own actions.
3. Those who serve are also learners and have significant control over what is expected to be learned.

Thus, service-learning is a constructivist process in which those being served create new understandings so that they can control their own destiny. Those providing service also interact with the community members to achieve new levels of understanding of community issues and of academic subjects in the context of applied settings. The nexus of both the practice and research on service-learning is found in the interaction among all stakeholders in the process. This understanding parallels the new understandings fostered by fourth-generation evaluation and embraces the foundational principles of qualitative and mixed-methods designs of research.

New Directions in Research

Given this foundational understanding, the focus of 21st-century research on service-learning is the numerous qualitative/interpretive and mixed-methods approaches. Multiple research paradigms are useful for service-learning investigations (Denzin & Lincoln, 1994). The literature describes more than 14 qualitative methods that focus on interpretive approaches, including critical theory (power relationships), case studies (individual programs and/or people), ethnography, participant observation, grounded theory, and biographical methods. Others practitioners use methods of data gathering that involve interviewing, observation techniques, personal experience, among several other approaches. Given this wide array of paradigms and methods of data collection, it is up to the researcher to select from these options the kind of design that is most suitable for the goals and objectives of the study.

One important element of conducting research on service-learning through a constructivist lens is context. Knowing the circumstances of the service-learning, where it is done, how it is done, and the outcomes attributed to the effort define the elements to be studied. According to Hecht (2003), context matters a great deal and must be considered in any research initiative. Four specific areas are noted: site context, background context, reflection context, and planning context. Research designs must address each of these areas and accommodate them through approaches such as regression models, hierarchical linear modeling, and approximation methods in quantitative paradigms. Interpretive/qualitative approaches can also accommodate the areas by using a multitude of design models that delve into the contextual factors that comprise the human interactions involved in the delivery of service-learning.

Yet many of the newer perspectives on service-learning research require methods and approaches that engage the participants in the creation and implementation of service-learning programs. The use of action research, studying the interactions of the process from multiple perspectives, seems best capable of capturing the complexity and nuances of the service-learning phenomenon.

Community-Based Research

One approach garnering wide support is community-based research (Strand et al., 2003). In this theoretical model, the research design and implementation process requires the involvement of community members. The role of the researcher is to help community members engage as active partners in the research enterprise and to facilitate development of their research skills so that they can continue the investigations after the "professionals" leave. Building on the foundational work in action research (Whyte, 1991), this approach engages college students and community members in continuous dialogue about what to study and how to study it. It requires active participation by community partners and embraces techniques that bring the process closer to the research approach described by Robert Coles (1993) in which research is conducted as a form of "witnessing." The best form of study involves engaging in the service-learning process alongside the participants so that the researcher can have similar experiences and observe the participants as they perform. This requires close engagement with those studied and is different from the separation and distancing required in high-quality quantitative studies.

Community-based research involves the following basic principles:

- Collaboration between academic researchers (professors and students) and community members
- Validation of multiple sources of knowledge and use of multiple methods of discovery and dissemination of the knowledge produced
- Goals of social action and social change for the purpose of achieving social justice (Strand et al., 2003, p. 8)

This community-based learning (CBL) effort is reminiscent of Robert Sigmon's (1979) charge for service-learning—to work for an empowered community that does service to embrace social justice. Many people describe service-learning as simply a pedagogy to learn how to apply academic subjects in real-world settings. This approach only describes half the service-learning agenda because without movement toward social justice, the service provided is relatively meaningless.

Strand et al. (2003) cite many examples of how community-based research works; as an example of "research with" not "research for," the authors tell of an effort at Hood College. Five students from a social science research course were conducting action research with a group of incarcerated women. As the students developed their interview questions, assistance from the instructor helped them move from traditional kinds of questions, such as "how many times have you been here?" to questions that focused more on opinions of inmates about drug-related services. As the story goes, the students didn't realize that the meaning of the change in focus meant they were actually talking to the group of incarcerated women. Students said:

> We need your help. We can't do the study without you. You are the ones best able to tell us what programs and services are out there, which ones are useful and which aren't, what you would like to see in the way of programs and services for women in your situation. (Strand et al., 2003, p. 151)

According to the authors, the atmosphere changed when a middle-aged African American woman, who had been exasperated with the process, broke into a half-smile and said: "Gee, no one ever asked us that before." Including community people in the process of developing research agendas and using local knowledge are cornerstones of service-learning practice and are essential components of effective service-learning research. Involving the women in the development of the project changed their perceptions of the research and allowed them to become part of the team.

In another example, a research consortium in Chicago (Chicago Policy Research Action Group, PRAG), consisting of 4 universities and 15 community-based organizations, or CBOs, developed and performed 10 to 15 projects at a time studying the processes and impacts of community-connected programs. Faculty, student interns, research assistants, and CBO staff developed research and carried it out in a collaborative manner. What made the consortium unique, and especially consistent with the principles of service-learning, is that it raised funds to carry out the research and put into practice policies that supported the transfer of knowledge-generating capacity to the community rather than fostering community dependence on university expertise (Strand et al., 2003, p. 170). This strategy fits nicely with Sigmon's (1979) notion that service-learning programs need to better equip community members to solve their own problems and develop the local expertise to carry out the evaluations and research needed by the community.

Empowerment Evaluation

The Chicago PRAG consortium is a prime example of another wave of research/evaluation change in the 21st century, that of "empowerment evaluation" (Fetterman, Kaftarian, & Wandersman, 1996; Fetterman & Wandersman, 2005). Under this approach to research and evaluation, the primary goal is to provide the training and support necessary for local community members to engage in self-assessment of their own programs. The purpose of empowerment work is to strengthen the skills, knowledge, and dispositions of the participants so that they can achieve a level of self-sufficiency and self-determination. This often involves acquiring research and evaluation knowledge and skills in the day-to-day actions of a community group or organization.

An example somewhat similar to the Chicago PRAG is the Community Coalition in South Central Los Angeles, an organization that uses principles of service-learning to address the challenges of inner-city life. The coalition especially deals with the continued conflict between city residents and the police around issues of drug, alcohol, and substance abuse. Outside evaluation/research professionals brought expertise in various evaluation and research approaches, including using quantitative designs, to enable the organizers to use data and research to bolster their positions and assist in making their cases to authorities in the city of Los Angeles. The empowerment approach changed the dynamics and brought researchers and evaluators into the process on an equal basis that respected the knowledge and skills of the community members and worked to help them learn new approaches to strengthen their organization and their causes. As the authors (Grills, Bass, Brown, & Akers, 1996) describe it:

> Some coalition members who were social service providers were particularly skeptical at first. They previously had negative experiences with evaluators who stood "above the folks" and critiqued with a misunderstanding of the target communities and had no understanding of their cultural or sociopolitical context. In this instance, however, the members quickly moved past the skepticism to share the viewpoint that the evaluator and evaluation component were an asset to their ongoing work and a means of empowerment. (Grills et al., 1996, p. 125)

Besides embedding evaluation and research into their operation, the organizers of the Community Coalition saw the entire process as a move to "enfranchise" community members and provide them with the tools and the knowledge to come to the table with city officials as "equals." Many of the citizens had lost faith in government and in the entire civic process. By having outside help in mastering the community's ability to conduct research and evaluation on the power relationships in the city, they were able to act in forceful ways to bring about social change and achieve social justice. The empowerment process used strategies and approaches that may differ slightly from community-based research (CBR), but the attention to social change and social justice is just what was called for through effective service-learning in community contexts. As Hecht (2003) reminds us, context is a critical element in service-learning research, and thus researchers, in this case, were able to learn from the community as community members learned from them.

Youth Participatory Research and Evaluation

The Community Coalition project in Los Angeles affected the enfranchisement of citizens; perhaps no group is more disenfranchised in most societies than young people are. As the International Youth Parliament (2003) study "Highly Affected, Rarely Considered: The International Youth Parliament Commission's Report on the Impacts of Globalization on Young People" captures in its title, youth are "highly affected and rarely considered." When it comes to involving young people in policy decisions, assessment of programs relating to their welfare, and participation in decisions affecting their lives, they often are denied the opportunity to be actively engaged. Even though the United Nations Convention on the Rights of the Child (1989) promises it, youth rarely have access to opportunities that provide control over their lives. One set of rights guaranteed in the UN Convention is the right to have a voice and opportunity to engage in self-determination in their life process, to be actively involved in expressing their point of view and in helping to shape the programs and activities that dominate their lives.

Although the world is slow to change, one way young people are gaining voice and self-determination is by becoming active participants in the evaluation process. According to Sabo (2003), this is a field in the making. Young people are participating in research and evaluations of their schools, their communities, and their after-school programs to understand how they work and how they can be improved to represent youth perspectives (Sabo, 2003).

Since the mid-1990s, increasing numbers of models and examples of youth-led research and evaluations have emerged in the United States and around the world. Participation has a pronounced effect on youth and their programs, and young people are engaging in service-learning-type projects in which they learn about the research/evaluation process and how to strengthen their voice in programs and policies that affect their lives.

The effort to engage youth in the research/evaluation process is spreading across the country, from Youth in Focus in San Francisco, to the University of Michigan School of Social Work in Ann Arbor, Michigan, to the Institute for Community Research in Hartford, Connecticut. Many different curriculum models accompany these projects (Checkoway & Richards-Schuster, n.d.; Institute for Community Research, 2000; Shumer, 2007; Youth in Focus, 2002), enabling youth to learn the skills and knowledge required to be researchers and evaluators and also helping them to learn the principles of service-learning by developing reciprocal relationships with the communities and people they study.

There are many examples of youth engaged in evaluation, some with internationally powerful people. Flores (2008, p. 91) describes the persistence of a 9-year-old researcher who met Kofi Annan, former Secretary General of the United Nations, and followed him until Annan agreed to allow her to interview him. She worked on her interview skills with her team, and then, later in the week, interviewed the Secretary General. She was well prepared and impressed him with her knowledge and skills; he was candid and respectful. The two engaged in discussion on equal terms.

Youth in Canada focuses on health issues as part of the Town Youth Participation Strategies (TYPS) project. The goal of the project, funded in part by Health Canada, is "to engage youth in the planning and operational decision making within the institutions that affect their lives and to ensure that youth have important roles in their respective communities to improve their futures" (Sabo, 2003, p. 25).

Local initiatives include youth research/evaluation activities from the start. The project has grown in size, and through a series of conferences and workshops, engages all participants in evaluation of program components, determining what worked and what could/should be shared with others to involve more communities in the process. Adhering to principles of service-learning, young people work collaboratively with adults and take the lead in the evaluation/research process. They have developed research/evaluation strategies and techniques and use these skills to produce reports that help shape plans for the future of the TYPS model and for networks of youth centers around the country.

In another example, faculty from the University of California, Los Angeles, Institute for Democracy, Education, and Access (IDEA) convened summer seminars to train a team of youth on critical research and critical learning through an apprentice program. The project brought together students (teens), teachers from elementary and secondary schools, and parents. Youth learned about issues of social justice, critical perspectives on the world, and collaborative ways to engage people through intimate contact (interviews, discussion, and participatory observation, for example). They began to develop knowledge and strategies to understand how to improve the lives of urban youth and research agendas to study schools in their home communities. Participants visited local classrooms, assessed textbooks and educational materials, interviewed teachers and other students, and examined technological resources to assess the condition of schools in Los Angeles. As a result of their study, students developed an Educational Bill of Rights and produced reports and PowerPoint presentations that influenced legislation in California related to the operation of schools. Some students even presented their research findings at the American Educational Research Association meeting in Chicago (2002). A few teachers adopted the idea of the apprentice program and started after-school programs focusing on critical research. Alumni from the program have traveled to New York to work with high school students who have started their own summer seminars, and others have gone to Boston and Brazil to help with the conditions of young people and social justice in those places.

Still other examples can be found in mainstream publications, such as *Educational Leadership* from the Association for Curriculum and Supervision Development. An entire volume (November 2008) is devoted to youth ownership of learning, with many examples of youth-led research that has produced positive change in schools (Brookhart, Moss, & Long, 2008; Mitra, 2008). In each instance, young people engaged in collaborative research efforts with adults to study issues in their schools and communities and to make changes based on their research. Youth participatory research and evaluation is becoming the tool, using principles of service-learning, to expand the knowledge and skills of young people as they work constructively to achieve social change and social justice.

Utilization Focused Evaluation and Research

Much of the discussion about new paradigms of research in the 21st century use models of both research and evaluation. Some might suggest that research and evaluation are not the same and should not be equated. For example, Michael Patton (2008) in his classic book on the subject suggests there is a difference between evaluation and research. He says:

> The difference between research and evaluation has been called by Cronbach and Suppes (1969) the difference between conclusion-oriented and decision-oriented inquiry. Research aims to produce knowledge and truth. Useful evaluation supports action.
>
> Patton, 2008, p. 40.

He goes on to cite Bickman's assessment of the difference between evaluation research and general evaluation by saying:

> Evaluation research differs from the more typical program evaluation in that it is more likely to be investigator initiated, theory based, and focused on the evaluation as the focus of study.
>
> Bickman, 2005, p. 141

Thus, evaluation research provides more power to the evaluation practitioner because he/she is responsible for weaving together all the program elements and for analyzing the results. This is quite the contrary to the more empowered, community connected work of service-learning programs and indicates that service-learning research needs to fall someplace in-between. It certainly needs to address issues of theory based, conclusion oriented inquiry, but as a phenomenon that requires social action and community partner empowerment as another product, it necessitates the combination of the two into action oriented research and evaluation that leads to practical use and social change.

Perhaps the connecting elements are what Patton describes as the non-negotiables in useful evaluations: systematic inquiry, intentional purpose, and data based (p. 41). Evaluation and research connect along the lines of empirically based inquiry that has focus, engagement of all those who have a stake in inquiry, and application of learning that results from study. Service-learning research for the 21st century requires a melding of evaluation and research to produce studies that are well grounded in theory and conclusion-based outcomes, yet modeled after action research that must always produce social engagement as well as community and individual change.

Conclusion

The research enterprise is changing in the 21st century. Research for community improvement, research/evaluation for social action and social justice, and newfound respect for community members as equal partners in the research enterprise are all changing the focus of research practice. The dominance of mathematically precise positivism and scientific methods is softening as alternative approaches introduce new measures of effective study: usefulness of the research to changing practice and the engagement of program participants in the actual development and conduct of the research and evaluation. As researchers such as Denzin and Lincoln (1994) have begun to dismantle some of the underpinnings of scientific, quantitative study, new approaches, most of which include principles of service-learning, are being adopted by more and more schools and communities. Community-based research, empowerment evaluation, utilization-focused research and evaluation, and youth participatory research and evaluation are changing the nature of investigation and putting important elements of service-learning in play at many levels. Although rigorous practice is still important, useful outcomes and an empowered citizenry are also necessary elements of a thriving democracy.

As service-learning expands its network of practitioners and policy advocates, conducting research and evaluation consistent with the principles of service-learning continues to offer new hope that service (through research) can lead to enhanced learning and provide meaningful social action and social change. At the beginning of this new century comes a renewed opportunity to construct meaning through research that engages citizens in the study of their lives and institutions. History will tell whether this shift produces more and better research and researchers, and whether society becomes more socially just as a result.

References

Bickman, L. (2005). Evaluation research. In S. Mathison (Ed). *Encyclopedia of Evaluation*. Thousand Oaks, CA: Sage.

Billig, S., & Eyler, J. (2003). The state of service-learning and service-learning research. In S. H. Billig & J. Eyler (Eds.), *Advances in service-learning research:*

Vol.3. Deconstructing service-learning: Research exploring context, participation, and impacts (pp. 253–264). Greenwich, CT: Information Age Publishing.

Bringle, R., Phillips, M., & Hudson, M. (2004). *The measure of service-learning: Research scales to assess student experiences.* Washington, DC: American Psychological Association.

Brookhart, S., Moss, C., & Long, B. (2008, November). Formative assessment that empowers. *Educational Leadership, 66*(3), 52–57.

Bruner, J. (1986). *Actual minds, possible worlds.* Cambridge, MA: Harvard University Press.

Bruner, J. (1990). *Acts of meaning.* Cambridge, MA: Harvard University Press.

Campbell, D., & Stanley, J. (1963). *Experimental and quasi-experimental designs for research.* Chicago: Rand McNally.

Cech, S. (2008, November 12). Program lets urban districts call the shots on research. *Education Week,* 10–11.

Checkoway, B., & Richards-Schuster, K. (n.d.). *Participatory evaluation with young people.* Ann Arbor: University of Michigan School of Social Work.

Coles, R. (1993). *The call of service: A witness to idealism.* New York: Houghton Mifflin.

Cresswell, J. W. (2003). *Research design: Qualitative, quantitative, and mixed methods approaches* (2nd ed.). Thousand Oaks, CA: Sage.

Denzin, N., & Lincoln, Y. (Eds.). (1994). *Handbook of qualitative research.* Thousand Oaks, CA: Sage.

Dewey, J. (1997). *Experience and education.* New York: Simon & Schuster. (Original work published 1938)

Encarta. (2007). Rigor. Retrieved October 5, 2007, from http://encarta.msn.com/dictionary_/rigor.html

Eyler, J. (2002). Stretching to meet the challenge: Improving the quality of research to improve the quality of service-learning. In S. H. Billig & A. Furco (Eds.), *Advances in service-learning research, Vol. 2. Service-learning through a multidisciplinary lens* (pp. 3–14). Greenwich, CT: Information Age.

Fetterman, D., Kaftarian, S., & Wandersman, A. (Eds.). (1996). *Empowerment evaluation.* Thousand Oaks, CA: Sage.

Fetterman, D., & Wandersman, A. (Eds.). (2005). *Empowerment evaluation: Principles in practice.* New York: Guilford Press.

Flores, K. S. (2008). *Youth participatory evaluation: Strategies for engaging young people.* San Francisco: Jossey-Bass.

Furco, A., & Billig, S. H. (2002). Establishing norms for scientific inquiry in service-learning. In S. H. Billig & A. Furco (Eds.), *Advances in service-learning research, Vol. 2. Service-learning through a multidisciplinary lens* (pp. 15–32). Greenwich, CT: Information Age.

Ginwright, S., Noguera, P., & Commarota, J. (Eds.). (2006). *Beyond resistance: Youth activism and community change.* New York: Rutledge, Taylor and Francis.

Green, J. C., Caracelli, V., & Graham, W. F. (1989). Toward a conceptual framework for mixed-method evaluation designs. *Educational Evaluation and Policy Analysis, 11*(3), 255–274.

Grills, C., Bass, K., Brown, D., & Akers, A. (1996). Empowerment evaluation: Building upon a tradition of activism in the African American community. In D. Fetterman, S. Kaftarian, & A. Wandersman (Eds.), *Empowerment evaluation.* Thousand Oaks, CA: Sage.

Guba, E., & Lincoln, Y. (1989). *Fourth generation evaluation.* Thousand Oaks, CA: Sage.

Hecht, D. (2003). The missing link: Exploring the context of learning in service-learning. In S. Billig & J. Eyler (Eds.), *Deconstructing service-learning: Research exploring context, participation, and impacts.* Greenwich, CT: Information Age.

Institute for Community Research. (2000). *Participatory action research: Curriculum for empowering youth.* Hartford, CT: Author.

International Youth Parliament. (2003). Highly affected, rarely considered: The International Youth Parliament Commission's report on the impacts of globalization on young people. Retrieved January 5, 2009, from http://iyp.oxfam.org/doc uments/ii.%20Background%20&%20Methodology.pdf

Levi-Strauss, C. (1966). *The savage mind* (2nd ed.). Chicago: University of Chicago Press.

Lewin, K. (1948). *Resolving social conflicts: Selected papers on group dynamics.* G. W. Lewin (Ed.). New York: Harper & Row.

Lewin, K. (1951). *Field theory in social science; selected theoretical papers.* D. Cartwright (Ed.). New York: Harper & Row.

Lynd, J. (1992). Creating knowledge through theater: A case study with developmentally disabled adults. *American Sociologist, 23,* 100–115.

Mayer, S. (1996). Building community capacity with evaluation activities that empower. In D. Fetterman, S. Kaftarian, & A. Wandersman (Eds.), *Empowerment evaluation.* Thousand Oaks, CA: Sage.

Mitra, D. (2008, November). Amplifying student voice. *Educational Leadership, 66*(3), 20–25.

Morrell, E. (2006). Youth initiated research as a tool for advocacy and change in urban schools. In S. Ginwright, P. Noguera, & J. Commarota (Eds.), *Beyond resistance: Youth activism and community change* (pp. 111–128). New York: Rutledge, Taylor and Francis.

Nelson, C., Treichler, P. A., & Grossberg, L. (1992). Cultural studies. In L. Grossberg, C. Nelson, & P. A . Treichler (Eds.), *Cultural studies* (pp. 1–16). New York: Routledge.

Patton, M. Q. (2008). *Utilization focused evaluation: The new century text* (4th ed.). Thousand Oaks, CA: Sage.

Sabo, K. (Ed.). (Summer 2003). *Youth participatory evaluation: A field in the making.* In *New Directions for Evaluation, 98.* Fairhaven, MA: American Evaluation Association.

Scriven, M. (1972a). Objectivity and subjectivity in educational research. In L. Thomas (Ed.), *Philosophical redirection of educational research: The seventy-first yearbook of the National Society for the Study of Education.* Chicago: University of Chicago Press.

Scriven, M. (1972b). Pros and cons about goal free evaluation. *Evaluation Comment: The Journal of Educational Evaluation* (Center for the Study of Evaluation, UCLA), *3*(4), 1–7.

Shavelson, R., & Towne, L. (Eds.). (2002). *Scientific research in education.* Washington, DC: National Academy Press.

Shumer, R. (2000, Fall). Science or storytelling: How should we conduct and report research in service-learning? In J. Howard (Ed.), *Michigan Journal of Community Service Learning.* Volume 1, Special Edition, pages 76–83.

Shumer, R. (2007). *Youth led evaluation: A guidebook.* Clemson, SC: National Dropout Prevention Center, College of Health, Education, and Human Development, Clemson University.

Sigmon, R. (1979, Spring). Service-learning: Three principles. *Synergist* (National Center for Service-Learning), *8*(1), 9–11.

Smith, L., & Martin, H. (Eds.). (2007). *Recent dissertations on service and service-learning topics: Volume IV, 2004–2006.* Scotts Valley, CA: National Service-Learning Clearinghouse.

Stake, R. (1975). *Evaluating the arts in education.* Columbus, OH: Merrill.

Stake, R. (2006). *Multiple case study analysis.* New York: Guilford Press.

Strand, K., Murillo, S., Cutforth, N., Stoecker, R., & Donohue, P. (2003). *Community based research and higher education.* San Francisco: Jossey-Bass.

Tashakkori, A., & Teddlie, C. (2003). *Handbook on mixed-methods in the behavioral and social sciences.* Thousand Oaks, CA: Sage.

United Nations (1989). The United Nations Convention on the Rights of the Child. General Assembly resolution 44/25 of 20 November 1989; *entry into force* 2 September 1990, in accordance with article 49.

Vygotsky, L. S. (1978). *Mind in society.* Cambridge, MA: Harvard University Press.

Whyte, W. F. (Ed) (1991). *Participatory Action Research.* Newbury Park, CA: Sage.

Youth in Focus. (2002). *Youth REP—step by step: An introduction to youth led research and evaluation.* Oakland, CA: Author.

Zeigert, A., & McGoldrick, K. (2004). Adding rigor to service-learning research: An armchair economists' approach. In M. Welch & S. Billig (Eds.), *New perspectives in service-learning: Research to advance the field.* Greenwich, CT: Information Age.

13

LIVING DEMOCRACY DAILY

Service-Learning and Active Citizenship

Walter Enloe

We, the People of Avalon, in order to provide for a safe and productive learning environment, promote the obtaining and usage of knowledge for the benefit of those around us, and to ensure general happiness, do ordain and establish this constitution for Avalon High School.

The 2001 Constitution of
Avalon High School, St. Paul, Minnesota

A Case Study in Public Service

This chapter presents a case study of a school created in 2001 in St. Paul, Minnesota, as part of the $4 billion Bill and Melinda Gates Foundation initiative to ensure that all students graduate from high school ready for college. Nationwide, just 70% of American students graduate from high school. Among African American, Hispanic, Native American, and low-income students, only 50% graduate. Avalon High School was created based on the assumption that when students have a sense of ownership of their work and the life-world of their school, and when academic service-learning is defined as servant leadership and active civic engagement, student achievement will increase.

Interdependent World

The changing world is increasingly complex and interdependent and is defined by ecological, technological, economic, political, and other frameworks. At the dawn of the 21st century, we face many daunting challenges, from global warming to social inequities, from tribal warfare to world conflict, from the threat of global ground zeroes like Hiroshima and the World Trade Center in New York. As Dr. Martin Luther King Jr. expressed in his last sermon days before his 1968 assassination: "The world is more and more of a neighborhood. But is it any more of a brotherhood? If we don't learn to love together as brothers and sisters, we shall perish together as fools (Washington, 1990, p. 245). In a world with increasing disparities between haves and have-nots, how can we prepare students to be responsible citizens locally and globally? How can we prepare them to lead, learn, and serve?

Recently, Minnesota's governor, following the lead of other states, initiated World-Class Students: From Nation Leading to World Competing (Minnesota Department of Education, 2008). Although Minnesota has a proud tradition of leading the nation in academic achievement, service-learning, and active citizenship, "our state and our students can no longer rely on our past success if we are to succeed in a more competitive global environment." The World-Class Students initiative "is designed to create a system of education for the 21st century, preparing Minnesota students to compete with students around the world." The World-Class Students initiative will

> help students to meet the demands of a more competitive global future by requiring every Minnesota high school student to do the following:
>
> 1. take at least one year of post-secondary education while in high school;
> 2. high schools must offer programs that support post-secondary access from the International Baccalaureate, Advance Placement, College in Schools, among others;
> 3. high schools must provide rigorous programs including career and technical courses in high demand fields and recognized by the business community; and
> 4. schools must forge community partnerships for meaningful work-based learning and internship." (Minnesota Department of Education, 2008)

Although these "competitive" initiatives are a response to an increasingly global, international-minded world, we must also understand that the global future demands what is at the heart of active citizenship and service-learning: local and global cooperation, collaboration, mutual respect and understanding, and problem solving and reflection. One of the most powerful lessons I learned from 8 years as principal of the International School in Hiroshima is that, if you are not developing empathy, cooperation, and mutual respect among children sitting next to each other, or across town or in another state, you will have little success developing such values for "strange lands and friendly peoples" across the globe.

In the following case study, I describe how, at the beginning of the new millennium, a small group of St. Paul, Minnesota, parents and supporters purposefully constituted the Avalon High School. This process involved building, maintaining, and sustaining a civil learning community using leadership teams, study groups and advisories, a school congress, restorative justice circles, peer mediation, and academic service-learning, all guided by a co-constructed school constitution and declaration of human rights and responsibilities. Avalon is one of the flagship learning communities of the EdVisions-Gates Project, funded in part by the Bill and Melinda Gates Foundation to create small "world-class" schools. (See the www.edvisions. com website for more information.

EdVision Schools

To judge a school's effectiveness on the international stage or in a local community, we need more than accountability in testing systems of literacy and reasoning. We also need to cultivate, support, and take into account the life-world of students, their attitudes toward living and learning, their behaviors, and their characters. "What we need if we are to judge schools effectively is a means by which schools can be assessed as cultures that create sets of relationships, norms of behaviors, and values and obligations that lead to the development of healthy and productive adults" (Newell & Van Ryzin, 2007, pp. 465–466).

For the past 5 years, EdVisions has been actively researching its schools using a number of assessment tools and formative evaluations, including the Hope Study, which measures the growth in dispositions for success in life, in particular those values meeting the developmental needs of adolescents: autonomy, belongingness, and competence.

EdVisions's experience "reveals that when certain concepts are built into a learning community—concepts that value 'personhood' over ruthless efficiency and encourage student self-directedness and teacher/student ownership instead of top-down hierarchies—then that community can indeed foster healthy development" (p. 466). EdVisions schools' "design essentials" are characterized by four main themes: (a) a student-centered democratic culture; (b) a self-directed, project-based learning program; (c) the use of authentic assessment; and (d) teacher ownership and accountability (p. 468). These characteristics are embodied in Avalon High School, as described later (Newell & Van Ryzin, 2007).

In sum, much has to be done to overcome the present fixation on assessing school effectiveness solely using standardized tests and other traditional measures. The educators at Avalon believe, as does Comer of the Yale Child Study Center Project, that improvement in school culture must come first, "or the relationships needed to engage students in a powerful way won't be created" (Comer, 2005, p. 762). A founding group of civic activists, pragmatic visionaries, and like-minded parents organized Avalon High School as a liberal arts school. This group hired an outstanding, dedicated staff and strove to create a small, people-centered secondary school of exemplary character. The school is characterized by a shared vision of student and teacher ownership and collaborative teaching and learning, with parents as full partners. The school's stakeholders co-created a highly innovative curriculum based on project-based learning and small seminars. The world is the classroom. More specifically, some of the founders committed to supporting the United Nations declaration of 2001–2010 as the International Decade for a Culture of Peace and Nonviolence for the Children of the World by becoming a living, local symbol of mindfulness and peacefulness. The Quaker tradition of circles of trust, the Native American tradition of restorative justice, the Hamline University law school's international reputation for alternative dispute resolution, and the school's primary consultant influenced the school's mission and vision as a world-minded service-oriented community.

The evolving mission of the school is as follows: "The Avalon School is a strong, nurturing community that inspires active learning, local action, and global awareness." Its core values statement is:

> Avalon expects and models respect for individuals, different cultures, the community, and the environment. The atmosphere is one of tolerance,

integrity, equity, and safety. Avalon believes it is the responsibility of individuals to be engaged, active participants in their local and global communities. Visitors to Avalon will immediately recognize the sense of purpose, quality, and commitment that energizes this community.

Following the Minnesota New Country School model, Avalon High School will become a teacher-owned school and a member of the EdVisions Teacher Cooperative, established in 1994. As of 2008, Avalon High School has reconstituted itself as a Teacher Professional Practice Organization (TPPO), an autonomous collaborative, and remains a strong affiliate of both the EdVisions Cooperative and the EdVisions regional Center for the Coalition of Essential Schools. In its original documents, Avalon's founders stated that they would "build a school culture and a set of values centered on excellence and active citizenship" with a "global perspective" and that its constituents would "develop leadership opportunities for all participants. All members of the school community will be involved in decision-making, and students will be given a real voice and stake in the school."

A few years earlier, several parent/founders (including the author of this chapter) had created Twin Cities Academy middle school in St. Paul (which the current and past mayors' children attended) as a school community emphasizing active citizenship. It became a learning place for building character and practicing active community involvement through enacting five core interrelated leadership and service values: active citizenship, respect, initiative, scholarship, and perseverance. We sought to integrate these leadership principles into the core mission and values of Avalon.

Active Citizenship

The creators of Avalon were also guided by the work of Harry Boyte and his partners (including teacher and civil rights activist Dorothy Cotton) at the University of Minnesota's Center for Democracy and Citizenship (CDC) and the leadership of Jim Keilsmeier at the National Youth Leadership Council (NYLC). I have deep-felt gratitude for apprenticing with democratic youth leaders as a partner and collaborator during the past 20 years. The active citizen and academic service-learning promoted by CDC and NYLC are often complementary. CDC's active citizenship executes everyday public work, including public problem solving by ordinary citizens in which governing is conceived for, by, and of the citizens (see the website www.

publicwork.org). NYLC's academic service-learning, for example, is defined as follows: "Picking up trash on a riverbank is *a service*. Studying water samples under a microscope is *learning*. When science students collect and analyze water samples, document their results, and present their findings to a local pollution control agency that is *service learning*" (National Youth Leadership Council website). Active citizenship and academic service-learning emphasize learning *through* experience and not simply learning *about* phenomena. Both are based on interconnecting students and the community by identifying specific learning goals and developing projects that meet them, or by identifying a project and then exploring the many ways it can be tied to learning objectives or curricula.

In consideration of active citizenship and academic service-learning, Avalon's founders emphasize the development of democratic character as an essential component of a democratic school learning community. Although this school emphasizes rigorous academics and best practices, it is grounded in core ethical, democratic virtues: honesty, respect, compassion, self-discipline, perseverance, and giving that is learned *through* and not *about*. School members live out these core virtues with purpose by word and by deed. Boyer (1995) captures the living (ecocultural, organic, systemic) nature of such a school learning community:

> But community just doesn't happen, even in a small school. To become a true community the institution must be organized around people. . . . What we are really talking about is the culture of the school, the vision that is shared, the ways people relate to one another. . . . Simply stated, the school becomes a community of learning when it is a purposeful place, a communicative place, a just place, a disciplined place, a caring place, and a celebrative place. (p. 18)

Democratic Service as Public Work

The teachers think that modeling democratic values daily is the best way to promote and perpetuate them so that they become integral to school culture. Democracy has value only when we recognize the humanity of each human being and her or his innate desire to be free and autonomous. Embodying the democratic virtues of civility and negotiation, collaboration and compromise, tolerance and mutual respect, Avalon develops active citizens through active learning and engagement. The teachers create learning and leadership conditions through school meetings, advisories, committees, projects, and seminars so that students can constitute themselves as a self-governing community.

In the first year of Avalon, students in a two-block civics seminar, advised by teacher Carrie Bakken, created the constitution of Avalon High School. The Avalon constitution is based in part upon a class constitution that was established in Bernie and Martha Schein's class at the Paideia School in Atlanta and that has evolved over several decades. In the initial stages, the students experienced many struggles reminiscent of the challenges faced by the creators of the United States Constitution and by many other young democratic institutions. Students argued about whether they should have a constitution, much less a congress or student government, and many meetings were spent "discussing" the central issue of adult authority and teacher power. After the civics seminar, students wrote the initial version of the constitution, which then underwent many drafts. Subsequently, the whole school voted to accept it. Since that time, the document has gone through several more revisions; today the constitution governs the school and defines how the students and staff work together. It tells members what their rights and responsibilities are as citizens of Avalon.

Avalon's constitution defines four branches of government: (a) the people individually and as a whole; (b) the legislative branch (student congress); (c) the judiciary (the Mediation Council consisting of peer mediators and the circle process group); and (d) the executive branch (the Avalon staff). Together they govern the school.

Another feature of the school's government that survived a rocky beginning before being amended to its present form is the judiciary branch. Initially, a group of dedicated students were appointed as judges in the judicial system. They waited patiently for court cases to be brought before them, planning to "sentence" each guilty offender with an appropriate punishment. But cases never materialized. One student discovered that the rest of the judges were beginning to conspire to fabricate cases, and the student brought this concern to the congress. The school realized that the traditional judicial process was not the way to address problems and offenses in this community.

They changed the constitution to incorporate peer mediation and circle processes into the judiciary branch, which today is known as the Mediation

Council. Peer mediators are students who are trained in mediation and who mediate issues that arise in the community between students or between students and staff. The circle process, based upon restorative justice philosophy, is another approach available to students and staff to identify issues and resolve conflicts. The school believed that congress and the circle process were such important parts of the community that they built meeting times into the weekly schedule for these groups. If students have issues they want to raise, they can present the issue to the circle for discussion. If the issue can be resolved in the circle, there is no further discussion. Sometimes circle issues are brought to congress and a bill may be created. In addition, individual students may bring issues and bills to congress.

When a bill is submitted to congress, the participants vote on it. In the past few years, students have submitted numerous bills to congress, and most have passed with some modifications. They include (a) a bill requiring Avalon to offer sex education seminars twice a year; (b) a bill allowing students to read outside their advisories' areas (during an all-school 30-minute reading period each day after lunch); (c) a bill to establish a school-wide mandatory advisory cleaning period 15 minutes before the end of the school day.

When a bill passes congress it is then submitted to the executive branch for approval. The executive branch can approve the bill, approve the bill with modifications, or reject the bill; the executive branch can also invite parents to discuss the bill or bring it to the school board before granting approval. If there are modifications to the bill, the bill then goes back to congress for approval. Once the bill is approved, it becomes law. This system of governance has allowed Avalon to build a strong community and face challenges with a team community approach. Students and staff know that when they have problems, they can discuss them with their advisor or any staff member, bring the issue to congress or circle, or ask for peer mediation. Students rely on one another to solve problems through myriad means, thereby helping each other deal with personal and social issues authentically, humanely, and often efficiently.

Two Concepts of Citizenship Service

Shigeo Kodama, a professor of educational thought at Ochanomizu University in Tokyo, has studied Avalon's governance process. In his study, "Two

Concepts of Citizenship" (Kodama, 2003), he distinguishes between citizenship as volunteer service and citizenship as political action:

> In volunteer activities [*sic*] young people do not have much time to think about the political meaning of their activity, and they are not given enough skill and competence of political action and judgment which are the indispensable factor of citizenship. Community service and volunteer activity will depoliticize the young people and prevent them from being active citizens.

He then describes how the advisors are teachers of academic subjects and facilitators of authentic community governance and leadership, encouraging students "to be active citizens in the public sphere." He contends that Avalon has two unique features. One is its institutional governance system, the EdVisions Cooperative, "a kind of governance system which is managed by the teachers themselves." The second is the Avalon constitution, which is the students' self-governance system and which is striking for its modeling of power relationships.

> According to the Constitution students in Avalon compose (the) Avalon Congress and make their decision(s). Teachers compose an executive branch and have a veto power to the students' decision(s). So in this system students not only have their own decision-making but also the power relationship between students and teachers could be visible. In this power relationship students could be trained as . . . active citizens. (Kodama, 2003, p. 38)

Professor Kodama notes that Avalon's approach to democratic governance derives from the work of Harry Boyte and his partners. In *Reinventing Citizenship* (Boyte & partners, 1995), Boyte argues that, unlike traditional civics education, where one learns passively without civility *about* democracy and its institutions and processes, Avalon's approach is for students and adults to learn *through* democratic practices by living democracy daily in ordinary affairs and everyday practices.

> Active, public citizenship begins and is grounded in our every day institutional environments—the places we live and work, go to school, volunteer, participate in communities of faith. It is public-spirited and practical: not

utopian or immaculate but part of the messy, difficult give-and-take process of problem solving. Citizenship links our daily life and interests to larger public values and arenas. Through citizenship we build and exercise our power" (Boyte & partners, 1995, p. 16).

Conclusion

Avalon strives to embody a community where government is not simply for the people (which is the current American representational, professional politics, in which the generic citizen is an informed voter), but rather of the people and by the people, a form of active citizenship.

This living democracy is a human ideal with all the constraints and opportunities inherent in the human condition. The founding of Avalon School was based in large part on Jean Piaget's theory of human development: his constructivist theory of learning, his activity pedagogy, his deep conviction that education should foster human rights and responsibilities (Article 26 Universal Declaration of Human Rights), and his commitment to student self-government (Piaget, 1948).

We believe very strongly that the basis for an authentic learning community is a school or learning organization in which the teachers are leaders and have ownership of their work lives, and lead, learn, and advise/teach together. We believe very strongly in a learning community where students are active learners and active citizens and are rightfully responsible for their actions of learning and leading. From EdVisions's reform efforts, we have learned that placing rigid curriculum, instruction, testing, and delivery systems in an environment that fails to meet adolescents' needs will not lead to long-term positive effects for students. The EdVisions experience leads us to believe that the new 3 Rs (relationships, relevance, and rigor) are more important than the old 3 Rs (reading, writing, and arithmetic). At EdVisions schools, "creating environments that allow for good relationships, relevant learning experiences, and rigorous assessment has created passionate, self-motivated, life-long learners" (Newell & Van Ryzin, 2007, p. 471). Avalon, a school in St. Paul, is such a citizen leader and service learning community.

References

Boyer, E. (1995). *The basic school.* San Francisco: Jossey-Bass.
Boyte, H. (2005). *Everyday politics: Reconnecting citizens and public life.* Philadelphia: University of Pennsylvania Press.

Boyte, H., & partners. (1995). *Reinventing citizenship: The practice of public work.* St. Paul: University of Minnesota Extension Service, www.extension.umn.edu/distribution/citizenship/DH6586.html

Cairn, R., & Kielsmeier, J. (1995). *Growing hope.* St. Paul: N.Y.L.C.

Collay, M., Dunlap, D., Enloe, W., & Gagnon, G. (1998). *Learning circles: Creating conditions for professional development.* Thousand Oaks, CA: Corwin Press.

Comer, J. (2005, June). Child and adolescent development: The critical missing focus in school reform. *Phi Delta Kappan, 28,* 28–34.

Dirkswager, E. (Ed). (2002). *Teachers as owners.* Lanham, MD: Rowman & Littlefield.

Education Evolving. (2005). *Listening to student voices.* Retrieved April 30, 2009, from http://www.educationevolving.org/studentvoices

Enloe, W. (1992) *Education 2000: Rural Minnesota in the world* (Vol. 1). Washington, DC: ERIC/CRESS Clearing House on Rural Education and Small Schools, U.S. Department of Education.

Enloe, W. (2002). *Lessons from ground zero.* St. Paul, MN: HU Press.

Friedman, T. L. (2005). *The world is flat: A brief history of the twenty-first century.* New York: Farrar, Straus, Giroux.

Greenleaf, R. (2003). *The servant leader within: A transformative path.* Mahwah, NJ: Paulist Press.

Kodama, S. (2003). Two concepts of citizenship. *Guidance and Education in High School* No.156.2003.3, Tokyo (original in Japanese, English summary used in this paper).

Kolderie, T. (1988). *What makes an organization want to improve? Ideas for the restructuring of public education.* University of Minnesota, Hubert H. Humphrey Institute of Public Affairs. Minneapolis, MN.

Martin, A., Bakken, C., Rude, C., & Enloe, W. (2005). Creating a democratic learning community: The Avalon experience. In *The coolest school in America* (pp. 121–132). Lanham, MD: Rowman & Littlefield.

Minnesota Department of Education. (2008). World class students. St. Paul, MN: Author.

Nathan, J. (1996). *Charter schools: Creating hope and opportunity for American education.* San Francisco: Jossey-Bass.

Newell, R., & Thomas, D. (2005). *Less, more, and better: A five year evaluation report from EdVisions schools.* Henderson, MN: EdVisions.

Newell, R., & Van Ryzin, M. (2005). Rigor, relevance, and relationships in educational reform: The story of the Hope Study. Retrieved April 30, 2008, from www.edvisions.edu.

Newell, R., & Van Ryzin, M. (2007). Growing hope as a determinant of school effectiveness. *Phi Delta Kappan, 88*(6), 465–471.

Newell, R., & Van Ryzin, M. (2008). *Assessing what really matters in school: Creating hope for the future.* Lanham, MD: Rowman & Littlefield.

Piaget, J. (1948). The right to education in the modern world. In J. Piaget (1973), *To understand is to invent,* Chapter 2. New York: Grossman.

Piaget, J. (1969). *The moral judgment of the child.* New York: Free Press. (Original work published 1936)

Thomas, D., Enloe, W., & Newell, R. (2005). *The coolest school in America.* Lanham, MD: Rowman & Littlefield.

Washington, J. (1990). A testament of hope. New York: HarperOne.

EPILOGUE

Marybeth Lima

The Association of American Colleges and Universities (AAC&U) panel that formed the basis of this book focused on service-learning issues now and into the near future. We created this book around these broad themes and we intend for this epilogue to summarize key concepts in service-learning that we believe will be important during the next 10 years. Although predicting the future is impossible, what follows is our best guess and resulting perspective.

The world is dynamic and the accelerating rate of change in the world is well established. One example is the amount of time it took for approximately 33% of Americans to own an automobile from the time it was invented (~75 years) compared to the amount of time it took for ~33% of Americans to own a radio (~35 years) compared to the time it took ~33% of Americans to own a cell phone (~20 years).

This accelerating rate of change will affect the academy, our communities, our country (we are using the United States as our reference point for this discussion, but we encourage readers to reference their home countries), and our world. We believe that the future of service-learning is contingent on our ability to react to the challenges created by change and our ability to "pro-act" to create opportunities in change.

Jean and I believe that support for service-learning and civic engagement will continue to increase in the academy and that universities will, to a greater or lesser extent, fulfill their missions for addressing major societal issues. Challenges for the academy include institutional efforts for the university to act as a reciprocal community partner, implementing a reward system for faculty members who engage in service-learning (see chapter 5), and regaining strength as a societal force for the greater good. These challenges may be difficult because of institutional inertia and the increasing corporatization of universities. We hope that service-learning scholars, service-learning center directors, community partners, and community stakeholders will keep the academy accountable for reciprocal community engagement efforts; appropriate reward systems; and dynamic, forward-thinking responses and solutions to critical issues.

Our communities are becoming increasingly diverse; our typical construct of diversity was conceived from a majority White perspective. Diversity meant including "others" (non-Whites); according to that limited definition, Whites are now becoming "others." Whites are projected to become an ethnic minority in the United States sometime in the next 40 years. We hope that service-learning and community partner scholars will join in the work described by Mitchell and Donahue in chapter 11 to improve our relationships and our lives through a sophisticated understanding of sameness, otherness, and respect.

Our communities are also becoming increasingly economically stratified. We challenge service-learning and community partner scholars to investigate and mitigate the economic structures that put profits ahead of people and serve to increase the gap between rich and poor. Cornel West (2004) sums this up well in his book *Democracy Matters*:

> The saturation of market forces and market moralities has indeed corrupted our system all the way up. Our leadership elite have themselves lost faith in the efficacy of adhering to democratic principles in the face of the overwhelming power of those market forces. . . . Our politicians have sacrificed their principles on the altar of special interests; our corporate leaders have sacrificed their integrity on the altar of profits; and our media watchdogs have sacrificed the voice of dissent on the altar of audience competition. (pp. 27–28)

We applaud the efforts of West and others like Rachel Willis (http://amerstud.unc.edu/people/willis.html), Paul Polak (see the book *Out of Poverty: What Works When Traditional Approaches Fail* and www.ideorg.org/), and Paul Krugman (http://web.mit.edu/krugman/www/) and encourage others to address this critical problem that affects the sustainability of our planet.

As I write this epilogue, Barack Obama has been elected to the presidency. Although our country faces unprecedented challenges, we anticipate renewed efforts with respect to community service in our country into the near future (see www.usaservice.org/content/home/). We encourage service-learning and community partner scholars to leverage these efforts accordingly.

Our world is becoming increasingly global, a concept well illustrated by Thomas Friedman in his books *The World Is Flat* and *Hot, Flat, and Crowded*. Service-learning and community partner scholars such as Jean Strait (chapter 10), Nadinne Cruz, Barbara Holland, Ed Zlotkowski, Andy Furco, Gerda Bender, Grace Ngai, Laura Johnson, and Julie Johnson-Pynn are establishing international models and methods of communication. We believe that increasing globalization will require all of us to continue to develop and make use of skills in cultural understanding, community context, conflict resolution, and negotiation.

Although we anticipate much change in the future, many features of our landscapes (community, country, and world) will remain constant. The need for complex problem solvers is consistent (if not increasing). We believe that service-learning and community partner scholars will continue to struggle with the questions raised by Jacoby in chapter 6: Will we perpetuate the status quo? What does it mean for service-learning to be institutionalized? Should service-learning be globalized (and if so, how)? We will also continue to struggle with issues like sustainability; economic tyranny; access to food, water, and medical care; and global warming.

In closing, the future holds complex challenges and opportunities; we are heartened by the unwavering ingenuity and commitment displayed by community partner and service-learning scholars to address such issues effectively.

References

West, C. (2004). *Democracy Matters: Winning the Fight Against Imperialism*. New York: Penguin Press.

CONTRIBUTORS

Jean Strait is an associate professor in undergraduate education at Hamline University, service-learning advocate, and both a national and international researcher of service-learning. She has been an elementary teacher, college professor, and the first director of faculty development for Minnesota Campus Compact. Currently, she is an engaged scholar for Campus Compact.

After Hurricane Katrina, Strait and her students began working with Martin Luther King Science and Technology Magnet School in the Ninth Ward in New Orleans. As of the date of this writing, three and a half years after the storm, MLK remains the only school that reopened in the Ninth Ward. Not only were Strait and her students first responders to the crisis, they have maintained a working relationship with several organizations through the creation of Each One, Teach One. Strait has taught and has partnerships in Ireland, Brussels, London, China, and most recently South Africa. She received her Ph.D. in Curriculum and Instruction from the University of Minnesota in 1994. She has served as a faculty member at Augsburg College, Minneapolis Community and Technical College, Century College, and Bemidji State University.

Marybeth Lima is a professor in biological and agricultural engineering at Louisiana State University, a registered professional engineer, and a nationally certified playground safety inspector. Lima has been working with the Baton Rouge community (primarily public schools) for 11 years to ensure that all kids have access to safe, fun playgrounds that the kids help to design. She believes that play is a right and not a privilege, and that children are the best playground designers; these beliefs have guided her service-learning teaching and research work with elementary school and college students and the larger community. The resulting LSU Community Project pairs elementary school and Lima's college students to design "dream playgrounds" created by the elementary school students. College students take these dream playground concepts, as well as input from teachers, parents, and community members, to design safe, fun, accessible playgrounds. After Lima and the schools complete fund-raising and grant writing, the design is built at the school by volunteers (primarily the college student designers) to promote learning and community spirit and to minimize construction costs. These sustained efforts have led to the design and construction of 18 playgrounds, primarily at Baton Rouge public schools. Marybeth's ultimate goal is to ensure that all public school playgrounds in Baton Rouge are safe, fun, accessible, and kid-designed. She received her Ph.D. in Food, Agricultural, and Biological Engineering from Ohio State University and has been a faculty member at LSU since 1996. Marybeth lives with her partner Lynn Hathaway and their two dogs and two cats.

Christine Allan is a principal lecturer in primary education at Leeds Metropolitan University, with particular interests in literacy and the internationalization of the curriculum. She has worked in primary schools for 19 years and was deputy head teacher in two of those schools. Her responsibilities have included leadership and coordination in English, mathematics, special educational needs, gifted and talented, and assessment. Allan spent 3 years as an education authority in the school improvement team, as a literacy consultant, before becoming a lecturer at Leeds Metropolitan University in 2001. Her research work includes effective literacy teaching, raising boys' achievement, and students' international experiences.

David M. Donahue, Ph.D., is an associate professor of education at Mills College in Oakland, California. He works with teacher credential students preparing to teach art, English, and history in secondary schools and graduate students investigating teaching and learning with a focus on equity in urban contexts.

He is one of 10 Engaged Scholars for New Perspectives in Higher Education and a special consultant to the California Campus Compact–Carnegie Foundation Faculty Fellows Program for Service Learning for Political Engagement. His research interests include teacher learning generally and learning from service-learning and the arts specifically.

Walter Enloe is professor of human studies at the School of Education at Hamline University and a board of directors member of EdVisions, Inc. He taught K–12 for 18 years at the Paideia School in Atlanta and Hiroshima International School, where he was principal teacher. Enloe has served on the board of the National Youth Leadership Council and has been a partner with the University of Minnesota's Center for Democracy and Citizenship since 1993.

Joseph Erickson is a professor of education at Augsburg College in Minneapolis, Minnesota. He is also a licensed psychologist in private practice. He earned his doctorate in educational psychology at the University of Minnesota. He was a member and former chair of the Minneapolis School Board.

In March 2006, Erickson was honored as one of the 100 District Leaders for Citizenship and Service-Learning by the Education Commission of the States' National Center for Learning and Citizenship for his leadership in civic education and commitment to community service-learning. He continues that work and conducts research primarily in effective teaching strategies, attitude change, and the use of technology for enhancing learning.

Andrew Furco is associate vice president for public engagement at the University of Minnesota, where he also serves as an associate professor in the College of Education and Human Development and as director of the university's International Center for Research on Community Engagement. His research focuses on experiential learning, civic engagement, and service-learning in primary, secondary, and higher education systems in the United States and abroad. He is a John Glenn Scholar for Service-Learning and recipient of the 2003 Award for Outstanding Contributions to Service-Learning Research and the National Society for Experiential Education's 2006 Researcher of the Year Award.

Melissa Kesler Gilbert is the founding director of the Center for Community Engagement at Otterbein College, where she also teaches courses in women's studies and sociology. She serves as one of 10 National Campus Compact Engaged Scholars and directs the Learn and Serve Great Cities ~ Great Service Higher Education Consortium, growing a culture of service across Ohio. She has provided extensive faculty development training to campuses across the country in the areas of partnership development and sustainability, service-learning pedagogy, reflection strategies, and outcomes assessment. Gilbert has published numerous articles and book chapters in the fields of feminist pedagogy and community-based learning.

Patrick M. Green, Ed.D., serves as the director of the Center for Experiential Learning (CEL) at Loyola University Chicago, which houses service-learning, academic internships, community-based Federal Work-Study, and the undergraduate research program. He also serves as a clinical instructor of experiential learning and teaches two general elective experiential learning courses, engaging students in both service-learning and internship experiences. Green received his doctorate in education from Roosevelt University, specializing in leadership in higher education, and has focused his research on experiential education. He currently serves with Campus Compact as an Engaged Scholar for New Perspectives in Higher Education.

Barbara A. Holland, Ph.D., is currently serving as pro vice-chancellor for the University of Western Sydney (Australia). She continues her affiliation with the National Service-Learning Clearinghouse and with the Center for Service and Learning at Indiana University–Purdue University Indianapolis. Her scholarly work has focused primarily on organizational change in higher education with an emphasis on the institutionalization and assessment of community-engaged teaching and research, and on community partnerships. In 2006, she received the Research Achievement Award from the International Association for Research on Service-Learning and Community Engagement.

Barbara Jacoby is senior scholar for the Adele H. Stamp Student Union— Center for Campus Life at the University of Maryland, College Park. In this role, she facilitates initiatives involving academic partnerships, assessment, scholarship, and student learning. She also serves as chair of the Coalition for Civic Engagement and Leadership at Maryland. She is the author or editor of six books, including *Civic Engagement in Higher Education, Service-Learning in Higher Education, Involving Commuter Students in Learning*, and *Building Partnerships for Service-Learning*, all from Jossey-Bass. Jacoby is a sought-after speaker and consultant on civic engagement and service-learning. She received her bachelor's, master's, and doctorate degrees—all summa cum laude—in French language and literature at the University of Maryland.

Mathew Johnson is an associate professor of sociology and environmental studies at Siena College in Loudonville, New York. In addition to his faculty responsibilities, Mathew serves the Office of the President in the roles of director of the Siena College Presidential Mission and Service VISTA Fellows Program, director of the Campus/Community Consortium for the Capital Region, director of the Siena College Center for Academic Service Learning, and faculty advisor to the Siena Bonner Service Leaders Program. His teaching and research focus on political and social organization of underrepresented communities in the United States and of indigenous communities in Latin America.

Micki Meyer serves as the director of the Office of Community Engagement at Rollins College in Winter Park, Florida, in the roles of advisor, teacher, collaborator, supervisor, and organizer. She is actively involved in higher education on state, national, and international levels with her work with Campus Compact, a nonprofit organization dedicated to educating college students to become well-equipped active citizens who are ready to develop creative solutions to society's most pressing issues. Through Campus Compact, Meyer serves as both an Engaged Scholar and Certified Scholar in Florida. She was presented with the 2007 Community Engagement Educator Award, the highest honor for a community engagement administrator in higher education in Florida.

Tania D. Mitchell is associate director for undergraduate studies and service-learning director in the Center for Comparative Studies in Race and Ethnicity at Stanford University, where she directs the academic program in public service, community development, and community-based research. She previously served as assistant professor for service-learning leadership at California State University–Monterey Bay. In 2006, she was recognized as an Emerging Scholar by the International Association for Research in Service-Learning and Civic Engagement (IARSLCE), and in 2008 as an Engaged Scholar by Campus Compact. Mitchell's teaching and research interests include service-learning pedagogy, college student development, and social justice.

Timothy Murphy is a senior lecturer in education studies at Leeds Metropolitan University. Previously, he worked as a researcher at the Centre for Excellence in Learning & Teaching (CELT) at NUI Galway, where he also worked for the Open Learning Centre and as a lecturer in education. He holds a doctorate in education from Teachers' College (Columbia University) in New York. He has strong interests (and publications) in civic education as well as academic staff development.

Ron Newell is the education director and director of research for EdVisions. He taught high school social studies for 28 years before joining EdVisions' Minnesota New Country School.

Julie Plaut currently serves as the executive director of Minnesota Campus Compact. Prior to assuming that position, she joined Campus Compact as director of Academic Initiatives in October 2007. She has also previously served as associate director of Minnesota Campus Compact and as an independent consultant to numerous nonprofit organizations focused on civic engagement and/or college access and success. Her work to advance higher education institutions' distinctive civic missions is grounded in an asset-based approach to collaboration and change and a deep commitment to creating just, democratic, and sustainable communities. Plaut received a Ph.D. in history from Indiana University and a B.A. in urban studies from Stanford University.

Margaret A. Post, Ph.D., is Director of the Donelan Office of Community-based Learning at the College of the Holy Cross (Worcester, Massachusetts). She holds a Doctorate in Social Policy from Brandeis University and a Master of Public Policy from the University of Minnesota. For more than 10 years, she has worked as a community organizer, educator, and scholar. Her research interests include the role of grassroots organizations in social policy change and the civic development of young people and new immigrants. In addition to teaching courses on organizing and public policy, Margaret regularly conducts trainings for a broad range of nonprofit and political organizations. In 2007, she received the K. Patricia Cross Future Leaders Award from the Association of American Colleges and Universities and the Bailis Family Social Justice Award from the Heller School at Brandeis University.

Lorilee R. Sandmann, Ph.D., is an associate professor in the Department of Lifelong Education, Administration, and Policy at the University of Georgia. Her research focuses on major institutional change processes to promote higher education community engagement and on criteria to define and evaluate faculty-engaged scholarship. She received her doctorate from the University of Wisconsin–Madison.

Robert Shumer lectures at the University of Minnesota on a variety of topics, including service-learning, civic engagement, constructivist curriculum, and research and evaluation. He has been an educator for 40 years, having served as a school teacher, librarian, and faculty member. He was the director of field studies development at UCLA and the founder and director of the National Service-Learning Clearinghouse. Shumer has written more than 30 publications on various topics related to education and civic engagement. He lives in Minnesota with his wife Susan and has three daughters and three grandchildren.

Elizabeth Carmichael Strong, MBA, serves Missouri State University as the Associate Director of the Office of Citizenship and Service-Learning (CASL), where she directs the University's service-learning program. That program includes Service-Learning Faculty Fellows, CASL Research Stipends, and Service-Learning and the First-Year Experience. Strong is one of 10 Engaged Scholars for New Perspectives in Higher Education, a Campus Compact initiative. Under her leadership, Missouri State's service-learning program has more than quadrupled the number of student participants and service hours. In 2007, she received the Staff Excellence for University Service Award. Her research interests include service-learning's role in cultural competency, ethics, and motivation.

Jon E. C. Tan is a senior lecturer and research coordinator in the field of education at Leeds Metropolitan University. He graduated from the University of York with a D.Phil. in social policy, and his work draws from a range of disciplines, including social welfare, education, and critical social theory. His current research in the area of professional learning and critical reflective pedagogies interconnects work with both practitioners in urban educational contexts and undergraduate and postgraduate students of teacher education. In recent years, in collaboration with co-author Christine Allan, Tan has conducted research focusing on student teachers' experiences of school practice placements in international settings.

Also available from Stylus

Learning through Serving
A Student Guidebook for Service-Learning Across the Disciplines
Christine M. Cress, Peter J. Collier, Vicki L. Reitenauer

"Finally, a companion reader for students in service-learning courses! It is filled with meaningful exercises to help students make sense of their service experience and relate it to the course content. This is an important contribution to the field of service learning and faculty should utilize this book to help students understand and make the most of their service-learning experience."—*Elaine K. Ikeda, Executive Director, California Campus Compact*

Intended as a textbook, this work reads like a conversation between the authors and the college student learner. The publication is student-friendly, comprehensive, easy to follow, and full of helpful activities."—*Journal of College Student Development*

Integrating Study Abroad Into the Curriculum
Theory and Practice across the Disciplines
Edited by Elizabeth Brewer, Kiran Cunningham
Foreword by Madeleine F. Green

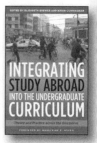

Is study abroad engendering the desired intercultural competencies and intellectual development?

To achieve this goal, this book proposes two strategies: Structure study abroad to bridge the separation of academic learning from experiential and intercultural learning; and integrate study abroad with the undergraduate curriculum.

In proposing this integration, the editors take into account the need for institutional change, and recognize faculty members' concerns about maintaining the integrity of the curriculum, teaching in areas outside their expertise, and keeping up with ever-evolving institutional missions.

This book opens with two chapters presenting different theoretical perspectives relevant to the integration of study abroad into the curriculum. The following nine chapters provide examples from a variety of disciplines, and within such contexts as distance learning, service learning, and the senior thesis.

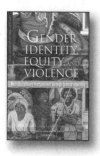

Service Learning for Civic Engagement Series
Series Editor: Gerald Eisman

As institutions of higher education embrace civic engagement, service learning has emerged as a most effective way to engage students in field experiences where they will confront profound questions about the relevance of academic learning to addressing community needs. Each volume in this new series is organized around a specific community issue, and provides multiple perspectives on both the theoretical foundations for understanding the corresponding issue, and purposeful approaches to addressing it. The contributors to these books—who represent disciplines in the sciences, humanities and social sciences—offer vivid examples of how they have integrated civic engagement in their courses, explain their objectives, and demonstrate how they assess outcomes.

Available titles:

Gender Identity, Equity, and Violence
Edited by Geraldine B. Stahly

Promoting Health and Wellness in Underserved Communities
Edited by Anabel Pelham and Elizabeth Sills

Race, Poverty, and Social Justice
Edited by José Z. Calderón

Research, Advocacy, and Political Engagement
Edited by Sally Tannenbaum

 22883 Quicksilver Drive
Sterling, VA 20166-2102

Subscribe to our e-mail alerts: www.Styluspub.com